AF522371

Information Networking Concepts in Library

Information Networking Concepts in Library

M. Ram

Information Networking Concepts in Library

ISBN 978-93-5111-244-0

Published in 2014 in India by

RANDOM PUBLICATIONS

4376-A/4B, Gali Murari Lal, Ansari Road
New Delhi-110 002
Phone : +91-11-43580356, +91-11-23289044
e-mail: randomexports@gmail.com, sales@randompublications.com, info@randompublications.com

Reprint 2021

Type Setting by : Keystoneprintads, Delhi-110051
Digitally Printed at : Replika Press Pvt. Ltd.

Preface

In this age of knowledge, libraries and information professionals are an essential part of any institution. As scholarly information is increasingly accessed and discovered online, away from the physical library, the profile of libraries and librarians needs to be raised in order to demonstrate the critical roles they play in both securing access to digital information and supporting research and teaching in new ways.

The ACU Libraries and Information Network enables professionals in the field to share professional expertise, knowledge and best practice with colleagues across the Commonwealth. Network members share opinions and experiences on issues such as the use of digital tools to create new research metrics, online learning, and new information access technologies. The Network, working in collaboration with the International Network for the Availability of Scientific Publications, has established the Publishers for Development initiative to help improve publishers' knowledge of developing country research environments and to strengthen the relationships between publishers and librarians.

Libraries always have performed some level of catalog maintenance, usually in card format, from simply filing cards and later withdrawing those as holding were removed, through maintaining a full syndetic structure that includes making cross-references and changing forms of entry as cataloging rules change. While an online environment offers increased access points, more flexible searching, and the ability to make global changes, new maintenance procedures need to be developed to take advantage of these capabilities. Computer revolution has overhauled the entire cataloguing and library networking system. Eminent issues are interpreted scientifically in this book. The language and concepts of this book that are written by the author of this book is easily understandable for each and every reader. Resulting from dependable sources this will prove an ideal reference work.

A network may fail in the early stages if there is not proper planning or if adequate funds are not available. Moreover, a common memorandum of agreement signed by the participating libraries at the institutional level is essential for the success of a network venture. On a more practical level, catalog data must be in a standard, machine readable form for it to be shared and exchanged. And, finally, a continuous flow of external assistance is crucial for the network's survival.

I thank all members of my team who have helped in the preparation of the book. My special thanks go to "Random Publications" who have published the book.

– M. Ram

Contents

1

Library and Information Science

THE ROLE AND PURPOSE OF THE PUBLIC LIBRARY

DEFINING THE PUBLIC LIBRARY

Public libraries are a world-wide phenomenon. They occur in a variety of societies, in differing cultures and at different stages of development. Although the varied contexts in which they operate inevitably result in differences in the services they provide, and the way those services are delivered, they normally have characteristics in common, which can be defined as follows.

A public library is an organisation established, supported and funded by the community, either through local, regional or national government or through some other form of community organisation. It provides access to knowledge, information and works of the imagination through a range of resources and services and is equally available to all members of the community regardless of race, nationality, age, gender, religion, language, disability, economic and employment status and educational attainment.

THE PURPOSES OF THE PUBLIC LIBRARY

The primary purposes of the public library are to provide resources and services in a variety of media to meet the needs of individuals and groups for education, information and personal development including recreation and leisure. They have an important role in the development and maintenance of a democratic society by giving the individual access to a wide and varied range of knowledge, ideas and opinions.

Education

The need for an agency available to all, which provides access to knowledge in printed and other formats to support formal and informal education, has been the reason for the foundation and maintenance of most public libraries and remains a core purpose for the public library. Throughout their lives people require education either at formal institutions, for example, schools, colleges and universities, or in a less formal context related to their employment and daily life. Learning does not end with the completion of formal education but is, for most people, a lifelong activity. In an increasingly complex society people will need to acquire new skills at various stages of their life. The public library has an important role in assisting this process. The public library should provide material in the appropriate media to support formal and informal learning processes.

It should also help the user to make use of these learning resources effectively as well as providing facilities that enable people to study. The ability to access information and make effective use of it is vital to successful education and, where possible, public libraries should co-operate with other educational organisations in teaching the use of information resources.

Where adequate library facilities exist to support formal education the public library should complement them rather than duplicating library provision available elsewhere. The public library should also actively support literacy campaigns, as literacy is the key to education and knowledge and to the use of libraries and information services.

Newly literate people need easy access to appropriate reading materials to maintain and develop their skills. In some countries the need for educational development is seen to be paramount and the focus of public libraries is to support formal education. There are, however, a variety of ways in which public libraries can support both formal and informal education. How this is achieved will depend on the local context and the level of available resources.

Information

It is a basic human right to be able to have access to and an understanding of information, and there is now more information available than ever before in the world's history. As a public service open to all, the public library has a key role in collecting, organising and exploiting information, as well as providing access to a wide range of information sources. The public library has a particular responsibility to collect local information and make it readily available.

It also acts as a memory of the past by collecting, conserving and providing access to material relating to the history of the community and of individuals. In providing a wide range of information the public library assists the community in informed debate and decision-making on key issues. In collecting and providing information the public library should, wherever possible, co-operate with other agencies to make the best use of available resources.

The rapid growth in the volume of available information and the continuing technological changes, which have radically affected the way information is accessed, have already made a significant effect on public libraries and their services. Information is very important to the development of the individual and of society, and information technology gives considerable power to those able to access and use it.

Despite its rapid growth it is not available to the majority of the world's population, and the gap between the information rich and the information poor continues to widen. A vital role for the public library is to bridge that gap by providing public access to the Internet as well as providing information in traditional formats. Public libraries should recognise and exploit the opportunities provided by the exciting developments in information and communications technology. They have the opportunity to become the electronic gateway to the information world.

Personal Development

The opportunity to develop personal creativity and pursue new interests is important to human development. To achieve this, people need access to knowledge and works of the imagination. The public library can provide access, in a variety of different media, to a rich and varied store of knowledge and creative achievement, which individuals cannot acquire on their own behalf.

Providing access to major collections of the world's literature and knowledge, including the community's own literature, has been a unique contribution of the public library and is still a vitally important function. Access to works of the imagination and knowledge is an important contribution to personal education and meaningful recreational activity.

The public library can also make a fundamental contribution to daily survival and social and economic development by being directly involved in providing information to people in developing communities; for example, basic life skills, adult basic education and AIDS awareness programmes. In communities with a high illiteracy rate the public library should provide services for non-literates and interpret and translate information where necessary. It should also provide basic user education.

CHILDREN AND YOUNG PEOPLE

The public library should attempt to meet the needs of all groups in the community regardless of age and physical, economic or social circumstances. However, it has a special responsibility to meet the needs of children and young people. If children can be inspired by the excitement of knowledge and by works of the imagination at an early age, they are likely to benefit from these vital elements of personal development throughout their lives, both enriching them and enhancing their contribution to society. Children can also encourage parents and other adults to make use of the library. It is also important that young people who experience difficulty in learning to read should have access to a library to provide them with appropriate material.

Public Libraries and Cultural Development

An important role of the public library is providing a focus for cultural and artistic development in the community and helping to shape and support the cultural identity of the community. This can be achieved by working in partnership with appropriate local and regional organisations, by providing space for cultural activity, organising cultural programmes and by ensuring that cultural interests are represented in the library's materials. The library's contribution should reflect the variety of cultures represented in the community. It should provide materials in the languages spoken and read in the local community, and support cultural traditions.

The Social Role of the Public Library

The public library has an important role as a public space and meeting place. This is particularly important in communities where there are few places for people to meet. It is sometimes called 'the drawing room of the community'. Use of the library for research and for finding information relating to the user's education and leisure interests, brings people into informal contact with other members of the community. Using the public library can be a positive social experience.

AN AGENCY FOR CHANGE

In carrying out its role in these key areas the public library is acting as an agency for social and personal development and can be a positive agency for change in the community. By providing a wide range of materials to support education and by making information accessible to all, the public library can bring economic and social benefits to individuals and to the community. It contributes to the creation and maintenance of a well–informed and democratic society and helps to empower people in the enrichment and development of their lives and that of the community in which they live. The public library should be aware of the issues that are being discussed within the community and provide information that will inform that debate.

FREEDOM OF INFORMATION

The public library should be able to represent all ranges of human experience and opinion, free from the risk of censorship. In some countries a Freedom of Information Act will help to ensure these rights are maintained. Librarians and governing bodies should uphold these basic human rights and resist pressure from individuals and groups to limit the material available in the public library.

ACCESS FOR ALL

A fundamental principle of the public library is that its services must be available to all and not directed to one group in the community to the exclusion of others. Provision should be made to ensure services are equally available to minority groups who for some reason are not able to use the mainstream services, for example, linguistic minorities, people with physical and sensory disabilities or those living in remote communities who are unable to reach library buildings.

The level of funding, development of services, the design of libraries and their opening hours should all be planned with the concept of universal access as a basic principle. The development of collections should also be based on the principle of access for all and include access to formats appropriate to specific client groups, for example, Braille and talking books for blind people. Information and communications technology should be used to allow access to the library's collections and those of other information sources, both from within the library or from remote sites.

LOCAL NEEDS

Public libraries are locally based services for the benefit of the local community and should provide community information services. The services and collections they provide should be based on local needs, which should be assessed regularly. Without this discipline the public library will get out of touch with those it is there to serve and will, as a result, not be used to its full potential. Librarians should, therefore, be aware of the changes in society arising from such factors as social and economic development, demographic change, variations in the age structure, levels of education, patterns of employment and the emergence of other educational and cultural providers.

LOCAL CULTURE

The public library should be a key agency in the local community for the collection, preservation and promotion of local culture in all its diversity. This can be achieved in a variety of ways, for example, the maintenance of local history collections, exhibitions, storytelling, publishing of items of local interest and developing interactive programmes on local themes. Where the oral tradition is an important method of communication the public library should encourage its continuation and development.

THE CULTURAL ROOTS OF THE PUBLIC LIBRARY

It is important to the long-term success of the library that it should be based on the culture, or cultures, of the country or area in which it operates. It is less likely to succeed if the form and structure of the public library are introduced from a country or area with a very different cultural background.

LIBRARIES WITHOUT WALLS

In developing policies to fulfil the role and purpose of the public library the emphasis should be on the services it provides. In meeting the needs of its community the public library will provide a range of services, some of which can be most effectively delivered from a library building. However, there will be many circumstances where it is more effective to provide the service beyond the walls of the library. Examples will vary in different societies but the principle of planning library development from a service rather than a building perspective is important in all public library policy development. The provision of services using information and communications technology also presents exciting opportunities to take library and information services direct to the home and the workplace.

A variety of forms of transport are used to deliver services to sparsely populated areas. The provision of library and information services to people unable to visit a library due to physical or sensory disability or lack of transport, for example, ensures that access to these services is available to all at their home or workplace regardless of their circumstances.

LIBRARY BUILDINGS

Library buildings play an important part in public library provision. They should be designed to reflect the functions of the library service, be accessible to all in the community and be sufficiently flexible to accommodate new and changing services. They should be located close to other community activities, for example, shops and cultural centres.

Wherever possible the library should also be available for community use, for example, for meetings and exhibitions and in larger buildings for theatrical, musical, audiovisual and media performances. A well used public library will make a significant contribution to the vitality of an urban area and be an important learning and social centre and meeting place, particularly in scattered rural areas. Librarians should, therefore, ensure that library buildings are used and managed effectively to make the best use of the facilities for the benefit of the whole community.

RESOURCES

To fulfil its roles satisfactorily the public library must have adequate resources, not just when it is established but also on a continuing basis, to enable it to sustain and develop services that meet the needs of the local community.

This means it should provide materials in all formats, up-dated regularly to meet the changing needs of groups and individuals, including newly-published and replacement materials. It should also provide adequate levels of staff with appropriate training and sufficient funds to support whatever methods of service delivery are needed for it to meet its vital role in the community.

THE LEGAL AND FINANCIAL FRAMEWORK

Public libraries are a community agency providing access at local level to a range of knowledge and information for the benefit of the individual and society as a whole. In order to maintain the level of service required to fulfil their functions public libraries should be supported by legislation and sustained funding.

THE PUBLIC LIBRARY AND GOVERNMENT

There are many different models of the relationship between public libraries and government. Equally, the laws that govern their activities and funding arrangements are varied and complex. In different countries, provinces, regions, states or municipalities are, either in whole or in part, responsible for library services.

As public libraries are a locally based service local government is often the most appropriate place in the government structure for them. However, in some countries public libraries are provided at regional or state level and the national library sometimes has responsibility for providing the public library service. There are instances of two or more levels of government co-operating in the provision of the service.

Alternative Structures

In some countries, although the local authority has nominal responsibility for the public library, it does not have the required funds and non-governmental organisations or private foundations undertake the practical operation of the public library services. However, to ensure sustained development and its role in the information network, the public library should be closely related to and funded by the appropriate level of government. The eventual aim should be to bring public libraries into the formal government structure operating under national legislation and with appropriate levels of funding.

National Information Policies

In order to make the most effective use of available library and information resources, and take full advantage of the opportunities offered by the development of electronic information sources, many countries are developing national information policies. Public libraries should be a key element in such policies and public librarians should ensure they are fully involved in their development.

PUBLIC LIBRARY LEGISLATION

Public libraries should be based on legislation, which assures their continuance and their place in the government structure. Public library legislation takes various forms. In some countries or regions the legislation is specific to public libraries whereas in others it is part of wider legislation which includes different types of libraries. Public library legislation is also varied in its provisions.

It can be simple, allowing the establishment of public libraries but leaving standards of service to the level of government directly responsible for the library, or more complex, with specific detail on what services should be provided and to what standard. Examples of public library legislation are available on the IFLA web site. Because governmental structures vary so much in different countries the form and detail of public library legislation is also likely to vary significantly. However, legislation governing public libraries should state which level of government is responsible for their provision and how they should be funded. It should also place them in the framework of libraries in the country or region as a whole.

Related Legislation

Public libraries are subject to a range of legislation apart from the specific legislation relating to them. This can include legislation on financial management, data protection, health and safety and staff conditions and there will be many other examples. Library managers should be aware of all legislation affecting the operation of the public library. They should also be aware of global trade negotiations, which can result in policies and agreements, which could have a serious impact on public libraries. In such cases librarians should take every opportunity to bring the effect of such policies on public libraries to the notice of the public and politicians.

Copyright

Copyright legislation, especially that relating to electronic publications, is of particular importance to public libraries. It is constantly subject to amendment and review and librarians should keep up-to-date with the legislation in relation to all media. Librarians should promote and support copyright legislation, which achieves an equitable balance between the rights of creators and the needs of users.

Public Lending Right

In some countries, public lending right legislation has been introduced which provides a payment to authors and others involved in the creation of a book, related to its provision in, and loan from, public libraries. It is important that funds for payment of public lending right should not be taken from libraries' funds for the purchase of materials.

However, public lending right, if separately funded, does provide support for authors without affecting public libraries' budgets. In some schemes it can also provide useful statistics on the loans of books by specific authors. Librarians should participate in the development of public lending right schemes to ensure they are not financed from library budgets.

FUNDING

Adequate levels of funding are crucial to the success of a public library in fulfilling its roles. Without suitable levels of funding over the long-term it is impossible to develop policies for service provision and make the most effective use of available resources. This can be seen in number of examples: a new library building without adequate funds to maintain it, collections of new books with no money for their replacement and computer systems without funds to maintain and update them. Funding is required not only when a public library is established, but should also be sustained on an assured and regular basis.

Priorities

A public library and the services it provides is a long-term investment on behalf of the community and should be funded appropriately. It is recognised that even in the wealthiest of societies it may not be possible to provide appropriate levels of funding for every service requirement. It is vitally important, therefore, that service development should be conducted on a planned basis with clear priorities.

This process is necessary whatever level of funding is available to the library service. To determine strategic planning and the maintenance of agreed priorities, written policy statements should be developed for services. They should be reviewed at regular intervals and revised where necessary.

Partnership

No public library, however large and well funded, can meet all the needs of its users on its own. Participation in partnerships and networks with other libraries and related organisations, and the provision of access to other sources of information, enables the public library to satisfy the information needs of its users by increasing the range of available resources.

Sources of Funding

A number of sources of funding are used to finance public libraries but the proportions of funding from each source will vary depending on local factors in each country.

The primary sources are:

- Taxation at local, regional or central level
- Block grants from central, regional or local level.

Secondary sources of income may include:

- Donations from funding bodies or private individuals
- Revenue from commercial activities, *e.g.*, publishing, book sales, sale of works of art and handicrafts
- Revenue from user fees, *e.g.*, fines
- Revenue from charges to users for individual services, *e.g.*, photocopying and printing facilities
- Sponsorship from external organisations
- Lottery funds for specific initiatives.

Charging the User

The *IFLA/UNESCO Public Library Manifesto* states: 'The public library shall in principle be free of charge'. Charging users for services and membership should not be used as a source of revenue for public libraries, as it makes the ability to pay a criterion in determining who can use a public library. This reduces access and therefore breaches the fundamental principle that the public library should be available to all. It is recognised that in some countries subscriptions to join the library or charges for specific services are levied. Such charges inevitably deny access to those unable to afford them.

They should be seen as an interim situation and not as a permanent feature of public library funding. It is common in some countries to ask users to pay a fee or fine when keeping an item after it is due for return to the library. This is sometimes necessary to ensure that items are kept in circulation and not retained for a long time by one user. The fine should not be set at a level that would deter anyone from using the library. Charges are also sometimes levied for personalised services, for example photocopying or use of a printer. These charges should also not be set at a level which will deter the user.

Funding for Technology

Public libraries must, whenever possible, make use of the new technologies to improve their services and provide new ones. This means a considerable investment in various kinds of electronic equipment, and a reliance on this equipment for the delivery of services. To continue to perform effectively equipment should be upgraded and replaced. This has significant funding consequences and a plan for the replacement and upgrading of technological equipment should be developed.

External Funding

Librarians should be imaginative in seeking external sources of funding for the public library. However, they should not accept funding from any source if, by so doing, the fundamental status of a public library as an agency available to all is compromised. Commercial organisations, for example, may offer funding with conditions which might prejudice the universal nature of the services provided by the public library.

THE GOVERNANCE OF THE PUBLIC LIBRARY

Public libraries should be governed by a properly established body made up largely of representatives of the local community including those elected either to the local council or to the library board. Library committees and boards should have rules of procedure and their proceedings should be open to the general public. They should meet on a regular basis and publish agenda, minutes, annual reports and financial statements.

Normally the governing body will be responsible for matters of policy rather than the day-to-day operation of the library. In all cases the chief librarian should have direct access to the meetings of the governing body of the library and work closely with it. Policy documents should be made available to the public and, where possible, steps should be taken to involve local citisens in the development of the public library. Public librarians must be fully accountable both to their governing bodies and local citizens for their actions by providing reports, holding public meetings and through consultation.

They must also maintain the highest professional standards in carrying out their duties and in advising the governing body. Although the final decisions on policy will be taken by the governing body and the librarian, ways should be sought to involve the local citizens who are the actual or potential library users. The concept of a 'library charter', which identifies and publicises the level of service the public library provides has been developed in some countries. This establishes a 'contract' between the public library and the users. Library charters have more credibility if they are developed in consultation with users.

THE ADMINISTRATION OF THE PUBLIC LIBRARY

Public libraries should be well managed and administered. The administration of a public library should be directed towardss improving the quality of service to the users and not as an end in itself. It should be efficient and accountable. To get best results the administrative and management staff of a large public library service should be multidisciplinary, involving staff with specialist skills, for example, librarians, accountants, public relations officers and system managers. It may also be necessary to draw on the expertise of staff of the parent authority or other related organisation in certain areas, for example, lawyers, payroll and pensions staff.

PUBLICITY AND PROMOTION

Public libraries operate in an increasingly complex society, which makes many calls on people's time and attention. It is important, therefore, that libraries publicise their presence and the range of services they provide. Publicity ranges from simple techniques, like signs on library buildings stating what they are, and leaflets advertising opening hours and services, to more sophisticated methods like marketing programmes and the use of web sites to promote the library's services and activities.

MEETING THE NEEDS OF THE USERS

To be successful in fulfilling its goals the public library service must be fully accessible to all its potential users. Any limitation of access, whether deliberate or accidental, will reduce the ability of the public library to fully achieve its primary role of meeting the library and information needs of the community it serves.

The following are important elements in delivering an effective public library service:

- Identifying potential users
- Analysing users' needs

- Developing services to groups and individuals
- Introducing customer care policies
- Promoting user education
- Co-operating and sharing resources
- Developing electronic networks
- Ensuring access to services
- Providing library buildings.

IDENTIFYING POTENTIAL USERS

The public library has to aim to serve all citizens and groups. An individual is never too young or too old to use a library.

The public library has the following potential target groups.

- People at all ages and at all stages of life:
- Children
- Young adults
- Adults.
- Individuals and groups of people with special needs:
- People from different cultures and ethnic groups including indigenous people
- People with disabilities, *e.g.*, blind and partially sighted, hearing impaired
- Housebound people
- Institutionally confined people, *e.g.*, in hospitals, prisons.
- Institutions within the wider community network:
- Educational, cultural and voluntary organisations and groups in the community
- The business community
- The governing body of the parent organisation, *e.g.*, local authority.

As resources are limited in even the wealthiest society it is not always possible to serve all users to the same level. The library must establish priorities based on an analysis of user needs and related to their access to alternative services.

ANALYSING NEEDS WITHIN THE COMMUNITY

It is important to establish who uses and who does not use the library service. It is also necessary to collect and analyse data that identifies those needs of individuals and groups within the community that can be met by the public library.

SERVICES TO USERS

The public library must provide services based on an analysis of the library and information needs of the local community. In planning services, clear priorities must be established and a strategy be developed for service provision in the medium to long term. Services should be developed for identified target groups and only provided if such groups exist in the local community. The services of the library should not be subject to any form of ideological, political, religious or commercial pressure.

Services must be able to adjust and develop to reflect changes in society, for example, variations in family structures, employment patterns, demographic changes, cultural diversity and methods of communication. They should take account of traditional cultures as well as new technologies, for example, support for oral methods of communication as well as making use of information and communication technology. In some countries the services that the public library must provide are defined in library legislation.

Service Provision

Public libraries provide a range of services, both within the library and in the community, to satisfy their users' needs. The library should facilitate access to its services for all, including those who have difficulty reading print.

The following services, which should be easily accessible to the user in a variety of formats and media, should be provided:

- Loan of books and other media
- Provision of books and other materials for use in the library
- Information services using print and electronic media
- Readers' advisory services including reservation services
- Community information services
- User education including support for literacy programmes
- Programming and events.

This is not an exhaustive list but an indication of some of the key services of the public library. The range and depth of provision will depend on the size of the library and the community it serves. Every library should aim to be an active participant in one or more networks, which will give the user access to a wide range of material, however small the access point.

Service provision should not be confined to the library building but also taken direct to the user where access to the library is not possible. In providing services, both within the library and beyond, use should be made of information and communications technology as well as the printed word.

Services to Children

By providing a wide range of materials and activities, public libraries provide an opportunity for children to experience the enjoyment of reading and the excitement of discovering knowledge and works of the imagination. Children and their parents should be taught how to make the best use of a library and how to develop skills in the use of printed and electronic media. Public libraries have a special responsibility to support the process of learning to read, and to promote books and other media for children. The library must provide special events for children, such as story telling and activities related to the library's services and resources. Children should be encouraged to use the library from an early age as this will make them more likely to remain users in future years. In multilingual countries books and audiovisual materials for children should be available in their mother tongue.

Services for Young Adults

Young people between childhood and adulthood develop as individual members of society with their own culture. Public libraries must understand their needs and provide services to meet them. Materials, including access to electronic information resources, that reflect their interests and culture should be provided.

In some cases this will mean acquiring materials that represent youth culture, in a variety of media that are not traditionally part of a library's resources, for example, popular novels, book and television series, music, video tapes, teenage magazines, posters, computer games, graphic novels.

It is important to enlist the help of young people in selecting this material to ensure that it reflects their interests. In larger libraries this material, with appropriate furniture, can form a special section of the library. This will help them to feel that the library is for them and help to overcome a feeling of alienation from the library, which is not unusual among this age group. Relevant programmes and talks to young adults should also be provided.

SERVICES FOR ADULTS

Adults will have different requirements of an information and library service related to the variety of situations they will encounter in their studies, employment and personal life. These requirements should be analysed and services be developed on the outcome of that analysis.

They should include support for:

- Lifelong learning
- Leisure time interests
- Information needs
- Community activities
- Cultural activity
- Recreational reading.

Services meeting these needs should also be available to children and young adults.

Lifelong Learning

The public library supports lifelong learning, working with schools and other educational institutions to help students of all ages with their formal education.

The challenge of providing educational support provides an opportunity for public libraries to interact and network with teachers and others involved in education.

The public library should also provide a range of materials on a variety of topics which will allow people to follow their interests and support their formal and informal education. It should also provide materials to support literacy and the development of basic life skills. In addition the library must provide study facilities for students who have inadequate or no access to these facilities in their homes.

The development in distance learning is having an impact on the public library. Distant learners, studying at home, are likely to make use of their local library as their primary source for material. Many will require access to the Internet which the public library should provide. Public libraries play an increasingly important role within the educational network and should provide space and access to materials to meet this demand.

Leisure Time Interests

People need information to support their leisure time interests and meeting this need by a range of resources in a variety of formats is another key role of the public library. Public libraries must be aware of the cultural, social and economic changes in the community and develop services that are sufficiently flexible to adjust to these changes. The public library should also help to preserve the culture, history and traditions of the local community and make them readily available.

The public library, by organising activities and exploiting its resources, should encourage artistic and cultural development in people of all ages. The library is also an important social centre for individuals and groups to meet both formally and informally. This is of special importance in communities where other meeting places are not available.

Information Services

The rapid development of information technology has brought a vast amount of information within reach of all those with access to electronic media. Information provision has always been a key role of the public library and the ways in which information can be collected, accessed and presented have changed radically in recent years.

The public library has a number of roles in providing information:

- Providing information about the local community and making it readily accessible, often in co-operation with other organisations
- Training people of all ages in the use of information and the associated technology
- Guiding users to the appropriate information sources
- Providing opportunities for disabled people to have independent access to information
- Acting as a gateway to the information world by making it accessible to all, thus helping to bridge the gap between 'the information rich' and 'the information poor'.

The dramatic development of the Internet has been largely unstructured and uncontrolled. The vast amount of information that can be accessed via the Internet is of variable quality and accuracy and a key role of the librarian is to guide users to accurate information sources, which will meet their requirements.

Services to Community Groups

The public library should be at the centre of the community if it is to play a full part in its activities. It should, therefore, work with other groups and organisations in the community. This will include departments of government and local government, the business community and voluntary organisations. An analysis of the information needs of these bodies should be conducted, and services be provided to meet these needs. This will not only help the organisations involved but will also demonstrate, in a practical way, the value of the public library to people in the community who are likely to have some influence on the future of the library service. Many public libraries, for example, provide an information service to local government politicians and staff, giving a practical demonstration of the value of the public library.

Services to Special User Groups

Potential users who, for whatever reason, are unable to use the regular services of the library have a right to equal access to library services. The library should, therefore, establish ways of making library material and services accessible to these users.

These will include:

- Special transport, *e.g.*, mobile libraries, book-boats and other forms of transport to serve those living in isolated areas.
- Services taken to the home of those people who are housebound.
- Services taken to factories and industrial premises for employees.
- Services for those confined in institutions, *e.g.*, prisons and hospitals.
- Special equipment and reading materials for those with physical and sensory disabilities, *e.g.*, hearing impaired and visually impaired people.
- Special materials for people with learning difficulties, *e.g.*, easy-to-read materials and cassettes.
- Services for immigrants and new citizens to help them to find their way within a different society and to provide access to media of their native culture.
- Electronic communication, *e.g.*, Internet catalogues.

Services for people with special needs can be enhanced by the use of new technology, for example, speech synthesisers for the visually impaired, online access catalogues for those in isolated areas or unable to leave their home, connections to remote sites for distance learning. Mainstream service provision, for example, public access catalogues (OPACs) can often be adapted to meet the needs of those with physical and sensory disabilities. Those who can benefit the most from technological developments are often the least able to afford the investment needed.

Innovative schemes should, therefore, be developed by the public library to exploit the new technology in order to make services available to as many people as possible. Services for ethnic groups in the community and for indigenous peoples should be developed in consultation with the group concerned.

They are likely to include:

- The employment of staff from the group in the library.
- Collections including the native literature of the group and reflecting the oral tradition and non-written knowledge of the people.
- The application of special conditions, developed in conjunction with local people, to culturally sensitive material.

Reading Promotion and Literacy

Reading, writing and the ability to use numbers are basic prerequisites to being an integrated and active member of society. Reading and writing are also the basic techniques needed for making use of new communication systems. The public library should support activities that will enable people to make the best use of modern technology. It should support other institutions that are combating illiteracy and promoting media competence.

It can achieve this by:

- Promoting reading.
- Providing appropriate materials for those with poor literacy skills.
- Working with other agencies in the community involved in combating illiteracy.
- Participating in campaigns to combat illiteracy and improve numeracy
- Organising events to promote an interest in reading, literature and media culture.
- Promoting and providing training in the use of computer technology
- Promoting awareness of new developments in the media market.
- Helping people to find the information they need in the appropriate format.
- Co-operating with teachers, parents and other contact persons to help new citizens acquire the necessary educational skills that will help them to manage their lives in the new context.

The public library provides a range of creative literature and can use promotional techniques to bring its variety and range to the attention of its users. It can also organise interactive programmes that enable users to exchange views about books that they have read.

CUSTOMER CARE

The policies and procedures of the library should be based on the needs and convenience of the users and not for the convenience of the organisation and its staff. Quality services can only be delivered if the library is sensitive to the needs of its users and shapes its services to meet those needs. Satisfied users are the best advocates of the library service.

The public library should have a positive policy of customer care. This means ensuring that in all policy planning, design of libraries and of systems, preparation of operational procedures and drafting of information and publicity material, a positive effect on the user should be a prime objective.

The following actions should be elements in a customer care policy:

- The image projected by all libraries must be neutral and objective.
- Staff should be courteous, friendly, respectful and helpful at all times
- There should be a regular programme of staff training in customer care.
- All staff should receive basic awareness training on how to deal with people with disabilities or from ethnic minorities.
- Jargon should be avoided in all forms of communication, verbal and written.
- Staff should have a friendly and informative telephone manner.
- Methods of communication with the users must be provided, *e.g.*, billboards, bulletins, web site.
- Library services should be properly planned, adequately prepared and reliable.
- The design of the library should be as convenient and inviting as possible.
- Opening hours should be convenient for the users.
- Open public access catalogues should be available on the Internet so that the user can access services from home and outside opening hours.
- There should be efficient renewal and reservation services.
- Services should be delivered beyond the library building when users' needs require it.
- Users should receive a response in the shortest possible time; letters and other forms of communication should be answered promptly and courteously.
- Equipment should be provided to make library use convenient, *e.g.*, drop-in boxes for returning materials out of hours, self-service issue and return equipment in the library, answering machines for communicating with the library out of hours.
- All printed information about services should be available in appropriate alternative formats, *e.g.*, large print, tape; they should also be available in minority languages.

- When resources allow, good quality electronic equipment should be provided in the library including special equipment for the partially sighted and hearing impaired.

User Participation

Customers should be involved in service development:

- By asking them through surveys what services they use and require.
- By analysing and responding to users' complaints.
- By monitoring users' reactions to services and new initiatives.
- By ensuring the input received from users is considered in the development of policy and procedures.
- By providing feedback to users about the effects of their input on service development.
- By providing suggestion boxes and a complaints and commendations procedure.

USER EDUCATION

The public library should help its users develop skills that will enable them to make the most effective use of the library's resources and services. Library staff must act as information navigators to help users of all ages to make the most effective use of information and communications technology, and programmes of user education should be developed.

As the new technologies become more commonly available, the role of the public library both in providing access to these technologies and in helping people learn how to make best use of them is of vital importance. Guided tours of the library should take place regularly to introduce people to the library building and services and how to use its tools, for example, catalogues and technical equipment.

These guided tours have to be carefully planned according to the needs of those taking part. Tours for groups should be organised in co-operation with the institution from which they come.

CO-OPERATION AND RESOURCE SHARING

Overall service to the community is enhanced when libraries develop links for exchanging information, ideas, services and expertise. Such co-operation results in less duplication of service, a combining of resources for maximum effect, and an overall improvement in community services. In addition, individual community members may in some cases be of great assistance in helping the library to carry out special tasks or projects.

Formal Links

The library should establish formal links with other organisations in the local community, for example, schools, cultural institutions such as museums, galleries and archives, literacy programmes, chambers of commerce or boards of trade. The links should be used to co-ordinate the resources and efforts of each partner and thereby jointly improve services to the community.

Relations with Schools

One of the most important institutional relationships for a public library is that with the local schools and the education system in the service area.

Types of linkages and/or forms of co-operation include:

- Sharing resources
- Sharing staff training
- Co-operative collection development
- Co-operative programming
- Co-ordination of electronic services and networks
- Co-operation in the development of learning tools
- Class visits to the public library
- Joint reading and literacy promotion
- Programme of web-awareness for children
- Sharing of telecommunications and network infrastructures
- Jointly arranged authors' visits.

Resource Sharing

Each library collection is in some degree unique. No collection can contain all the materials that the members of its public require. Libraries, therefore, can greatly enhance services to their users by providing them with access to the collections of other libraries.

Libraries can participate in resource-sharing schemes at any level, local, regional, national and international, involving libraries of a wide range of organisations with information resources. The library should also make its collection available for loan to other libraries through participation in a network, for example, in a union catalogue or in a local network of information providers, such as schools, colleges and universities.

Bibliographic Records

The library should classify and catalogue its resources according to accepted international or national bibliographic standards. This facilitates their inclusion in wider networks.

Borrowing from Other Libraries

In order to meet the information needs of users the library should borrow materials from other libraries both within the same organisation and beyond.

The library should establish interlending policies, which address such issues as:

- Lending materials to other public libraries
- The type of materials it is prepared to lend or not to lend
- The length of time for which materials will be lent

- When it will request materials from other libraries
- Methods of shipment
- How the costs of the service will be met
- Action to be taken if materials are lost or damaged.

ELECTRONIC NETWORKS

Public libraries are instruments of equal opportunity and must provide a safety- net against alienation and social exclusion from technological advance by becoming the electronic doorway to information in the digital age.

They should enable all citizens to have access to the information that will enable them to manage their lives at the local level, to acquire essential information about the democratic process and to participate positively in an increasingly global society.

The library should provide access to the resources of the library and to those of other libraries and information services through the creation and maintenance of and participation in effective electronic networks at all levels from local to international.

This can include participation in community networks, programmes to develop technologically advanced communities and electronic networks linking two or more agencies. They should also be part of national information policies.

User Access

The library should provide free public access to the Internet/world wide web to enable all citizens, regardless of economic means, to have access to information available in electronic form. It should have at least one public-access workstation with Internet access and a printer that is not shared with staff.

Remote Access

The library should exploit information and communications technology to enable the public to gain access to as many of its electronic resources and services as possible from their home, school or workplace. If possible they should be made accessible 24 hours a day, seven days a week. Making the library catalogue available on the Internet increases its accessibility to the public, and to other libraries, and improves the quality of the service.

Staff Access

Library staff should have access to the Internet/world wide web to enable them to provide better reference and readers' advisory service to users. Staff should have regular training in using the Internet.

Information Navigator

The public library's role is becoming one of mediator, of being the public's electronic doorway to digital information and of helping citizens cross the 'digital divide' to a better future. The librarian's role is increasingly one of 'information navigator' ensuring that the user gets accurate and reliable information.

ACCESS TO SERVICES

Physical accessibility is one of the major keys to the successful delivery of public library services. Services of high quality are of no value to those who are unable to access them. Access to services should be structured in a way that maximizes convenience to users and potential users.

Location of Service Outlets

Public library service outlets should be located for the maximum convenience of residents of the community. If possible they should be near the centre of transport networks and close to areas of community activity, for example, shops, commercial centres, cultural centres. Where appropriate the public library may share buildings with other services such as arts centres, museums, art galleries, community centres and sports facilities. This can help to attract users and achieve capital and operational economies. The outlet should be highly visible and easily reached by foot, public transport, where available, or by private vehicle. In well-developed urban and suburban areas a public library should be available within a journey by private vehicle of about 15 minutes.

Opening Hours

In order to provide the best possible access to the library service, the library must be open at times of maximum convenience to those who live, work and study in the community.

LIBRARY BUILDINGS

In general when planning a library, the librarian and governing body should consider the following elements:

- The function of the library.
- The size of the library.
- Designated spaces.
- Design features.
- Accessible shelving.
- Sign-posting.
- The ambience of the library.
- Electronic and audiovisual equipment.
- Safety.
- Parking.

The Function of the Library

The library should have adequate space to implement the full range of library services that are consistent with the library's strategic plan and that meet local, area or national standards/guidelines.

The Size of the Library

The amount of floor-space required by a public library depends on such factors as the unique needs of the individual community, the functions of the library, the level of resources available, the size of the collection, the space available and the proximity of other libraries.

Because these elements will vary significantly from country to country and between different building projects it is not possible to propose a universal standard on the space required for a public library.

Designated Spaces

The library should include space for services to adults, children and young adults and for family use. It should aim to provide a range of materials to meet the needs of all groups and individuals in the community. The range of functions provided and the space available for each will depend on the size of the library.

In planning a new library the following should be considered for inclusion:

- The library collection including, books, periodicals, special collections, sound recordings and video cassettes and other non-print and digital resources.
- Reader seating space for adults, children and young adults to use for leisure reading, serious study, group work and one–one tutoring; quiet rooms should be provided.
- Outreach services: space should be provided to house special collections and preparation areas for outreach services.
- Staff facilities, including work space rest space for eating and relaxing during breaks and meeting rooms where staff can meet with colleagues and supervisors in private.
- Meeting room space for large and small community groups, which should have separate access to the washrooms and to the exterior to enable meetings to be held while the library is closed
- Technology, including public access workstations, printers, CD-ROM stations, copiers, microfilm/fiche readers, public typewriters and facilities for listening to recorded sound.
- special equipment, including atlas cases, newspaper racks, self-service book circulation, dictionaries, wall-mounted display racks, display stands, filing cabinets, map cases, etc.
- Sufficient space for ease of circulation by both public and staff; this can be 15 per cent–20 per cent of public areas and 20 per cent–25 per cent in staff areas.
- In larger libraries a café area for the public is a desirable facility.
- Space must be allowed for the mechanical services of the library, *e.g.*, elevators, heating, ventilation, maintenance, storage of cleaning materials, etc.

Design Features

The library should guarantee easy access for all users and in particular persons with physical and sensory disabilities.

The following features should be included in the planning of a new library:

- The exterior of the library should be well lit and identified with signs clearly visible from the street.
- The entrance of the library should be clearly visible and located on that part of the building that most users approach.
- The library should focus on eliminating barriers to use.
- There should be no design features that limit the ability of an individual or groups to use any part of the library.
- Care should be taken to avoid steps as much as possible in both interior and exterior design.
- Lighting levels should comply with those stated in international or national standards.
- Libraries that occupy two or more floors should provide elevators that are close to the library entrance and that easily accommodate wheelchairs and child strollers.
- The library should provide facilities for the return of library materials when the library is closed; after-hours deposit boxes should be both theft and waterproof.
- A library should undertake an 'accessibility' audit on a regular basis to confirm that there are no barriers to easy use.
- Local, national or international standards on making public buildings accessible to the disabled should be followed, wherever possible.

Accessible Shelving

Materials should be displayed on open shelves and arranged at a height within easy reach for users. All shelving should be adjustable and preferably on lockable wheels so that it can easily be moved. The furniture in the children's section should be appropriately sized. Shelves should be of accessible height and width for persons using a wheelchair.

Sign-posting

The library's exterior signs not only identify the particular function of the building but are also the library's most basic form of publicity. Signs should therefore be carefully planned to communicate an appropriate image of the library. Internal areas of the library and parts of the collection should be clearly identified by signs of a professional standard so that users can easily find them, for example, the library catalogue, magazines, reference services, the children's area, washrooms, Internet stations, copy machines, etc.

Signs should also be posted in Braille where necessary. Where appropriate, signs should be provided in languages used by ethnic groups in the community. A sign displaying the opening hours of the library should be clearly visible from outside the library. Talking kiosks could also be considered to help all users find their way in the library. Directional signs should be erected in nearby streets and town centres to guide the public to the library.

The Ambience of the Library

The library should provide a physical setting for the library service that is inviting to the public and that provides:

- Adequate space to store and display the library collection.
- Adequate, comfortable and attractive space for the public to make proper and convenient use of the library's services.
- Sufficient space for the library staff to carry out their duties in an efficient and comfortable setting.
- Adequate space and flexibility for the future.

The climate of the library should be maintained at a comfortable temperature, using efficient heating and air conditioning. Humidity control helps to protect the stock as well as increasing the comfort of the library. Larger libraries may include a café open either throughout the opening hours of the library or for special occasions. Such facilities are sometimes contracted out to a commercial provider.

Electronic and Audiovisual Equipment

As a major function of the public library is to bridge the gap between the information rich and the information poor, it has also to provide access to the necessary electronic, computer and audiovisual equipment. This will include personal computers with Internet access, public access catalogues, microform readers, tape recorders, slide projectors and equipment for the visually and physically handicapped. Wiring should be up-to-date and easily accessible for alterations at a later date. It should also be inspected regularly.

Safety

Every effort should be made to ensure that the library is safe for the public and the staff. Smoke and fire alarms should be provided and security protection for staff and resources. The location of fire extinguishers and emergency exits should be clearly marked. Staff should be trained in first aid and first aid supplies be made readily available. Evacuation drills should be carried out regularly. The library manager in co-operation with the emergency services should prepare a disaster plan to be put into action in the event of a serious incident, for example fire.

Parking

Where users travel to the library in private vehicles there should be sufficient safe and well lit parking either at or close to the library with appropriately identified spaces for persons with disabilities. If bicycles are a common mode of transport, secure cycle racks should be provided outside the library.

COLLECTION DEVELOPMENT

The public library should provide equality of access to a range of resources that meets the needs of its users for education, information, leisure and personal development. The library should provide access to the heritage of its society and develop diverse cultural resources and experiences. Constant interaction and consultation with the local community will help to ensure this objective is achieved.

COLLECTION MANAGEMENT POLICY

Each public library system requires a written collection management policy, endorsed by the governing body of the library service. The aim of the policy should be to ensure a consistent approach to the maintenance and development of the library collections and access to resources. It is imperative that collections continue to be developed on an ongoing basis to ensure that people have a constant choice of new materials and to meet the demands of new services and of changing levels of use.

In the light of today's technological advances, the policy must reflect not only a library's own collections but also strategies for accessing information available throughout the world. The policy should be based upon library standards developed by professional staff related to the needs and interests of local people, and reflecting the diversity of society. The policy should define the purpose, scope and content of the collection, as well as access to external resources.

Content of the Policy

The policy may proceed from statements of universal applicability that are relevant to all library services, through more general statements that are relevant to particular countries, or regions, to statements that are specific to particular library services and could include the following elements.

Universal

- Article XIX of the Declaration of Human Rights.
- IFLA statement on freedom of access to information.
- Statements on intellectual freedom, free access to library collections.
- Freedom of information.
- Consideration of the International Copyright Convention.
- IFLA/UNESCO Public Library Manifesto.

General

- Purpose of the collection management policy and its relation to the corporate plan of the library service.

- Long and short term objectives.
- Access strategies.
- History of the collection and/or library service.
- Identification of relevant legislation.

Specific

- Analysis of community needs.
- Priorities of the library service.
- Parameters of the collection, including special collections and collections for special needs, such as multicultural material, literacy and resources for people with disabilities.
- Selection and discard principles and methods.
- Budget allocation.
- Responsibility within the organisation for collection development, selection and discard.
- Access to electronic resources including online access to periodicals, databases and other information sources.
- The role of the library as an electronic gateway to information.
- Co-operative relationships with other libraries and organisations.
- Preservation and conservation policies.
- Auditing requirements: accessioning, recording, control, discard, sale or disposal.
- Financial accountability.
- Donations policy.
- Complaints procedure.
- A resource management plan assessing the current and future needs of the collections.
- Review and assessment of the policy.

This is not an exhaustive list but an indication of some of the issues that may be included.

RANGE OF RESOURCES

The public library should provide a wide range of materials in a variety of formats and in sufficient quantity to meet the needs and interests of the community. The culture of the local community and society must be reflected in the resource collection. Public libraries must keep abreast of new formats and new methods of accessing information. All information should be as readily available as possible, irrespective of format. The development of local information sources and resources is vital.

Collections

The following categories of library materials may be represented in a typical public library, although this list is not exhaustive:

- Fiction and non-fiction for adults, young adults and children.

- Reference works.
- Access to databases.
- Periodicals.
- Local, regional and national newspapers.
- Community information.
- Government information, including information by and about local administrations.
- Business information.
- Local history resources.
- Genealogical resources.
- Resources in the primary language of the community.
- Resources in minority languages in the community.
- Resources in other languages.
- Music scores.
- Computer games.
- Toys.
- Games and puzzles.
- Study materials.

Formats

The following formats may be included in a public library collection although this list is not exhaustive and new formats are continually appearing:

- Books, both hard and soft covers.
- Pamphlets and ephemera.
- Newspapers and periodicals including cuttings files.
- Digital information through the Internet.
- Online databases.
- CD-ROM databases.
- Software programmes.
- Microforms.
- Tapes and compact discs (CDs).
- Digital versatile discs (DVDs).
- Videocassettes.
- Laser discs.
- Large print materials.
- Braille materials.
- Audio books.
- Electronic books.
- Posters.

COLLECTION DEVELOPMENT

Collections complement services and should not be seen as an end in themselves, unless their specified primary purpose is the preservation and conservation of resources for future generations. Large collections are not synonymous with good collections, particularly in the new digital world. The relevance of the collection to the needs of the local community is more important than the size of the collection.

Collection size is determined by many factors, including space, financial resources, catchment population of the library, proximity to other libraries, regional role of the collections, access to electronic resources, assessment of local needs, acquisition and discard rates, and policy of stock exchanges with other libraries.

Criteria for Collections

The main criteria for collections should be:

- A range of resources that cater for all members of the community.
- Resources in formats that enable all members of the community to make use of the library service.
- Inflow of new titles.
- Inflow of new books.
- A wide range of fiction categories and of non-fiction subject coverage
- Provision of non-print resources.
- Access to external resources such as libraries of other institutions, electronic databases, local societies, government departments or the community's knowledge of oral cultures.
- Discard of old, worn and outdated books, non-print resources and information sources.

COLLECTION MAINTENANCE PRINCIPLES

Public libraries of any size will contain materials in a variety of formats. Collection maintenance applies equally to all materials whatever their format. Materials on open access should be in good physical condition and contain current information.

A smaller, high quality stock will result in more usage than a large stock with a high proportion of old, worn and outdated books, in which newer titles can be lost among mediocre stock. Using outdated reference material can result in the user being given inaccurate information.

Materials in electronic formats complement book collections and will replace them in certain areas. Reference works and periodicals on the Internet and on CDs are viable alternatives to printed formats.

Acquisition and Discards

The library collection is a dynamic resource. It requires a constant inflow of new material and outflow of old material to ensure that it remains relevant to the community and at an acceptable level of accuracy. Acquisition rates are more significant than collection size. The acquisition rate is often determined largely by the size of the resource budget.

However, it can also be affected by other factors, for example:

- The number of books published in local languages.
- The population served.
- The level of use.
- The multicultural and linguistic diversity.
- Age distribution of the population.
- Special needs such as people with disabilities or older persons.
- Access to online information.

The size and quality of the stock should reflect the needs of the community.

Reserve Stocks

It may be necessary to maintain a collection of older and lesser-used books on shelves not directly accessible to the public. This should only contain books that have a current or future use and that cannot be replaced or found in any other format. This may include special subject collections that are used on a regular, if limited, basis and out-of-print fiction.

Books that contain outdated information or are in poor condition and can be replaced, should be discarded and not held in a reserve stock. It is efficient to maintain a cooperative reserve with other libraries. The maintenance of a reserve stock should be a regular and on-going activity. The availability of a wide range of information on the Internet and electronic databases reduces the need for public libraries to keep extensive reserve stocks.

Interlending

No library or library service can be self-sufficient in stock, and an efficient and effective interlibrary loan system should be an essential part of every public library service. Within a library service with several outlets a regular programme of exchange of stock between libraries makes maximum use of the stock and provides users with a greater variety of titles from which to choose.

STANDARDS FOR BOOK COLLECTIONS

The following proposed standards relate to book collections. Local and financial circumstances could lead to variations in these proposed standards. Where resources are severely limited these may be regarded as target figures and medium and long-term strategies should be developed to work towards achieving these standards in the future.

In the smallest collections materials for children, adult fiction and adult nonfiction may be provided in equal proportions. In larger collections the percentage of non-fiction titles will tend to increase. These ratios can vary according to the needs of the local community and the role of the public library.

Relevant collections to serve the needs of young adults should be developed. Where the library has a strong educational role this is likely to be reflected in the composition of the stock. Where reliable population figures are not available alternative methods of developing standards are needed. The estimated size of the community served, the size of the library, and the number of current and anticipated users can be used as a basis for developing standards for the size of the collection. Comparisons with a number of existing libraries serving communities of a similar size and make-up can be used to determine a target figure for the size of the collection and the resources needed to maintain it.

STANDARDS FOR ELECTRONIC INFORMATION FACILITIES

The development of standards for the provision of electronic information facilities is at an early stage.

Current standards include the following:

- An assessment is required of the demographics of the community in the catchment areas of proposed new library developments to determine the initial mix of collections. The development of local and regional standards should be undertaken to take account of variations in the catchment population to be served by the new library. The following recommended standards relate to book provision. Additional standards will be required for other media.

Establishment Phase

A basic collection should be established in new libraries to serve the needs of the general population within the catchment area. A sufficient range and depth of resources to meet general needs should be the aim at this stage rather than comprehensive coverage. The interlibrary loan system should be at its peak utilisation during this phase to supplement the developing collections. In some countries materials from a national or provincial centre are used to supplement the local stock. Where this is not achievable a modest growth plan should be implemented to establish this minimum base stock over a period of three years. Access to electronic information sources should also be included in this phase of development.

Consolidation Phase

The objective under this phase is to achieve growth in the stock size, range and depth. Special conditions of the population are taken into account and collections developed to meet the more in-depth needs of the population served. The book discard factor comes into play and the collection growth rate decreases as discards begin to offset acquisitions.

Steady-state Phase

The collections meet the needs of the community in depth, range and quantity. The quality of collections is maintained by acquisition rates matching discard rates. New formats are accommodated within the collections as they become available and access is provided to the widest possible range of resources through the use of technology.

Content Creation

The service should become a content creator and a preserver of local community resources. Content creation includes publication of information booklets and the development of web content by providing access to information about the library or held by the library in printed formats. This positions the library as an electronic gateway by the creation of links to useful web pages.

ACQUISITION AND DISCARD RATES

The following examples suggest the size of book stock for communities of different sizes.

Scenario 1:

- Established library service serving 100 000 population.
- Median book stock of 200 000 volumes.
- Annual acquisition rate of 20 000 volumes.

Scenario 2:

- Established library service serving 50 000 population.
- Median book stock of 100 000 volumes.
- Annual acquisition rate of 11 250 volumes.

Scenario 3:

- Established library service serving 20 000 population.
- Median book stock of 40 000 volumes.
- Annual acquisition rate of 5000 volumes.

Small Libraries and Mobile Libraries

The general acquisition rates would be inadequate to meet the needs of small libraries and mobile libraries where stock numbers are limited. All libraries require a certain minimum stock in order to provide a sufficient range of books from which users may make their selection. The acquisition rate of 250 books per 1000 population may not be relevant in the smallest service points, where physical limitations may reduce stock levels below the minimum recommended level of 2500 volumes. In these cases the acquisition rates, renewal rates or exchange rates should be based upon the collection size rather than the population served, and be in the order of 100 per cent or more per annum. An efficient interlibrary loan system is essential in these situations.

Special Collections

General acquisition and discard rates may not be relevant to some parts of the collection or to particular special collections or where special circumstances prevail. In these cases the collection policy must reflect the special needs.

Particular examples of these exceptions are:

- *Indigenous Resources* – the public library has a role in maintaining and promoting collections of resources related to the culture of indigenous people and ensuring access to them.
- *local History Resources* – material relating to the history of the locality should be actively collected, preserved and made available.
- Libraries in Communities with a high proportion of particular groups, *e.g.*, children, retired people, young adults, indigenous peoples, ethnic minorities or unemployed people should reflect the needs of these groups in their collections and services.
- Reference Collections – older reference material may need to be retained to provide historical data for research.

HUMAN RESOURCES

Staff are a vitally important resource in the operation of a library. Staff expenses normally represent a high proportion of a library's budget. In order to provide the best possible service to the community it is necessary to maintain well trained and highly motivated staff to make effective use of the resources of the library and to meet the demands of the community. Staff should be available in sufficient numbers to carry out these responsibilities. The management of library staff is itself an important task. All staff should have a clear understanding of the policy of the library service, well-defined duties and responsibilities, properly regulated conditions of employment and salaries that are competitive with other similar jobs.

THE SKILLS OF LIBRARY STAFF

The public library is a service aimed at all members of the community who will have varied and changing needs. Public library staff will require a range of skills and qualities, including interpersonal skills, social awareness, teamwork and leadership and competence in the practices and procedures of the organisation.

The fundamental qualities and skills required of public library staff can be defined as:

- The ability to communicate positively with people.
- The ability to understand the needs of users.
- The ability to co-operate with individuals and groups in the community.
- Knowledge and understanding of cultural diversity.
- Knowledge of the material that forms the library's collection and how to access it.
- An understanding of and sympathy with the principles of public service.
- The ability to work with others in providing an effective library service

- Organisational skills, with the flexibility to identify and implement changes.
- Imagination, vision and openness to new ideas and practice.
- Readiness to change methods of working to meet new situations.
- Knowledge of information and communications technology.

STAFF CATEGORIES

The following categories of staff are found in public libraries:

- Qualified librarians.
- Library assistants.
- Specialist staff.
- Support staff.

In some countries there is an additional category of library technician, or para-professional, with an intermediate level of qualifications. Staff in all categories may be appointed on either a full-time or part-time basis. In some countries two or more people share a single post, a practice known as job-sharing. This provides the opportunity to appoint and retain experienced staff who may not be able to work full-time.

Qualified Librarians

Qualified librarians are professional staff who have undertaken a course of study in librarianship and information studies to degree or post-graduate level. A librarian designs, plans, organises, implements, manages and evaluates library and information services and systems to meet the needs of the users of library and information services in the community.

This will include collection development, the organisation and exploitation of resources, the provision of advice and assistance to users in finding and using information and the development of systems that will facilitate access to the library's resources. Qualified librarians will have regular contact with members of the community that they serve.

In order to fulfil its functions staff with expertise in specific areas, for example, children's librarians, information officers and reference librarians should form part of the professional team. The following is a list of some of the duties of the qualified librarian.

This list is not exhaustive nor is it likely that the qualified librarian will undertake all these activities simultaneously:

- Analysing the resource and information needs of the community.
- Formulating and implementing policies for service development.
- Planning services to the public and participating in their delivery.
- Retrieving and presenting information.
- Answering reference and information enquiries using appropriate material.
- Assisting users in the use of library resources and information.

- Developing services to meet the needs of special groups, *e.g.*, children
- Creating and maintaining databases to meet the needs of the library and its users.
- Designing library and information services and systems to meet the needs of the public.
- Developing acquisition policies and systems for library resources.
- Managing and administering library and information systems.
- Cataloguing and classification of library materials.
- Promoting library services.
- Evaluating library services and systems and measuring their performance.
- Selecting, evaluating, managing and training staff.
- Budgeting.
- Strategic planning.
- Participation in planning the design and layout of new and refurbished libraries and of mobile libraries.
- Keeping up-to-date with current developments in librarianship and information services including the relevant technologies.

Library Assistants

The duties of the library assistant include routine circulation functions and operational library tasks such as shelving, shelf-checking, processing library materials, data entry, filing, secretarial support and basic level reader enquiry work.

Library assistants are the staff the public will come into contact with most frequently. It is essential, therefore, that they should have a high level of interpersonal and communication skills and receive appropriate training.

Specialist Staff

Large public library services may employ specialist staff to carry out specific functions, for example, computer system managers, administrative, financial, training and marketing staff. Specialist staff may have a qualification in their specialism rather than in librarianship.

Support Staff

Support staff include caretakers, cleaners, drivers and security staff. They carry out important functions, which contribute to the smooth operation of the library service. They should be regarded as an integral part of the library's staff.

The Composition of the Staff

The composition of the staff should, as far as possible, reflect the make-up of the population it serves. Where, for example, there is a significant number of people from a particular ethnic group within the community, the library staff should include members of that group. This demonstrates that the library is a service for all members of the local community and will help to attract users from all sections of the public.

ETHICAL STANDARDS

Public library staff have a responsibility to maintain high ethical standards in their dealings with the public, other members of staff and external organisations. All members of the public should be dealt with on an equal basis and every effort must be made to ensure that information provided is as full and accurate as possible.

Librarians must not allow their personal attitudes and opinions to determine which members of the public are served and what materials are selected and displayed. The public must have confidence in the impartiality of the library staff if the library is to meet the needs of all members of the community. Library associations in some countries have developed codes of ethics, which can be used as models to introduce similar codes elsewhere.

THE DUTIES OF LIBRARY STAFF

The operation of a library should be a team effort with a close working relationship between all members of staff. It is important, however, that staff are used primarily for tasks related to their skills and qualifications. It is a wasteful use of scarce resources, for example, for qualified librarians to regularly carry out routine circulation functions. For the same reason it is not necessary to have a qualified librarian in every library regardless of size or circulation rate.

Small libraries open for limited hours do not require the continuous presence of a qualified librarian. They should however be under the supervision of a member of the qualified staff. All users should have the opportunity of access to a qualified librarian. Staff should have a written contract at the time of their appointment, which clearly states their duties and responsibilities. These should not be changed without consulting the member of staff involved.

STAFFING LEVELS

The number of staff required in each library service will be affected by a range of factors, for example, the number of library buildings, their size and layout, the number of departments within each building, the level of use, services provided beyond the library and requirements for specialist staff.

Where some services are provided or supplemented by a regional or national central agency this will have an impact on the number of staff required at local level. The level of available resources is also a critical factor.

Allowing for these and other local differences the following basic staffing level is recommended:

- These are basic recommended levels, which will be affected by local circumstances. Where reliable population figures are not available staffing levels can be related to the size of the library, the range of its functions and the number of users. Another method of developing an appropriate staffing level for a library service is to carry out bench-marking with libraries of comparative size and similar characteristics.

EDUCATION OF LIBRARIANS

Qualified librarians will have undertaken a degree or post-graduate course in librarianship and information studies at a school of librarianship. To ensure that they remain in touch with the latest developments, librarians should maintain a process of continuing professional development on a formal and informal basis. It is important that public librarians maintain close links with the schools of librarianship in their country and are fully aware of course content. Whenever possible they should participate in the work of the schools, for example, by contributing lectures, assisting in interviewing of prospective students and other appropriate forms of co-operation.

TRAINING

Training is a vital element of the activities of a public library. There must be a planned and continuous programme of training for staff at all levels, which should include both full-time and part-time staff.

The rapid developments in information technology make the need for regular training even more essential, and the importance of networking and access to other information sources should be included in training programmes. Specialist and support staff should receive induction training in the functions and purpose of the public library and the context in which it operates. In budgeting for the implementation of new systems, an element should be included for training.

In large library services a post of training officer should be created to plan and implement the training programme. To ensure funds are available for training a set percentage of the budget should be earmarked for this function. This level of funding for training should be maintained at times of budget reductions as the need for a well-trained staff is very important in such circumstances.

Mentoring

An effective and economical method of training is to introduce a system of mentoring. New staff work with a more experienced colleague who provides guidance and training. The mentor should be able to advise the new member of staff about issues relating to their work and employment. A checklist of the training provided by the mentor should be maintained to ensure that it is carried out effectively.

Contacts

In addition to in-service training staff should be given opportunities to attend short courses and conferences relevant to their ability to carry out their work. They should be encouraged to be active members of the relevant library association, as this creates links with other library staff and provides opportunities for an exchange of ideas and experience. It may also be possible to arrange staff exchanges with staff in other libraries, either in the same country or in a similar library in another country, which can be a valuable experience for all those involved.

Career Development

In order to motivate and retain skilled staff opportunities for career development should be available at all levels. A scheme of performance appraisal should be in place that provides staff with an evaluation of current performance and guidance in improving and developing their skills. It also presents an opportunity to review career progression.

WORKING CONDITIONS

All library staff should have satisfactory working conditions and the conditions of employment should be clearly stated in the contract given to the new member of staff when they are employed. Salaries should be at a level appropriate to the level of work being undertaken and competitive with other similar jobs in the community.

Health and Safety

The health and safety of staff must be a high priority and policies and procedures put in place to reduce risks.

Consideration should be given to:

- Good working conditions for staff.
- Ergonomically designed furniture and equipment.
- Availability of technical aids for employees with special needs and disabilities.
- The drawing up of evacuation plans and their testing on a regular basis.
- Identified health and safety risks being rectified at the earliest opportunity.
- Ensuring that all equipment and cabling conforms with recognised safety standards.
- The establishment of a staff health and safety committee.

- Appointment and training of staff as first-aid officers and fire wardens.
- Provision of safety devices for staff, particularly when staff work at nights or away from the library.
- Providing advanced driver training for staff who drive library vehicles
- Protective clothing when required.
- Limiting the weight of cartons and loads on book trolleys.

Public libraries are often open for long hours including evenings and weekends. In creating work schedules for staff every effort should be made to ensure that their working hours provide them with adequate time off at appropriate times for social activity. It is vital that good labour relations are maintained and fostered with staff.

Anti-social Behaviour

In any building freely accessible to the public, staff will occasionally encounter users who behave in an unpleasant and anti-social manner. Staff should be trained in how to deal with such situations and have alarm systems that can alert other staff. Senior staff should be immediately available to assist staff and full records of such occurrences should be kept. A support system involving other staff and people from other agencies, for example, social workers, should be developed to help library staff deal with these situations.

VOLUNTEERS

Where a library uses volunteer help from individuals in the community to assist library staff, a written policy should be in place defining the tasks of these volunteers and their relationship to the library operation and staff. Volunteers should not be used as a substitute for paid staff.

THE MANAGEMENT AND MARKETING OF PUBLIC LIBRARIES

A successful public library is a dynamic organisation working with other institutions and with individuals to provide a range of library and information services to meet the varied and changing needs of the community. To be effective it requires experienced, flexible and well trained managers and staff able to use a range of management techniques. This chapter deals with the key elements of public library management.

MANAGEMENT SKILLS

Management of a public library involves a number of different skills:

- Leadership and motivation.
- Maintaining effective relationships with governing and funding bodies.

- Planning and policy development.
- Building and maintaining networks with other organisations.
- Budget negotiations and management.
- Management of library resources.
- Staff management.
- Planning and development of library systems.
- The management of change.
- Marketing and promotion.
- Community liaison and lobbying.

Leadership and Motivation

The library manager has a vital role in advocating the value of public libraries as an integral part of an international, national and local infrastructure. He/she must promote public libraries to politicians and key stakeholders at all levels in order to ensure they are aware of the importance of public libraries and to attract adequate funding for their maintenance and development.

The library manager must ensure that governing authorities are informed of new developments that may impact on public library services and are made aware that the library service is a key player in providing access to the delivery of new services. The library manager is responsible for the motivation of staff and bringing energy, vitality and strength into the library service and its staff.

The manager also plays a key role in managing the development of physical facilities and ensuring that the most effective use is made of resources, including information technology, to enable the library service to meet the library and information needs of the community.

Relationships with Governing and Funding Bodies

To achieve its goals the public library needs adequate and sustained funding. It is very important that the library manager establishes and maintains a close and positive relationship with the bodies that govern the library service and provide its funding.

The library manager as head of the public library service should have direct access to and involvement with the board or committee that is directly responsible for the library service. As well as formal meetings there should be regular informal contacts between the library manager and members of the governing body, and they should be kept well informed about the library service and current and future developments.

Planning and Policy Development

Planning ensures that:

- The library responds to the needs of the community.
- The governing body, management and staff understand what the library is trying to achieve.

- Community funds are spent in an effective and responsible manner.
- Continuity of service is maintained regardless of changes of personnel.
- The library expands the expectations of the community as new services are developed.
- The library is able to respond effectively to change.

The determination of public library goals, short and long term objectives, strategies and performance measurement is necessary to ensure equitable, effective and efficient library service provision with access for all sectors of the community. Strategic and operational plans require formulation, documentation and adoption. Planning should not take place in isolation but in conjunction with the governing and funding bodies, the library staff and the actual and potential clients served.

A strategic plan must be user-focused and should include the following elements:

- Review of achievements.
- Examination of needs.
- Identification of priorities and short term goals.
- Development of strategies for achieving goals.
- Identification of critical success factors.
- Budget allocation.
- Deployment of resources to achieve optimum performance.
- Measurement and evaluation of input and output performance.
- Reassessment of needs and policies.

Operational Planning

An operational plan is necessary to ensure that the activities of the library service are focused on achieving the priorities and goals identified in the strategic plan.

The plan should reflect the following elements:

- A focus on service to users.
- The implementation of the priorities and goals of the strategic plan.
- The formation of operational elements of the agreed strategies.
- The development of clearly identified goals with manageable and achievable time frames.
- The definition of achievable outputs for the level of inputs.
- The participation of library staff who carry out the activities.
- The allocation of responsibility to identified staff members for achieving outputs.
- A programme for monitoring, evaluating and amending the plan at regular intervals.

By-laws or local legislation, specific policies and procedures may be needed and should be properly formulated, documented and communicated to all those involved. Business and marketing plans, market research, community needs analyses and surveys of users and non-users should form part of the management process. Planning for the future should advocate positive change and flexibility and aim to minimize the impact of transition on services, staff and users. To achieve effective change, all stakeholders must be involved in the change process.

BUILDING AND MAINTAINING NETWORKS

The library manager must ensure that networks are developed and maintained at national, regional and local level, using information and communications technology wherever appropriate. This enables a very wide range of resources to be brought to the user at a local level.

The library manager should also develop good working relationships with other agencies in the community, for example, schools, other local government departments and voluntary organisations for the benefit of the users, and to confirm the public library's role at the centre of community activity. The library manager should, wherever possible, ensure that the library takes an active and positive role within the corporate structure of the parent organisation.

FINANCIAL MANAGEMENT

Financial management and financial planning are vitally important to ensure that the library operates efficiently, economically, and effectively.

In order to achieve these aims the library manager should:

- Look for ways of improving levels of funding from national, state or local government or from other sources.
- Prepare 3–5 year business plans based on the library's long term plans, including bids for the required funds.
- Allocate funds to support activities identified in the library's policy statement and based on the priorities previously determined.
- Establish partnerships, where appropriate, for co-operative purchasing to maximize the use of available funds.
- Undertake activity-based costing to determine the cost of activities and programmes and to facilitate future planning.
- Maintain a policy for the sustainable renewal of plant and equipment.
- Evaluate and implement automated techniques, wherever appropriate, to improve efficiency and effectiveness.
- Introduce systems that will ensure that all staff with responsibility for any part of the budget will be fully accountable for the expenditure of funds for which they are responsible.
- Improve staff productivity and efficiency.

MANAGEMENT OF LIBRARY RESOURCES

A major element of a library's budget is expenditure on library materials. The library manager should ensure that these funds are spent properly and in accordance with the agreed priorities of the library and that the materials are maintained and made available so that they can be of maximum benefit to the library user.

STAFF MANAGEMENT

Library staff are a vital element of the library's resources and staff salaries are normally the largest part of the library budget. It is very important that the management of staff should be sensitive, consistent and based on sound principles if staff are to work most effectively and with high levels of motivation and job satisfaction.

The following are important elements of staff management:

- An equitable procedure for staff appointments. Job and person specifications should be drawn up prior to a post being advertised. Interviews should be conducted in a way that is fair to all applicants. Appointments should be based solely on professional judgement and suitability for the post and not be prejudiced by any other factors.
- Good communication between staff at all levels. Managers should review internal communication systems regularly to make sure staff are well informed about the policies and procedures of the library service.
- The opportunity for staff to participate in the development of policy and operational procedures. Initiative should be encouraged to make the best use of the skills and experience of staff. By bringing staff into the decision-making process they will feel they 'own' the policies and procedures of the service.
- The principles of affirmative action, including the creation of nominated positions for special needs areas, may be adopted.

PLANNING AND DEVELOPMENT OF LIBRARY SYSTEMS

To make the most effective use of resources the public library will require a variety of systems, for example circulation control, financial management, internal communications. The library manager should ensure that appropriate systems are introduced, making use of specialist staff for their development where necessary. Staff must be given adequate training in the use of such systems, the effectiveness of which must be reviewed regularly.

THE MANAGEMENT OF CHANGE

In common with many other organisations public libraries are going through a period of unprecedented and ongoing change as a result of the rapid development of information technology and social and demographic change. This presents tremendous opportunities for the public library, as information provision is one of its primary roles. It also presents challenges to managers and staff to ensure that change can be introduced with the maximum effectiveness and the least stress on staff and the organisation. Library managers must be aware of the issues arising from continuous and fundamental change and establish methods of dealing with them.

Planning for the Future

Library managers should be aware of developments both within and outside librarianship that are likely to have an impact on service development. They should make time to read and study so that they can anticipate the effect of changes, particularly technological, on the future shape of the service. They should also ensure that policy-makers and other staff are kept informed of future developments.

DELEGATION

The library manager in charge of the public library service has ultimate responsibility for the service, in conjunction with the governing body. However, all library staff with responsibility for any resources of the library, whether materials, staff or library premises, have a managerial role, and this should be recognised by the library manager and the member of staff concerned. They should be given appropriate managerial training and participate in the policy development of the library whenever possible. Managerial responsibility should be delegated to staff at an appropriate lower level. It should be made clear what responsibilities are being delegated and what the reporting mechanism to senior managers is. Staff must be given training to enable them to carry out the delegated responsibilities effectively. A planned system of delegation makes best use of the skills and experience of a wide range of staff and provides opportunities for professional development. It also increases the number of people fully involved in the development and operation of the library service, improves job satisfaction and prepares staff for promotion when opportunities arise.

MANAGEMENT TOOLS

A wide range of management tools can be used in a public library. Their relevance will depend on a number of factors, for example, the cultural context, the size and character of the service, the management style of other departments in the same organisation and available experience and funding.

The following are however important tools for public libraries in almost any situation:

- Community needs analysis.
- Monitoring and evaluation.
- Performance measurement.

Community Needs Analysis

In order to provide services that meet the needs of the whole community, the public library has to establish the extent of those needs. As needs and expectations will change, this process will need to be repeated at regular intervals, perhaps every five years. A community needs assessment is a process in which the library collects detailed information about the local community and its library and information needs. Planning and policy development are based on the results of this assessment and in this way a match between services and needs can be achieved. In some countries the preparation of a community needs assessment is a legislative requirement of the local authority.

The information to be collected will include:

- Socio-demographic information about the local community *e.g.*, the age and gender profile, ethnic diversity, educational level.
- Data about organisations in the community, *e.g.*, educational institutions, health centres, hospitals, penal establishments, voluntary organisations.
- Information about business and commerce in the locality.
- The catchment area of the library, *i.e.*, where library users live in relation to the library.
- Transport patterns in the community.
- Information services provided by other agencies in the community.

This is not an exhaustive list and further research would be required to establish what information is needed to form a community needs assessment in each situation. However, the principle of preparing a community profile, which will enable the librarian and the governing body to plan service development and promotion on the needs of the community, is an important one whatever the local context.

The assessment should be complemented by regular customer surveys to establish what library and information services the public wants, at what level, and how they judge the services they receive. Survey work is a specialist skill and, where resources are available, a more objective result will be gained if the survey is carried out by an external organisation.

Monitoring and Evaluation

As the library service moves towards its goals, management must be accountable in terms of financial control and the monitoring and evaluation of library activities. Management must continually monitor the performance of the library service to ensure that strategies and operational results are achieving the set objectives. Statistics should be collected over time to allow trends to be identified. Community needs and satisfaction surveys, and performance indicators are valuable tools in monitoring the achievements of the library. Techniques should be developed to measure the quality of the services provided and their impact on the community.

All programmes and services should be evaluated on a regular basis to ascertain whether they are:

- Achieving the objectives and declared goals of the library.
- Actually and regularly provided.

- Meeting the needs of the community.
- Able to meet changing needs.
- In need of improvement, new direction or redefinition.
- Adequately resourced.
- Cost effective.

Procedures and processes operating within the library also require constant evaluation and revision to increase efficiency and effectiveness.

Performance Indicators

The availability of reliable performance information is a necessary tool for evaluation and the improvement of efficiency, effectiveness and quality of service. The collection of statistics related to resources, staff, services, circulation, activities, etc., will provide data for planning, show accountability and assist informed management decision-making. The following key performance indicators may be used to evaluate and monitor the achievement of the library's objectives.

Usage indicators:

- Loans per capita.
- Total library visits per capita.
- Membership as a percentage of the population.
- Loans per item, *i.e.*, turnover resources.
- Reference enquiries per capita.
- Loans per opening hour.
- Number of accesses to electronic services and other non-print materials.

Resource indicators:

- Total stock per capita.
- Provision of terminals/personal computers per capita.
- Provision of online public access computers (OPACs) per capita.

Human Resource Indicators:

- Ratio of full time equivalent (FTE) staff to population
- Ratio of professional staff to population.
- Ratio of full time equivalent (FTE) staff to library use.

Qualitative indicators:

- User satisfaction surveys.
- Enquiries satisfied.

Cost indicators:

- Unit costs for functions, services and activities.
- Staff costs per functions, *e.g.*, books processed, programmes.
- Total costs per capita, per member, per visitor, per service point, etc.

Comparative indicators:

- bench-mark statistical data against other relevant and comparable library services, internationally, nationally and locally.

In addition to the collection and analysis of input and output service statistics, the unstated needs of non-users should be established by carrying out market research including the use of focus groups and community surveys. Where reliable population statistics are not available it becomes more difficult to develop reliable performance indicators. Use can be made of estimated population totals, the comparison of costs with user and visitor statistics and bench-marking with other libraries with similar characteristics.

Performance Measurement

Performance measurement has been used in public libraries for some years. Measurements or performance indicators are established to measure the input to libraries, that is the resources devoted to the whole or particular services, and the output: what is achieved as a result of the activity being carried out.

For example, the establishment of an enquiry service for users requires the input of staff, materials, equipment and floor space. The output is the number of enquiries received, the number satisfied, the level of use made of the resources and the use of other services, for example, the reservation service, arising from the original activity. These measures can then be compared each year to see if the effectiveness of the library service is improving. Computer technology makes performance measurement a simpler task and enables sophisticated models of library use to be established and used in service development.

Performance measurement should be a planned process carried out with consistency over a period of time. Further information about library performance indicators can be found in ISO 11620:1998 *Information and documentation. Library performance indicators*. Another way of gaining a useful indication of the success of a library service is to compare key input and output measurements with other public libraries of similar size and characteristics. This is usually known as benchmarking and is a useful adjunct to performance measurements carried out internally.

MARKETING AND PROMOTION

Library managers can use marketing techniques to enable them to understand the needs of their users and to plan effectively to meet those needs. The library should also promote its services to the public to ensure that they are kept informed of the services provided to meet their library and information requirements.

Marketing and Promotion Policy

The library should have a written communications, marketing and promotions policy to enable it to undertake a planned promotion of its services to the public. The policy should include a marketing and communication strategy and methods of evaluating promotional programmes.

Marketing and Promotion Plan

To enable the library to achieve its marketing strategy, a coherent marketing and promotion plan should be developed based on the agreed policy.

It could include the following elements:

- Making positive use of print, electronic and communications media.
- Displays and exhibits.
- Effective interior and exterior sign-posting.
- Regular publications and the preparation of resource lists and pamphlets.
- Reading and literacy campaigns.
- Designing campaigns to meet the needs of people with physical and sensory disabilities.
- Book fairs.
- Library web sites.
- Links to and from related web sites and portals.
- Friends of the library groups.
- Annual library week celebrations and other collective promotional activities.
- Special years of celebration and anniversaries.
- Library listings in the telephone book and other community directories.
- Fund-raising activities and campaigns.
- Public-speaking activities and liaison with community groups.
- Special library publications, *e.g.*, history of the library, history of the community.

This list is not exhaustive and other elements can be added depending on local circumstances.

Working with the Media

Library staff should be trained to use communication media to promote the library service and respond to media enquiries. They should be able to write articles for local newspapers and prepare press releases. They should be familiar with the techniques of speaking and being interviewed on radio and television.

They should also be able to promote the library and its services via computer and telecommunication networks including the creation of library web sites.

Community Support

The library managers must ensure that the community is aware of the importance of the library service. Municipal, regional and national funding bodies should be made fully aware of the important place that the library occupies in the community, and support its development.

Gaining Community Support

The library should have an agreed policy and a sustained programme for developing community support.

This can include:

- Maintaining a 'friends of the library' organisation for fund-raising and general support.
- Working with community advocates in support of major initiatives such as new buildings and services.
- Forming liaisons with community groups to enhance parts of the collection or strengthen specific services.
- Working with groups that wish to speak out on behalf of the library service and its development.
- Participation by library staff in activities aimed at increasing awareness of the variety and value of the library service.

The support of the community also depends on the library delivering the services it has promised to deliver.

Advocacy

The library should have established and adopted written policies that define its role in generating public support for the library service. A well informed public can provide valuable support for the public library service and actively promote it within the community. Getting people to talk positively about the library and its services is one of the most effective marketing tools. Lobbying involves interaction with decision-makers to secure specific objectives at an appropriate point in the legislative, policy-making or budget process.

Working with Governing Bodies

Library managers should meet at least annually with the library's principal governing and funding body to review the library's services, development plans, achievements and obstacles. Librarians should look for as many opportunities as possible to involve its governing body in its major activities. Events such as the opening of a new library, the launching of a service, the installation of public Internet access, the opening of a new collection and the inauguration of a fund-raising drive can be used for this purpose.

Participation in Community Life

One of the most effective promotional strategies is the participation of wellinformed library staff and committee or board members in community activities.

Examples include:

- Presenting book and activity reviews on radio and television.

- Working with adults and children's literature and cultural groups.
- Writing a newspaper column.
- Supporting literacy organisations and campaigns.
- Participating in the activities of local organisations.
- Assisting with school-based initiatives.
- Participating in local history and genealogy societies.
- Being a member of a service organisation, *e.g.*, Rotary.
- Visiting local organisations to promote the library service.

Evaluation

The library should carry out a regular evaluation of its marketing and promotion programme and ensure the results of the evaluation are taken into account when planning future programmes.

2

Content-Based Information Retrieval and Libraries

INTRODUCTION

The explosion of literature in the form of micro documents on the one hand and the growing number of users demanding more specialised literature/ information on the other hand have led to information scientists to develop an efficient information retrieval systems for the realisation of retrieval suspend on advances in technology and its associated techniques.

Database creation of the library resources and the sophistication in indexing techniques has eased the problems of storing and handling of large volumes of data. At the best, it enhanced the retrieval of the items. Therefore, the focus of the information scientist for the recent past few decades is on the design and development of more powerful information search and retrieval systems.

INFORMATION SYSTEMS

Computer based information system is categorised into:

- Information Storage and Retrieval systems.
- Database Management systems.
- Management Information Systems.
- Decision support systems.

All these systems exhibit similarities to some extent in the area of information processing but differ in their functionalities.

OBJECTIVES OF THE INFORMATION RETRIEVAL SYSTEM

M.L. Pao, "user's input is an important consideration to be incorporated in setting the overall objective of the system for service point of view", as follows:

- Information content of information resources collected.
- Utility of information resources.
- Users.
- Documentary resources.

- Performance resources.
- Economics.

Information retrieval (IR) is the main purpose of any library. The librarian is a nodal point in the IR process and in the traditional library.

INFORMATION SEARCH AND RETRIEVAL IN DIGITAL LIBRARIES

Information search and retrieval of an object from digital library software is a vital feature of the system. The search enables quick retrieval of information. Search services help users to select relevant information from digital library. Digital library's service provides fast access to exact information which is looking for. The success of a search service in digital library relies on the implementation of a powerful retrieval engine and a flexible user interface for metadata support. The Search interface allows users to do "across database" searching without having to modify a query. Search service also covers searching beyond text to multiple media formats, including images, sound and video.

The retrieval formats should be flexible and should provide users to manipulate the search process and results by retrieving search history, adjusting search strategies, editing and sorting search results and choosing preferable delivery formats. Users should also be able to get statistical analysis of the searches they have carried out. Many digital libraries provide different search options to users based on the metadata fields along with the facilities for federated search across a number of digital libraries.

Most digital libraries offer search by Boolean operator, keyword, and phrase and field searches. In the case of information retrieval, evaluation is often focused on the effectiveness of a result set in a specific search. Browsing and searching are two major paradigms for exploring digital libraries. Boolean, proximity and truncation searching are commonly used in digital libraries. They are often provided as separate services. Searching is popular because it is useful when appropriate search keyword are unavailable to users.

The use of Information Retrieval is motivated by an information need. This information need can be explicitly or implicitly verbalised. In a 'real world' setting the person seeking information (*i.e.*, the user) formulates such a question and poses it to an expert. The expert calls upon his internal representation of the knowledge space and external documents and formulates answers. From the answers received the user extracts relevant points and gives feedback to the expert. This "conversational loop" can also be found in the use of an Information Retrieval System (IRS).

As the IRS is not capable to understand the information need, thus, an abstraction matching in the IRS is needed. This abstraction is called query. Analogously to the expert, the IRS formulates an answer based upon the internal representation of the knowledge space and external documents. The answer is composed of documents perceived relevant or links to such documents.

Boolean Model

This simple retrieval model, which was adopted by many early commercial bibliographic systems, is based on set theory and Boolean algebra. The advantages are the intuitiveness of the concept of a set and the precise semantics of Boolean expressions, which form the queries. The major drawback of the model is that the retrieval is based on a binary decision leaving relevancy of the search result. Moreover it is often not simple to translate an information need into a Boolean expression. In this model, index terms are either considered present or absent in a document, resulting in binary weights. Due to this binary value for relevancy, no partial match to the query is defined. So, if a document includes only one index term it is considered not relevant. As a result, the Boolean model often retrieves very less or too many documents.

Vector Model

The vector model heeds the fact that the use of binary weights is limiting and proposes a framework that allows a partial match. Non- binary term weights are used to compute a degree of similarity. The resulting set of documents retrieved is returned in decreasing order of this degree of similarity. Though various term weighting techniques exist, only the main idea of the most effective techniques shall be discussed. The basic idea is to separate a document collection into two parts to satisfy the information need. One of the parts is composed of the objects related to the information need while the other is not. To accomplish this separation clustering techniques are utilised. Two sets of features are used to discern sets of related elements from those that are not.

The first set of features describes the intra-cluster similarity while the second describes inter-cluster dissimilarity. The improved retrieval performance resulting from the term-weighting scheme is one of the main advantages of the vector model. The second main advantage is the partial matching strategy and the fact that the cosine ranking function sorts the documents according to the degree of similarity to the query. Efficient implementations for the vector model are possible. Finally, the vector model allows easy relevance feedback. Disadvantages of the vector model include the fact that the term "independency" is not fully given. In fact, real term independency might hurt the retrieval process. Moreover, syntactic information remains unconsidered.

Generalised Vector Space Model

The term "independence" in the classic vector space model is addressed by the generalised vector space model. The independence is interpreted as pair-wise orthogonality among the index term vectors that forms the vector space. Wong *et al.*, proposed an alternate view which leads to the generalised vector space model. In this model, the index term vectors are assumed linearly independent but are not pair wise orthogonal. As such, they are not as like in the classic vector space model where the vectors compose the basis of the space. They are composed of smaller components derived from the collection. These pair wise orthogonal so called min-term vectors compose the bases of the space. The main advantage of the generalised vector space model is the dependence of the index term. However, this dependence is still a controversial issue. Thus, the advantage of the generalised vector space model in practical situations is not yet proved. The main drawback is the high cost of computation due to the fact that the number of min-terms might be proportional to the number of documents in the collection.

INFORMATION RETRIEVAL CONCEPTS IN DIGITAL LIBRARIES

Digital libraries rely on effective retrieval methods with easy access to the information. Thus, the success of digital libraries is depends on the quality of retrieval. Research in the IR has traditionally been important in the research pertaining to the digital libraries. One important topic in this context is the search in distributed collections. As the document collection is managed by different organisational units or even the document collections of different digital libraries are used, the interfaces and functionality of these systems are supposedly inhomogeneous. Gutl part of the difficulties in this context are the variable IR methods and interfaces, like representation and relevance ranking, as well as the scope of the search results.

Another difficulty is the merging of the individual results and the inter-system ranking. The second important topic in this context is the multimedia content in document collection. Baeza-Yates *et al.*, states the need for suiting query languages for different media, like a visual query for image search. In a multimedia environment, the task is even more complex, as the combined search in different media, as Gutl points out.

BROWSING FEATURES

The browsing feature is important for retrieval of neither information that is nor already known in part. Browsing enables people to look through a digital library and discover things that they had no previous knowledge of.

Users should be able to browse digital objects by:

- Author/ Creator/ Contributor.
- Title of the document/ article/ book.
- Issue Date/ Date of Publication.
- Collection.
- Communities.
- Subject browsing.
- Publisher wise browsing.
- Table of contents browsing.
- Multi-dimensional browsing.

SEARCHING FEATURES

Searching in any digital library is one of the important aspects. Hence, it is necessary to know what type of search features are supported by the software.

While, evaluating the software it is necessary to do functional testing of the software, i.e., determining the extent to which a digital library, in whole or in part, is able to perform desired operations.

- Full text searching.
- Boolean (AND, OR, NOT) searching.
- Basic Search.
- Advanced search.
- Truncation/Wild card searching.
- Exact words/phrases searching.
- Proximity searching.
- Stemming search.
- Fuzzy search.
- Phonetic search.
- Case sensitive.
- Case insensitive.
- Boosting the term.
- Range searching.
- Expand search.
- Lateral search.
- Multilingual search.
- Refine search.

QUALITY OF SEARCH RESULTS

Generally IR systems have to cope with a vaguely described information need of the user; the results of an IR process are not exactly matches to this information needs, but are ranked by relevance. The evaluation of the precision of this answer is called information retrieval evaluation. Besides, the performance measures generally important for a software system, like response time, space, and the like, this retrieval performance is the key to an IR system.

Information retrieval evaluation is performed by querying a standardised reference collection. These reference collections consist of a set of documents, a set of example information needs, and corresponding sets of relevant documents. The relevant documents for example information requests are determined by experts. For a given retrieval strategy, the documents retrieved are compared to the set of relevant documents determined by experts. The similarity between these two sets is quantified by the test collection's evaluation measure and leads to the goodness of the tested retrieval strategy.

RECALL AND PRECISION

Recall and precision are basic evaluation parameters. The drawback of recall and precision is the fact that the examination of all documents of the answer set is assumed. This, however, is contrary to the usual fact that the user is presented only a part of the retrieved documents, ranked by the degree of relevance.

Thus, the recall and precision values vary as the user proceeds through his examination of the retrieved documents. In order to record this development, a precision versus recall curve is plotted. Usually recall and precision values resulting from averaging various queries are used to compare the performance of IR systems.

Such average recall versus precision plots trade the advantage of a better overview on the overall retrieval performance for that fact that single mavericks remain undetected. In various situations, such as, to discover the superiority between the single value summary of the recall and precision plots. One possibility is to calculate the Average Precision at Seen Relevant Documents. To that end the precision figures obtained are averaged after each new relevant document which is observed.

CONCLUSION

Digital libraries present still another new environment for information retrieval, presenting new and different challenges and an expanded research agenda. Some of these challenges arise from the nature of the content in digital libraries, others from the nature of the tasks performed and the characteristics of the users of digital libraries. Like the Web, digital libraries incorporate mixed data types. The data may be structured, semi structured, or unstructured; and incorporate text, images, video, and audio information. Information retrieval from this mix of structure and formats is relatively unstudied, since research has usually been based on an assumption of a homogenous collection, and metadata, where available, has been treated as unstructured text.

How do we incorporate evidence from these multiple sources to create an ordered list? Since digital libraries are by definition often distributed or federated systems, another level of complexity is added by the need to make retrieval from multiple sites and multiple collections transparent to the user. Given multiple sites, we need to give priority for search to sites with the highest probability of success. Searching on multiple sites leads to a data fusion problem as the system must integrate and rank information from different datasets, with different data and metadata. Furthermore the importance and challenges of distributed document collections have been analysed. Though the Web may appear as a distributed digital library at the first glance, there are numerous differences. Information Retrieval system which presents the basic layer applied in conceptualisation processes and discussed the models of the IR system.

3

Factors Influencing the Number of Computers in Libraries

INTRODUCTION

Good things come in small packages. The old adage holds true for this new contribution to the field of library and information science by Wilson. At just under 200 pages, this book is densely packed with the information that library technicians and assistants need to understand the impact that computers and the Internet have had on library systems and procedures. The State Library of New South Wales in Sydney, Australia, is the current location for Wilson's professional work and where she manages the digital and library systems. Clearly, her years of experience have informed her writing. A colleague encouraged her to put her extensive knowledge and experience in information technology and library systems into book form. In doing research for her book, she discovered older texts on library automation and realised the paradigm-shifting impact that the Internet has had on library operations.

As Wilson states in her preface, the "audience for this book is both practicing and new library technicians and library assistants." As with any discipline, library and information science has its own set of acronyms and field-specific jargon. By including acronym and abbreviation definitions with other terminology, Wilson attempts to remove the barriers to understanding.

Wilson begins her book with a discussion of the history of the Internet and its protocols and applications. The service areas in which the Internet is used in library settings are then reviewed, and public services, reference services, technical services, and collection development are covered. In fact, the overall strategy Wilson has employed to arrange the contents of her book follows this format. Chapter titles include "The Internet," "Integrated Library Management Systems," "Acqui-sitions," "Cataloguing," "Circulation," "Serials," and "The Online Public Access Catalogue." Organizing the information in the book in this manner is helpful for readers, as new and changing technological innovations and systems are applied to each service area in which a library technician or assistant might work.

A chapter on resource sharing explains the world of consortial arrangements for the sharing of library materials and automated systems for interlibrary loan of print as well as electronic sources. Two very informative chapters are instructive on successful search processes and skills for both online databases and the Internet, including some brief explanations for creating Web-based content with codingin hypertext markup language (HTML).

Finally, "Future Directions," looks at the trends in the use of computers in libraries. Wilson predicts the continued emphasis on the digitization of collections and the ensuing increased access to the collections by the public at large. Challenges in access and licensing will need to be addressed by developing new ways to preserve and manage those electronic resources. Libraries may consider purchasing integrated library management systems that are more open sourced in nature.

Bibliographic standards, including MARC, may be revised and expanded to increase their applicability. As the use of the online public access catalogue (OPAC) continues to decline, libraries will need to come up with new and innovative ways to deliver responses to users' information requests, such as through the creation of portals.

Wilson has an interesting take on the reference desk versus information desk quandary. She states that efforts in the 1990s to "rename reference and research departments and desks as Information Services have reversed". She sees the focus of each as separate, with information residing in the physical structure and reference and research assistance moving beyond the physical building into the online environment.

Lastly, library technicians and librarians alike must make efforts to keep up with the changing technologies required in their individual settings. This reviewer conducted an informal survey with two instructors who teach in library technician programmes, one in a face-to-face environment and the other through a correspondence course format. The instructor of the "in-seat" course on computers in libraries is using Wilson's book for the first time. She also will draw from the *Neal-Schuman Library Technology Companion: A Basic Guide for Library Staff* by Burke. Her opinion is that the Burke book is more comprehensive but more expensive.

The correspondence course instructor was not familiar with Wilson's book. He used *Introduction to Automation for Librarians* by Saffady. However, he felt that it contained too much detail for his students' needs. He has also chosen Burke's book for his course. The Burke book provides questions for review at the end of each chapter, as does Wilson's, but Burke places his list of recommended readings with the chapters, instead of in a bibliography at the end. The content of Burke's book does not seem to be as practically organized. Wilson's treatment, arranged by service area, is much more approac-hable and useful.

While this book is highly recommended for use as a textbook in library technician programmes,its scope is necessarily, and as claimed, an introduction to the topic. To truly understand and take to heart all that was presented in this volume, one must transfer the knowledge to practice.

Development of Digital Libraries in India: Socio–economic Problems and Prospects

Information and Communication Technology (ICT) has revolutionized the information management activities in the academic libraries during the past few years developing the Information Society. The Information society demands that all the relevant technologies; that are involved in Access to Information, Information collection, information processing, consolidation, repackaging and retrieval be merged so as to evolve an integrated system; capable of providing diversified services. Advances in Computer Storage and telecommunication methods, online access to databases, electronic journals, electronic knowledge banks, direct document delivery, teletext, teleconferences, bulletin boards, Radio Frequency Identification Systems, Compact discs, Digital Versatile Disks, Networks including Internet, Smart Cards etc. are revolu-tionary developments in the last two to three decades that have brought a great change in the collection, communication, storage and management of information. As a result, the organization structure and functions of the libraries are changed. The libraries are termed as Conventional Libraries, Digital Libraries and Hybrid Libraries.

DIGITAL LIBRARIES

The digital libraries may be defined as the new way of carrying out the functions of libraries, encompassing new type of information resources new approaches to acquisition; new methods of storage and preservations; new approaches to classification and cataloguing; intensive use of electronic systems and networks; and dramatic shifts in intellectual, organizational and electronic practice. Digital library is system providing a community of users with coherent access to a large, organized repository of information and knowledge.

The digital library is not just one entity, but multiple sources seamlessly integrated. The digital libraries endow with a structural and planned entrance to information stuffing in a dispersed environment and assist users in searching evaluating and utilizing resources irrespective of their format. Improved information retrieval and enhanced document delivery capabilities are widely acclaimed strength of digital library in a networked environment through internet and internet in library and information center.

The US Association of Research Libraries Identified Five Elements Common to All Definitions of Digital Libraries:

- The digital library is not a single entity;
- The digital library requires technology to link the resources;

- Linkages between digital libraries and information services are transparent;
- Universal access to digital library must be a goal;
- Digital library collections are restricted to document surrogates but include digital artifacts that have no printed equivalent.

To use the digital format, the user population must be literate, preferably computer literates with Internet facilities. Further, there is adequate resources such as Electricity power generation in the country, higher standard of living, proper telecommunication facilities etc. Today, in developing country like India the numbers of digital libraries are growing. Further, in various academic libraries, conversion and digitization of the collection from print to electronic format is also progressive. But there are many social, economical and political problems, which have become obstacles to the development of the digital libraries in India.

SOCIO-ECONOMIC PROBLEMS

Of Course any of the nations in the world, is not completely free from its own problems like unemployment, Poverty, Illiteracy, Crime etc. In other words, every nation is having its own problems. Similarly, India is also having certain Political, Economical and Social problems. These problems are the hindrance to the development of the digital libraries in India. They are discussed as under:

PROSPECTS AND DEVELOPMENTS

The Government of India, Union Territories and State Governments already, formulated and executed various plans and policies to curb the growth rate of population, Literacy programmes, increase in standard of living, to achieve full employment, developing Agriculture and industrial sector, Improvement in Power Production and Supply, to increase the exports, etc., due to such efforts, India is developing in all respects.

Even though many of social, political and economic problems proved to be obstacles and problems for the development of the digital libraries in India, the Government of India and different state governments initiated Information Technology projects to develop the application of Information Technology in administration and planned to educate the people. Of course, it is not possible to discuss all the measures and policies undertaken by the Government of India for encouraging use of ICT and web in India.

Following are a few policies of the Government of India and developmental trends in promoting use and development of the Information and Communication Technology, electronic media and Information Sector. The Prime Minister of India constituted a National Task Force on Information Technology and Software Development in May 1998 with the purpose of formulating a long term National IT Policy to convert India into an IT software superpower.

As it is not possible to mention all the developments, the developments stated in the following paragraphs are the only a few achievements made in different departments and parts of the Central Government:

- A Land Information System has already started using Geographic Information System (GIS) and remote sensing to help the farmers to plan their activities and facilitate decision making and planning at the local level. Government is also planned for a System known as "Agriculture Online" for the exchange of Ideas and Information between farmers, Agricultural Scientists, traders and exporters.
- The higher education institutions consisting of 310 Universities and academic institutions 16,000 affiliated colleges were networked with the help of INFLIBNET, an Inter-University Centre of UGC. In 28th December 2003, UGC-INFONET Electronic Journal Consortia was started by INFLIBNET and at present it is providing 4000+ Research Journals to 100+ Universities in India Online. The INFLIBNET is conducting regular training programmes in different applications of ICT to the information professionals. Now a days, every Indian University is using internet for its activities such as Admissions, Exams, Results etc.
- Postal Department got computerized and several new services based on Internet were introduced. E-Post is a new service available at 204 Post Offices at present in a few States — Andhra Pradesh, Gujarat, Goa, Kerala, and Maharastra to cater the postal service to the persons who do not have a PC or internet facilities. E-Bill post is a multipurpose web based facility for paying telephone bills, mobile phone bills, Electricity bills etc, online. Speed Net is another internet based tracking and tracing service for the customer at Speed Post Counters. The computerization and VSAT connectivity for the postal service is under progress.
- India has the fifth largest telecom network in the world comprising of 61.09 million telephone connections (basic and mobile) and over 1.48 million public call offices. There are over 16 million cellular subscribers in the country, growing at the rate of about 1 million per month. The number of digital electronic exchanges was around 300 increased to 36,772 in July 2003.
- The software and IT industry has grown significantly during 2003-04 by emerging as one of the fastest growing sectors with a growth rate of over 30.5% and an export value of US$12.5 billion. According to the National Association of Software and Services Companies (NASSCOM) estimate in 2002-03, the total revenue from the India IT market was ₹317 billion against ₹291 billion in 2001-02. The Indian IT and electronics industry recorded a production of ₹80,884 Crore during 2001-02 as compared to ₹68,450 Crore during 2000-01

showing a growth of 18 per cent. Software export alone has jumped by approxi-mately 10 per cent to ₹36,500 crores during 2001-02 from ₹3,700 Crore during 1996-97 with a compound annual growth of about 60 per cent.

- The Government of India computerized different departments under E-Governance programme. The departments are Customs and Excise department, Banks, Railways, Air Transport, Income Tax, and Telecommunications etc. so as to facilitate Online Transactions. Similarly the Electronic Voting Machines were introduced in Elections.
- Government also taken up development programmes in Mass Media, such as Television, Radio, Newspapers and Magazines. Electronic Media developed in such a way that the actual situations at various polling booths in Lok Sabha Elections 2004 were telecasted live through Video-Conferencing. Many of the News Channels in Television using Video Conferencing for Live Telecast of the News and Other events.
- The Collections of many of the Academic Libraries and Special Libraries were digitized already and can be accessible through the networks. Several Information Systems and Networks are developed connecting libraries. NISSAT developed several Metropolitan Area Networks such as ADINET, BONET, CALIBNET, DELNET, etc. The Other networks are INFLIBNET, ERNET, SIRNET, etc. Through networking of the Libraries, many libraries are sharing their resources online.
- On September 20, 2004 Geo-Synchronous Satellite Launch Vehicle (GSLV) is launched from Sriharikota and put EDUSAT, the educational Satellite. The EDUSAT is set to bring about revolutionary changes in distance education, converting homes into virtual classrooms. Through EDUSAT, a teacher from a television studio can simultaneously address hundreds of students in different schools and colleges in the various parts of the country if the educational institutions have a terminal to receive the programme. The EDUSAT has 12 transponders, which are capable of generating regional beams covering different parts of India. It is estimated that programmes from EDUSAT can reach 1,000 class rooms and 50,000 students.
- According to Essential Science Indicators (ESI) during 1997-2001, India produced 76,970 papers as against 1,14,894 by China. The Number of Scientific papers is just one measure of state of research in the country.
- India has joined a select club of six advanced countries with the Pune-based Centre for Development of Advanced Computing (C-DAC) developing the country's Super computer. CDAC developed

'Param Padam' a super computer which promises the creation of a seamless computing platform for supercomputing at an affordable price in the international market.

- India also ahead in production and export of the electronic products,

The Impact of Information Technology on Library Anxiety: The Role of Computer Attitudes

Computers and information technologies have experienced considerable growth over the past two decades. As such, familiarity with computers is rapidly becoming a basic skill and a prerequisite for many tasks. Although not every college student is equally prepared for the rising demand of computer skills in the information age, computer literacy is increasingly becoming a gatekeeper for students' academic success.

Gaps in computer literacy and skills can leave many students behind not only in their academic achievement but also in their future job-market success. The unprecedented pace of technological change in the development of digital information networks and electronic services in recent years has helped to expand the role of the academic library. Once only a storehouse of printed materials, it is now a technology-laden information network where students can conduct research in a mixed print and digital-resource environment, experience the use of advanced information technologies, and hone their computer skills. Yet, many students are struggling to cope with the changes brought on by the rapid advances of information technologies.

Academic libraries of various sizes have spent a large percentage of their material budget on electronic commercial content, and the trend will continue. These days, college students are faced with the choices of ever-changing modes of electronic accessing tools, interfaces, and protocols along with the traditional print resources in the library.

The fact that the same journal article may be available in multiple vendors' aggregator sites (such as EBSCOhost and Gale Group) makes the navigation through these bibliographic databases more complex and challenging. Relevant sources must be identified and navigation protocols must be learned before appropriate information and contents can be found. Furthermore, students still have to search the library online catalogue to find out if the journal or book is available in the library and, if not, know how to make an interlibrary loan request either on paper or electronically.

Anxiety levels can be high and patience levels can be low at varying times of conducting library research. That students experience various levels of apprehension when using academic libraries is not a new phenomenon. Indeed, the phenomenon is prevalent among college students in the United States and many other countries, and is widely known as library anxiety.

Mellon first coined the term in her study in which she noted that 75 per cent to 85 per cent of undergraduate students described their initial library experiences in terms of anxiety. Feelings of anxiety stem from either the relative size of the library; a lack of knowledge about the location of materials, equipment, and resources of the library; how to initiate library research; or how to proceed with a library search. Library anxiety is an unpleasant feeling or emotional state with physiological and behavioural concomitants that come to the fore in library settings.

Typically, library-anxious students experience negative emotions, including ruminations, tension, fear, and mental disorganization, which prevent them from using the library effectively. A student who experiences library anxiety usually undergoes either emotional or physical discomfort when faced with any library or library-related task. Library anxiety may arise from a lack of self-confidence in conducting research, lack of prior exposure to academic libraries, the inability to see the relevance of libraries to one's field of interest, and lack of familiarity with library equipment and technologies.

Library anxiety is often accorded special attention because of its debilitating effects on students' academic achievement. Although many students continue to experience high levels of library anxiety, it is likely that the new technologies and electronic databases in libraries have led to students experiencing other forms of negative affective states. In particular, it is likely that library anxiety experienced by students is, in part, a function of their attitudes towards computers.

Consistent with this assertion, Mizrachi and Shoham and Mizrachi reported a statistically significant relationship between library anxiety and computer attitudes. They noted in their research that home and work usage of computers, computer games, word processors, computer spreadsheets, and the Internet are all related to the dimensions of library anxiety found among Israeli students to varying degrees. Similarly, Jerabek, Meyer, and Kordinak found levels of computer anxiety to be related to levels of library anxiety for both men and women. These studies focused exclusively on undergraduate students.

However, no study has examined this relationship among graduate students, a population that uses the academic library more than any other student population. Over the past fifteen years, a large body of research literature on computer attitudes has been generated. In particular, many researchers have studied the relationship between computer attitudes and computer use. The importance of beliefs and attitudes towards computers and technologies is widely acknowledged.

Students' computer attitudes arguably impact their willingness to engage in computer-related activities in colleges and universities where effectively using library electronic resources represents an increasingly important part of college education. Negative computer attitudes may inhibit students' interests in learning to use the library resources and thereby weaken their academic performance levels, while at the same time elevating levels of library anxiety. McInerney, McInerney, and Sinclair observed that negative perceptions about computers among student teachers may accompany feelings of anxiety, including worries about being embarrassed, looking foolish, and even damaging the computer equipment.

Further, there is often a negative relationship between prior experience with computers and computer anxiety experienced by individuals. Until recently, library anxiety has only been interpreted in the context of the library setting—that is, a phenomenon that occurs while students are undertaking library tasks. Researchers defined library anxiety as "an uncomfortable feeling or emotional disposition, experienced in a library setting, which has cognitive, affective, physiological, and behavioural ramifications."

At the same time, unprecedented technological advancement has had a profound impact on the products and services offered by academic libraries. Students now are able to conduct sophisticated library searches from the comfort of their homes. It is clear that the construct of library anxiety needs to be expanded in the new library and information environment, incorporating into its definition other variables that are relevant for the changing library and information context. Because many library users spend a significant portion of their time using computer-based technologies to conduct information searches, it is natural to ask, to what extent does library anxiety stem from students' prior attitudes and experiences with computers and library technologies?

However, with the exception of the studies conducted by Mizrachi and Shoham and Mizrachi on Israeli undergraduate students, this link has not been examined. Thus, the present study investigated the relationship between computer attitudes and library anxiety in the rapidly changing library and information environment. As such, the current enquiry replicated the works of library activists by examining the degree to which computer attitudes predict levels of library anxiety among graduate students in the United States. It was expected that findings from this study would help to increase the understanding of the construct of library anxiety. Indeed, research in this area has become critical in higher education where educators are responsible for graduating students with the skills necessary to thrive and to lead in a rapidly changing technological environment in the twenty-first century.

METHOD

Participants

Participants were ninety-four African American graduate students enrolled in the College of Education at a historically Black college and university in the eastern U.S. All participants were solicited in either a statistics or a measurement course at the time that the investigation took place. In order to participate in the study, students were required to sign an informed-consent document that was given during the first class session of the semester. The majority of the participants were female. Ages of the participants ranged from twenty-two to sixty-two years (Mean = 30.40, SD = 8.75).

Instruments and Procedure

All participants were administered two scales, namely, the Computer Attitude Scale (CAS) and the Library Anxiety Scale (LAS). The CAS, developed by Loyd and Gressard, contains forty Likert-type items that assess individuals' attitudes towards computers and the use of computers.

This instrument consists of the following four scales, which can be used separately:

- Anxiety or fear of computers;
- Confidence in the ability to use computers;
- Liking or enjoying working with computers; and
- Computer usefulness.

Loyd and Gressard reported coefficient alpha reliability coefficients of.86.91.91, and.95 for scores pertaining to computer anxiety, computer confidence, computer liking, and total scales, respectively.

For the present study, the score reliabilities were as follows:

- Computer anxiety.84 (95 per cent confidence interval CI =.79.88);
- Computer confidence.81 (95 per cent CI =.75.86);
- Computer liking.89 (95 per cent CI =.85.92); and
- Computer usefulness.76 (95 per cent CI =.68.83).

The LAS, developed by Bostick, contains forty-three 5-point Likert-format items that assess levels of library anxiety experienced by college students.

It also contains the following five subscales:

- Barriers with staff;
- Affective barriers;
- Comfort with the library;
- Knowledge of the library; and
- Mechanical barriers.

A high score on any subscale represents high levels of anxiety in that area.

Jiao and Onwuegbuzie, in their examination of the score reliability reported on LAS in the extant literature, found that it has typically been in the adequate to high range for the subscale and total-scale scores.

Based on their analysis, Onwuegbuzie, Jiao, and Bostick concluded that "not only does the produce scores that yield extremely reliable estimates, but also these estimates are remarkably consistent across samples with different cultures, nationalities, ages, years of study, gender composition, educational majors, and so forth."

For the current investigation, the subscales generated scores for the combined sample that had a classical theory alpha reliability coefficient of:

- .89 (95 per cent CI =.85.92) for barriers with staff,
- .84 (95 per cent CI =.79.88) for affective barriers,
- .53 (95 per cent CI =.37.66) for comfort with the library,
- .62 (95 per cent CI =.48.73) for knowledge of the library, and
- .70 (95 per cent CI =.58.79) for mechanical barriers.

Analysis

A canonical correlation analysis was conducted to identify a combination of library anxiety dimensions (barriers with staff, affective barriers, comfort with the library, knowledge of the library, and mechanical barriers) that might be simultaneously related to a combination of computer-attitude dimensions (computer anxiety, computer liking, computer confidence, and computer usefulness).

Canonical correlation analysis is used to examine the relationship between two sets of variables whereby each set contains more than one variable. In the present investigation, the five dimensions of library anxiety were treated as the dependent multivariate set of variables, and the four dimensions of computer attitudes formed the independent multivariate profile. The number of canonical functions (factors) that can be produced for a given dataset is equal to the number of variables in the smaller of the two variable sets.

Because the library-anxiety set contained five dimensions and the computer-attitude set contained four variables, four canonical functions were generated. For any significant canonical coefficient, the standardized canonical-function coefficients and structure coefficients were then interpreted. Standardized canonicalfunction coefficients are computed weights that are applied to each variable in a given set in order to obtain the composite variate used in the canonical correlation analysis.

As such, standardized canonical-function coefficients are equivalent to factor-pattern coefficients in factor analysis or to beta coefficients in a regression analysis. Conversely, structure coefficients represent the correlations between a given variable and the scores on the canonical composite (latent variable) in the set to which the variable belongs.

Thus, structure coefficients indicate the degree to which each variable is related to the canonical composite for the variable set. Indeed, structure coefficients are essentially bivariate correlation coefficients that range in value between-1.0 and +1.0 inclusive. The square of the structure coefficient yields the proportion of variance that the original variable shares linearly with the canonical variate.

EMERGENCE OF DIGITAL LIBRARY SERVICES IN INDIA

The digital library is an electronic or virtual library where information is selected, acquired, processed, organised, stored and retrieved in digital form. The developed countries have already digitized their libraries. The developing countries are in the process of digitization of their libraries.

The users of digital libraries are the universal users who should have facility to access to all created and acquired digital sources of information in the form of electronic text, image, map, sound, video and multimedia. Thus the digital libraries are attributed to electronic databases and capable of handling large data and servicing users effectively in resource sharing environment.

DIGITAL LIBRARY INFRASTRUCTURE

A digital library has certain technological requirements such as:

- Locally developed database
- Local library system with adequate personal computers having LAN and CD-ROM Drives.
- Electronic mail service
- Network connection to have access to other data bases
- Various functions to coordinate, manage the entry and retrieve data.
- Multimedia Kit
- Well trained manpower
- Computer Hardware with Audio-Visuals, Video Conferencing Kit, Pentium Web Server, Laser Printer, Scanner, Barcode Scanner, Barcode Printer, Digital graphic printer and UPS.
- Software and its accessories.

The super structure of digital library rests on some important factors like:

- The human need for information especially that is timely and relevant and
- Accumulation of information, and all the supporting infrastructure that includes research community, professional associations, libraries and publishers, advances in methods and technology leading to developments in net working, information science, information storage and retireval, hyper-media, human-computer interaction, artificial intelligence and other areas of computer science that make digital libraries a possible proposition.

Digital Library Services

Always library services are followed by library works. But now the advancement in information technology has brought changes in the concept of traditional library work as well as service. The recent trend and change in the information related field especially in collection, storing, processing and dissemination of information have resulted in to the evolution of digital libraries. Now most of the reference books like encyclopaedias, dictionaries, directories, hand books, etc. are published in electronic form. Similarly about 50% of the existing secondary resources like abstracting and indexing services are available in electronic form for example, Chemical Abstracts Service, Index Medicus, Engineering Index. At present most of the digital libraries have been highlighted mainly on providing access to diverse digital information resources. The provision of personalized reference and information services is considered as one of the important characteristics of the library and information profession.

However reference services include:

- Either finding the required information on behalf of users, or assisting users in finding information themselves;
- Instruction in the use of library resources and services, and
- User guidance in which users are guided in selecting the most appropriate information sources and services.

In this changing scenario, reference works of modern libraries are influenced by a set of related technical and economic factors, especially the increasing use of technology and techniques. To cite some examples, the recent developments in the INTERNET and in Web Technologies have brought significant changes in the concept of traditional reference services and a number of web-based "expert services", that are now offered by many non-library organisation. Information services are provided to the users on demand as well as anticipating the user needs including various forms of current awareness and selective dissemination of informa-tion services. Such services are provided to the users to keep them abreast of the latest developments in their field of interest through on-line search services in digital information environment, even by the non-library organisations like Dialog.

PERSONALIZED SERVICES

Most of the researches on digital library development have focused on access to and retrieval of digital information but they have overlooked the personalized service aspects, as primary goal of library information services. However the technology and information resources, on their own, can not make up an effective digital library. On priority basis the personalized services in a digital library environment would help the users to find information resources available in a digitally chaotic world.

In a Delphy study it was revealed that:

- The primary roles library professionals play in digital libraries include organization of macro and micro-documents, selection and acquisition and acting as gateways to the provision of information services, and
- The best reasons of developing a digital library include: increasing access to information serving and users needs and bringing organization to the unstructured universe of electronically available information.

However there is a demand for end-user instruction on the use of digital libraries and the digital library professionals who are subject specialists should help users to formulate disciplinary search strategies and provide assistance in developing new digital information resources.

Web-based reference and information services

Several reference and information services are now available on the web and many of these services are provided by non-library organization. Also a web site that provides a categorized listing of libraries that offer real-time reference services using specific software, live interactive communication tools, call centre management software, bulletin board services and other INTERNET technologies. Of course, most of these services are designed for registered users of some specific libraries in-digital information environment. HodgKin has made an aggregation approach to reference and information services. According to which more than one reference sources is made accessible digitally and also it is more practicable in terms of visibility and profitability than a single reference source.

Further:

- It's reference service becomes much better known to professional users and thus easier to find, by providing access to several reference works,
- By tackling a number of reference works at a time, the publishers can achieve economics of scale in production and development
- The user's search session is likely to be much more powerful and fruitful.

Online reference and information services can be broadly categorized into three groups:

- Those from publishers, database search services and specialized institutions
- Those provided by libraries and/or experts through the INTERNET and
- Where the users need to conduct a search and find information through the web.

Also they have listed several online information services that belong to the first category comprising various current awareness, and SDI services, for example:

- Contents pages services from commercial publishers, such as Elsevier's Contents Direct Service and IDEAL Alert from Academic Press.
- Information on new books available for free from publishers and vendors, such as Wiley Book, Notification Service from Wiley, and Amazon.com.
- SDI services from online search services providers, such as Dialog (Dialog Alerts)
- Current contents and ISI Alerting Services from ISI and so on.

However some of these services, particularly the contents page services from publishers of journals, are free, while for others, such as Dialog Alerts, or Current Contents from ISI, users need to register and pay for the services. There are also some web-based reference services where users need to conduct a search in order to answer their reference query.

For example:

- The Internet Public Library,
- Britannica,

- The Electric Library and
- The Internet Library for librarians.

Most of these web-based reference services are available free of charge but some charge a small amount as fee. For example, the Electric Library charges an annual subscription fee.

SEARCH ENGINE SERVICES

Sherman made a comparision among three web-based reference services like:

- Ask Jeeves basically a search engine, is useful for complex questions and is a good choice for searchers who lack Boolean or other searching skills, because of its strong natural language parser and question-and-answer template structure. The users can ask a question on a given topic and it comes up with a list of questions on the same or similar topics; the users can select any of those predefined questions and then it provides further answers. It processes each query syntactically and semantically and then its answer processing engine provides the question template response. When the users click on a response, the answer-processing engine retrieves the answer template that contains links to the answer locations. Thus Ask Jeeves can help users to select a query from a pre-defined set of queries on a given topic. So it is considered as a useful model for reference and infor-mation services in digital libraries.
- The Electric Library is an excellent choice for a serious researcher in need of timely content from a wide array of otherwise unavailable sources. It provides access to various on line reference sources and allows users to either select a specific source or conduct a search on a range, or all, of the sources.
- Information please is a suitable tool for students and other researchers, as an authoritative source of facts and pointers for further investigation.

Moreover Chowdhury and Chowdhury have suggested some other useful search engine services like:

- Web help.com that claims to offer real time search assistance with a real live expertany time, day or night,
- About.com is a service that shows a number of pre-defined categories related to a search topic given by the user.

For example, a simple search on 'e-commerce' not only produces a list of sites, but also provides a set of topics related to e-commerce, such as e-commercedefinition, e-commerce security, the advantages and disadvantages of e-commerce, e-commerce statistics and so on.

DIGITAL REFERENCE SERVICES FOR GENERAL PUBLIC

Today web-based digital reference services are being provided by a network of public libraries. The users make their query on an enquiry page and it is automatically routed to one of the participating libraries which records it as an e-mail message to the user containing necessary and available information. For example, the British Library, London provides special reference services for business, scientific, technical, medical, patent and environmental information which range from answering simple queries up to complex questions involving on line data base searches.

Of course some of these services are free if users put simple queries, but for complex queries users need to pay at the prescribed rate which covers the costs of staff time, on-line searching and value added tax (VAT). The British Library provides STM (Science, Technology and Medicine) Search Service for which users need to pay. Similarly New York Public Library (Digital Library), American Library of Congress, Alexandria Digital Library, Berkeley Digital Library, Bibliotheque Nationale de France, Victoria State Library, Vatican Library, etc. are some other libraries which provide digital reference services for users.

DIGITAL REFERENCE SERVICES OF ACADEMIC LIBRARIES

Web based reference services are also now being provided by academic libraries, Recently a study report on web-based reference services reflects the current practices of digital library services in seventy academic libraries of USA.

The study shows that university libraries allow their patrons to put reference questions in a variety ways: 99% offer e-mail reference, 96% offer reference services by appointment while 29% of the libraries offer real-time virtual reference. These libraries use *customer relationship management* (CRM) software packages for providing web-based reference services in the virtual reference environment.

CO-OPERATIVE DIGITAL LIBRARY SERVICES

The rising cost of digital reference sources and its proper processing by the trained manpower and also the initial infrastructural investment for introducing new services in libraries have influenced different organisations to choose a co-operative model of digital reference services. As a result some co-operative projects have been launched for providing web-based reference services to the users who can ask for such services from a remote location at any time.

The Library of Congress, USA has launched the collaborative digital reference service with a mission to provide the users, anywhere anytime through an international digital network of libraries.

This network has three main components consisting of:

- Member Profiles
- Request Manager-Software for entering, routing and answering reference queries; and
- Knowledge Base-a searchable database of questions and answer sets.

In this network a participating library sends a question to the system on behalf of a user and the system looks in to the knowledge base for a match. Then a reply is sent to the relevant library through e-mail.

Incase the question and its corresponding answer is not found in the knowledge base, then it is passed on to the Request Manager where using the profiles of participating libraries and their information resources collection, expertise etc, relevant query is passed on to an appropriate library. This library receives the query, finds an answer and sends back reply to the results store and answer to the knowledge base.

Thus the Knowledge Base and Request Manager become able to provide reference service in digital environment. However, the Library of Congress and OCLC have developed a co-operative "Question Point" the advanced generation of *collaborative Digital Reference Service* (CDTS) in June 2002 which integrates local as well as global electronic reference networks.

PRESENT SCENARIO IN INDIA

All the six IITs (Indian Institute of Technology) created as centres of excellence for higher training, research and development in science, engineering and technology, have automated their libraries and now they have access to more than one thousand electronic journals. The Central Library IIT, Delhi has switched over to the Silver Platter's Electronics Reference Library (ERL) technology for providing access to bibliographic databases subscribed on CD-ROM. The technology facilitates simultaneous and integrated access to ERL complaint reference databases to multiple users across the LAN/WAN Via TCP/IP.

This library offers network-based CD-ROM search services from the CD-ROM databases subscribed in the central library. Most of its databases have now been transferred to ERL technology and its CD-NET system has been installed for searching of CD-ROM databases on the campus intranet.

This Library has started subscribing to the web-based full-text electronic journals with availability of high speed INTERNET connection and about 1330 electronic journals are accessible full text.

In most of the higher learning and research institutes in India such as:

- The Regional Engineering Colleges (RECs),
- Tata Institute of Fundamental Research (TFIR),
- Indian Institute of Science (IIS),
- Indian Statistical Institute (ISI),
- Indian Agricultural Research Institute (IARI),
- Institute of Veterinary Research of India (IVRI),
- All India Institute of Medical Science (AIMS),
- Indian Institute of Management (IIMs),
- Institute of Physics, Institute of Life Science,
- Shaha Institute Nuclear Physics,
- The Medical College Libraries etc., have automated their library systems.

Some of them are in the process of digitization of rare and valuable documents. Digital library services in India are in developing stage. At present most of the university libraries have taken steps to provide web-based reference and information services in digital environment in addition to their traditional library services.

These services include:

- Access to library catalogues and union catalogues.
- Access to bibliographic databases
- Access to subject gate ways in specific disciplines
- Providing links to web sites
- Accessing and procuring e-reference sources
- Subscribing to e-journals
- Reference services provided by librarians and experts on the web
- Document delivery services
- On-line current awareness services
- Digitization of library resources, considering their intellectual value.

The University Grants Commission (UGC) of India has launched the major initiative for setting up nation wide communication network for Indian universities called UGC-Infonet. Each university was to establish a LAN in its campus linking all the teaching departments including library.

ERNET of India and INFLIBNET Centre, Ahmedabad are conducting a series of training programmes for technical staff of each participating university library for managing and maintaining the network at their premises. The INFLIBNET Centre will administer and monitor the E-Journal programme and will have independent electronic access to all the publications to help with the process. The INFLIBNET Centre has carried out training programmes in various places to spread awareness and to develop expertise in the University community in the use of E-Resoures under the networked environment. The INFLIBNET Centre has developed and also recently released library automation software package new version for university libraries (SOUL) for building up digital library services.

Soul is Windows based user friendly software, based on client server architecture with multi-user and multi language facilities which supports internationally known standards such as CCF, AACR-II andMARC-21, etc. Thus INFLIBNET centre is patronizing for digitization of college and university libraries and encouraging e-subscription and e-learning in Indian Universities and colleges.

The DELNET (Delhi Library Network) created as a metropolitan network in 1988, has changed its name to Developing Library New Work (DELNET) in 2000. The main objectives of DELNET are to promote resource sharing among its member libraries, develop a network of member libraries, collect store and disseminate information, offer computerized information services in digital environment

The DELNET presently avails the high speed satellite communication facilities of NIC spread across the country and its 620 member libraries can access about 35 lakh bibliographic records in machine readable form. Also it maintains an online union catalogue of books available in its member libraries in CCF format. Its union catalogue is continuously updated. DELNET has been networking the libraries of about 400 affiliated institutes of AICTE, New Delhi. DELNET presents two management software packages *i.e.* DELMARC and DELPLUS.

4

Computers in the Children's Section of the Public Library

INTRODUCTION

In The Historical Society of Cotuit, Sheila Bourbeau writes: "A library is books and somewhere to put them and some people to want them there". Yet increasingly, this simple definition doesn't apply to the modern public library. More often, today's public libraries are bustling community centers, offering not only books, but also computers with online catalogues, databases, various software, and internet access.

Indeed, computer use in the public library is becoming more prominent and pervasive. Moreover, technological services are available to a wider audience of adults and children than ever before. In particular, computers with educational or recreational software and internet access are especially popular in the children's section of the public library. Given this recent shift towards computer use in the children's section, it is essential that library and information science professionals examine the way in which these services are implemented, utilized, and promoted.

Children's librarians are in a unique position to provide observations and suggestions regarding the role of computers in the children's section of the public library. In addition, they are more likely to be able to identify trends in computer use. Collecting their impressions signifies an important step towards offering better computer services to children in the public library. Through personal interviews, this research project considers children's librarians' perceptions of the following: quality of computers and computer software; staff knowledge of and involvement with computers; procedures for computer use; patron use of computers; and children's librarians' attitudes and responses to computer use in the children's section of the public library.

Ultimately, this study's findings have the potential to benefit both children's librarians and their young patrons by highlighting ways computer services are successful and ways in which they require improvement. This research project employed a flexible, rather than a fixed design. More specifically, it comprised a set of individual case studies. In Real World Research, Colin Robson defines the case study approach as a "strategy for doing research which involves an empirical investigation of a particular contemporary phenomenon within its real life context using multiple sources of evidence". Further, this study focused on a "small number of individuals with some features in common".

These common features included: location; workplace; and job description. Because multiple libraries and librarians were represented in this study, the results are more reliable and more generally applicable. Moreover, this approach provided multi-layered, qualitative, and empirical evidence. Personal interviews constituted this study's research method. Robson explains that personal interviews offer a "flexible and adaptable way of finding things out," providing potentially rich and illuminating material. Further, he suggests that personal interviews promise several advantages, including "modifying one's line of enquiry" and "following up interesting responses and investigating underlying motives in a way that postal and other self-administered questionnaires cannot".

This study is based on personal interviews, each lasting approximately a half an hour in length, with four children's librarians from North Carolina public libraries. In addition, physical observations provided a visual dimension to this study.

The process for initiating this research project involved several steps: first, after submitting a proposal, UNC's Institutional Review Board granted permission to conduct a study involving human participants; second, four children's librarians at North Carolina public libraries were invited to participate in the study; and finally, research participants were asked to sign informed consent forms at the time of their scheduled interviews. Three out of four sessions were taped with a handheld recorder to ensure precision and complete-ness. Interviews consisted of both closed and open-ended questions related to five broad headings: computers, staff, procedures, patrons, and attitudes and responses.

This study produced a combination of quantitative and qualitative data. A small portion of this data, such as the number of computers available in the children's section, was quantitative in nature. The majority of data collected, however, was qualitative. Since the purpose of this research project was to gather a sample of children's librarians' perceptions of computers in the children's section of the public library, the qualitative results of this study were emphasized.

An interpretive and flexible editing approach, rather than a quasi-statistical, template, or immersion approach, was utilized for analysis. Informal coding was applied to the results of the personal interviews, highlighting "similar phrases, patterns, themes, relationships, sequences, differences between sub-groups, etc." Finally, the emergence of these relationships was used to describe trends in children's librarians' perceptions of computers in the children's section of the public library, as well as to identify strengths and weaknesses in practice.

RESULTS AND DISCUSSION

LIBRARY A

Library A offers two non-OPAC computers specifically designated for children. While posted signs stipulate that these computers are intended for users between the ages of two and fourteen, other patrons are allowed to use them as well. At one time, these computers were located at the entrance to the children's section, making them immediately visible to incoming patrons. Now, the computers are still within view of the children's information desk, but they occupy a less central part of the children's section.

As Children's Librarian A explains: "... the problem we were having with our old location was that it was so prominent, that as soon as kids entered the children's section, they'd be drawn, like a television, to the computers, and they often would have to be pulled away." Indeed, because the computers are so popular, the library is planning to add at least two more to the children's section in the near future.

Moreover, although the current computers are perhaps only two or three years old, both will be replaced in the next year in accordance with the town's computer replacement policy. Further, as gifts of the Gates Foundation, Library A's computers came with a variety of software, including Microsoft's Office package, Encarta Encyclopedia, three Arthur games, three Barney games, three Magic Schoolbus games, Living Tales, Success Builder Algebra and Geometry, Experiment Science, and Big Science Ideas.

Most of the games range in age appropriateness from two to ten years old, while the more educational software is appropriate for young adults. Currently, Library A's children's section does not have a budget for computers since both computers were gifts. Library A's children's section is staffed by three full-time and two part-time librarians. While acknowledging that "you could use one person just to do the computer cue," Children's Librarian A stresses that she would like more staff for activities unrelated to computer use, such as community outreach.

She describes monitoring computer use as a "pretty constant" staff responsibility, but "not excessive." She mentions one instance in which this task becomes problematic: "The only time it's troublesome is when you get a lot of people coming in, and you have a whole lot of people on the wait list, and people are up and down, and you're trying to find the person who's next." Library A uses a manual sign-in procedure and limits patrons to thirty minutes on the computer at a time.

Children's Librarian A explains: "We have a list, a purple sheet at the desk ... where patrons are supposed to, if it's their first time, read the guidelines for use, and then sign in with the adult name, if the child is nine or younger, the child's name, age, and the time they're starting to use the computer, and which computer they're on." If other patrons are already using the computers, this sign-in sheet acts as a wait list. When a computer becomes available, staff in the children's section call on patrons who are waiting.

For this reason, most of the interactions Library A's children's staff have with the computers consist of "keeping an eye on the clock and showing people where to sign in." Children's Librarian A describes the procedure for using computers as relatively problem-free, although there are "complications sometimes." Usually, these complications arise when a patron does not sign in, but expects to be able to use a computer when it becomes available. For this reason, Children's Librarian A would like an automated sign-in procedure installed eventually, mentioning a company called Library Guardian that offers software with a timing component.

While noting that this type of procedure requires patrons to have their library cards with them to access the computers, she suggests that this system would be advantageous overall. In the mean time, she comments: "For the most part, our procedure works pretty well, and we haven't been able to think of how we might improve on it." Library A does not have a strict age requirement for computer use, although they suggest that children be at least two years old. Children's Librarian A feels that this recommen-dation is appropriate, if only because children under two do not have the manual dexterity to use a mouse successfully.

Still, she points out that "some two year olds really will just sit and listen to the whole Stellaluna story [a read-along story programme]...And other [children] just want to bang on the keyboards!" Children who are nine years old and younger are required to be with an adult in the library building, so they are also required to be supervised by an adult on the computer. Children's Librarian A agrees with this policy, too, noting that the children's section has had a problem with parents leaving their children at the computers unattended. In terms of written policy regarding computer use, Library A has a safe child policy, guidelines for using the computers, rules of conduct, and an internet use policy.

Children's Librarian A designed the safe child policy to apply to the computers in the children's section specifically, "covering all your basic safeguards," which was approved by her library director. This policy is posted beside the sign-in sheet at the children's information desk, as well as beside the computers. Computer use in the children's section at Library A is constant. Children's Librarian A estimates that many children would stay on the computers longer than their allotted thirty minutes if possible. When asked if she would prefer to see her young patrons spending their time in other ways, like reading books and attending programmes, Children's Librarian A says she feels "pretty good" about the level of computer use. She explains that her library supports a strong base of readers: "I think a lot of people who are coming, that are using the computers, are also big readers...we're real lucky to have readers." In addition, she suggests that many patrons who would not ordinarily visit the library are drawn in by the computers.

She describes a scenario in which a nanny told her: "I used to try to bring the kids, and they never really wanted to come here, but now that you have the computers, it gets them excited to come and visit the computers, and then once I have them here, we can also grab some books." She hypothesizes that computers may be related to the children's section's dramatic rise in circulation statistics. She thinks that the Barney and Arthur games are the most popular applications because even the youngest children are able to play them. She feels that almost all the games and read along stories are both age appropriate and appealing to children. On the other hand, she criticizes the Magic Schoolbus programmes, which attract younger children, but are intended for six to eleven year olds.

She estimates that three to five year olds spend the most time on the computers. Although she does not have a preference for which age group uses the computers most or least, she wishes that the educational software, such as the Encarta Africana, were available more often: "I'd like to see the more educational products, which are really great, being used more, and they would be helpful to upper elementary, middle school students, but I think that most of the time [when] the elementary and middle school students walk by, they see Arthur and Barney there, [and] they assume that's all there is." Children's Librarian A lists several reasons for having computers in the children's section.

- First, she suggests that the public library has an obligation to provide access to computers to patrons who don't have them at home.
- Second, she argues that the computers act as a gateway, drawing in patrons that might not visit the library otherwise, in effect, increasing "use of the library by having different resources.
- "Third, she asserts that computers are a "really great service [the library] can provide." For example, she mentions being able to offer free word processing for children to complete homework assignments, rather than having to refer them to a for-profit business, like Kinko's.

When asked what she considers to be the mission and goals of children's services, she explains: "I think it's to get kids excited about reading... and [to] get kids excited about learning." She feels that the inclusion of computers in the children's section is in keeping with these mission and goals. While pointing out that there are some patrons who disapprove of "technology in general or things changing in general," she feels that it is useful to have computers in the children's section at Library A. Indeed, her impressions of computers are positive: "On the whole, I think that most people are happy that we have [computers], and making your public happy and satisfied with the services you offer is obviously what's going to keep you in business."

LIBRARY B

Library B offers six non-OPAC computers specifically for children in the children's section. Like Library A, these compu-ters are intended primarily for children's use, but they are also available to adults. Located immediately adjacent to the children's information desk, four of the six computers are internet access only, while the other two are for word processing. A printer is also available for patron use. When asked if the children's section would benefit from a greater number of computers, Children's Librarian B asserts that they are able to meet their patrons' needs successfully with their six current computers: "We have the ability to see how many reservations we might have for people waiting [for a computer], and we don't have a waiting line."

While it does not offer any educational software, Library B does subscribe to several online sources, such as Gale Source's Biography Resource Center and World Geography Online, that arrive via the internet. Children's Librarian B notes that while children would probably enjoy "wilder video games," the amount of software the library offers meets the standards specified in the library's mission statement. Finally, Library B's children's section does not have a budget of its own for computer technology, but rather is encompassed by the library's Computer Operations budget. Two full-time librarians, one part-time librarian, one full-time library assistant, two part-time library assistants, and several floaters staff Library B's children's section.

Children's Librarian B explains: "To meet the daily needs of [the patrons that] come through the door, we do our best to balance, so we do OK," but implies that she would like more staff. She estimates that the children's staff spends about ten per cent or less of its work day "giving directions" about the computers. She notes, however, that before the implementation of their current automated sign-in procedure, they were devoting a much higher percentage of their time to this activity: "... we were spending probably a third of our time everyday monito-ring computer use, because we signed everybody up at the desk, and we also were trying to place limitations on how long they could use the computers, so we were spending a lot more time paying attention to it, and now we don't."

At Library B, the procedure for using computers in the children's section is the same as the procedure used in the adults' section. Children's Librarian B explains: "We require our users to bring a library card, and to use that library card to sign themselves up at an available computer ... If all the stations are busy, then they come to a library staff member who can make a reservation for them, and they will get the next available opening." Although young patrons sometimes forget their library cards, Children's Librarian B claims that this system "works very well." She reflects that at one time, the staff in the children's section acted as a "reservation station," signing children up manually for time on the computer. Now, they find that having children sign themselves up requires certain skills that act as "kind of a test" of appropriateness.

In effect, the automated sign-in procedure helps screen out children who are physically or develop-mentally unready to use the computer without an adult. Further, she notes that the automated sign-in procedure frees up staff in the children's section to spend valuable one-on-one time with patrons who need assistance: "It allows us to be able to spend time with the people who can really take advantage of the expertise we have." There is no age requirement for using the computers in the children's section at Library B.

Children's Librarian B explains that at one time there were certain guidelines they required patrons to read before using the computers, specifying that "if you were a non-reader, that you have a reader with you." Children's Librarian B feels that their new policy works well. She argues that just as children are not required to be supervised in the stacks, they should not be required to be supervised at the computer unless their behaviour demonstrates that they need such supervision: ". . . if they show that they don't have the skills to use [the computer], then we ask that they [do it with] an adult or someone that can help."

While Library B does not have a standard acceptable use policy, there is a statement on the automated sign-in page that patrons must click on or agree to before accessing the internet. This statement was developed by the county library system, and appears on all branch computers. Children's Librarian B estimates that the average child spends thirty to sixty minutes on the computer in the children's section of Library B, while pointing out that patrons can spend up to three hours on the computers. She explains that she would like to see "more of a mix" between computer use and other library-related activities, especially reading.

When asked what computer applications are most popular among her patrons, Children's Librarian B mentions several game sites. She does not feel comfortable evaluating "how good they are at what they are," but says that children seem to enjoy them. She thinks that six to twelve year olds spend the most time on the computer, noting that young children "think they want to [use the computer], but then they get on there, and it's not quite what they thought it was."

Finally, when asked which age groups she would like to see spending the most and the least amount of time on the computer, Children's Librarian B claims to have no preference. Children's Librarian B suggests that having computers in the children's section supports the library's mission and goals: "Our mission statement is to promote the love of reading and foster the pursuit of knowledge, and [computers are] an avenue of knowledge." Further, she sees the inclusion of computers in the children's section as a positive extension of library services, not only because it is an expectation that public libraries provide computers, but also because children get excited about them. In addition to the formal interview, Children's Librarian B shared some unique insights about computers afforded by her long-time career in the public library system. She mentions some of her past frustrations related to computer use in the children's section. First, she describes observing staff struggling with the way children use computers.

She explains that children's librarians are trained to help children "find information to support homework or to support a hobby or a special interest," but that children rarely use the computers for these purposes. Second, in the past, she recalls being irritated at the computers freezing up, particularly on game sites: "... [it got] to the point where you were spending much more than a third of your time shutting them down, starting them up, and you [felt like asking], 'Why are we doing this?' We didn't have Scrabble, we didn't have pinball, and now we're spending a lot of time doing this."

Third, she touches on the issue of appropriateness, mentioning that older children sometimes use chat rooms in an unacceptable manner. She points out that although Library B uses filtering software, this mechanism "limits sites," but not "what people can type." Interestingly, she says that she and her staff have been very satisfied with filtering: "It's relieved a lot of responsibility from our staff, of having to watch and watch and watch, which has been nice. And we all did not want it. We did not want filtering at all, we felt like that would be the wrong way to go, but once it came, nobody wanted to go back."

LIBRARY C

Unlike the other libraries represented in this study, Library C does not have any non-OPAC computers in the children's section. Instead, it offers six computers for both children and adults. Four are available beside the adults' information desk, while two others are located inside a small private room. Children's Librarian C explains that this branch was, at one time, slated for renovations that would have expanded the physical space, thus allowing room for both a children's desk and computers in the children's section.

In the mean time, however, one of the computers in the back room does include several "animated games," as well as the online Encarta Encyclopedia for children. Library C employs only one full-time children's librarian. Children's Librarian C explains that one part-time position is informally assigned to children's services, but that "it's a little problematic because [the part-time employees] don't always come as a person that has any experience and training in children's [services], and they don't really emphasize that when they advertise, so. . . I have to sort of go with the flow."

She says that she would like more staff, especially for programming. When asked how much time staff spends directing children to computers and offering instruction, she explains that because they don't have "software that self-times," staff is constantly assisting patrons with the computers. She claims, however, that staff spends a "really, really small" amount of time offering more extensive help, such as helping a child with a paper. Library C utilizes a manual sign-in procedure and limits computer use to thirty minutes.

Children's Librarian C reflects that in terms of procedure, the time limit poses the biggest challenge: ". . . we only have four [computers], and you know, it's becoming more and more popular. People come here first thing in the morning to use the computers." She considers the potential benefits of an automated sign-in procedure, noting that it might be less work for Library C's small staff, but suggests that "it's kind of hard [to judge] until you get there." At Library C, children under eighteen are not allowed to use the computers without adult supervision or signed parental consent.

Children's Librarian C explains that at one time the age requirement was sixteen, but they raised it because all of Library C's computers have unfiltered internet access. She mentions that the county's central branch has software that blocks certain internet sites according to age, but explains that Library C chose not to adopt this option because so many adults need full access to the internet. Library C does have an acceptable use policy, developed by the county library system, which is posted by the sign-in sheet at the adults' information desk. To answer the series of questions about patrons, Children's Librarian C relies partly on her weekend experience at the county's central branch, where she has observed greater computer use.

She argues that because the children at the county's central branch come from a lower socioeconomic level that "it's a little bit more fascinating to them, and it's a little bit harder to tell them to get off because, you know, it's kind of new and exciting." At Library C, she suggests that many patrons have computers at home. She worries that her young patrons don't find books to be as exciting as computers: "I guess my fear is that they're just so hooked into it, and it's sort of an interactive thing that they don't really get involved in the whole book thing." In spite of these concerns, however, she feels that Library C needs more computer opportunities for children.

She says that children at Library C use the computers most often for homework and to play games. She estimates that older children, from nine years old to the early teens, use the computers most often. In contrast, she thinks that eight to twelve year olds spend the most time on the computers at the county's central branch.

When asked what age groups she would like to see spending the most amount of time on the computers, she says five to six year olds, because they stand to gain the most from these interactions: ". . . people talk about kids improving their reading skills when they're just learning to read, and you know, I've heard some good results from that, so I think that's something that could be an opportunity for them."

Conversely, she feels that older children "often gravitate towards the computer when the book is right there." Also, at the county's central branch, she mentions older children printing off "music to rap songs" and "all kinds of stuff that's kind of a waste of time." She wishes that older children "could just be more inclusive in using books" and not be so quick to "discount" them. Children's Librarian C feels that inclusion of computers in the children's section would complement the mission and goals of children's services. She tempers this response, however, by suggesting that children's use of computers should be "controlled." She argues that the children's section would require space for a children's information desk in order to provide support and supervision for computers designated solely to children.

She stresses that children, like adults, should have access to computers. Further, she asserts that computers have the potential to "help with reading or help with homework," by providing "timely," as well as "obscure" information. Ultimately, she agrees that her impressions of computer use are generally positive, emphasizing that she thinks children should "definitely have access [to computers] and more so than [they do at Library C]."

LIBRARY D

Library D offers one non-OPAC computer specifically designated for children in the children's section. Unfortunately, this computer is at least three years old, and therefore breaks often due to hard and frequent use by young children. Children's Librarian D notes that it would be nice to have more computers, especially since children enjoy using the computer, but feels that space and shelving are more pressing issues. In addition to the designated children's computer, a Gates and a bilingual computer, both purchased with Smart Start money, are popular among children. In fact, Children's Librarian D explains that most new computers come to Library D through grants, such as Gates or LSTA, because although the county has a computer replacement policy, there is currently no budget. Reading games and read along programmes are most popular with children, although Children's Librarian D stresses that the children's section would benefit from having new and different story CD-ROMs.

At Library D, the staff hours for the children's section are split into two jobs, so that there is one full-time librarian and one part-time librarian. Children's Librarian D feels that she does not have enough staff to meet the demands of the children's section. When asked how much time staff spends monitoring computer use, Children's Librarian D says that "it's like twenty four-seven, all day, everyday," because patrons often run into problems when using the computers. Further, she characterizes the demands of monitoring computer use as "labour-intensive" and "bothersome," because she believes that patrons spend too much time on activities like e-mail, which aren't research-oriented.

Unlike the other libraries in this study, Library D's procedure for computer use in the children's section is first come, first serve, with no time limit, although there's an informal thirty minute rule when other patrons are waiting. For the other computers with internet access, there is a manual sign-in procedure, which Children's Librarian D describes as "staff-intensive." Interestingly, while acknowledging that patrons are "pretty good" about following these procedures, she hints that they could be improved, but admits that staff is reluctant to confront patrons. There is no age requirement for using the computer in the children's section at Library D because it only offers educational CD-ROMs. Twelve year olds and younger can use the computers with internet access with a parent, while thirteen year olds and older may use them independently with signed parental consent on file. Children's Librarian D feels that these requirements are appropriate, not only for safety reasons, but also because she thinks that children do not need to spend "all their time" on the computer.

Further, she stresses that librarians are not babysitters, noting that internet use opens up a number of safety and legality issues. Library D does have an acceptable use policy. While the county and state set certain guidelines that must be followed for determining this policy, the library itself is responsible for particular details, such as age requirements. This policy is posted with support documentation at the adults' information desk. Children's Librarian D describes the amount of time children spend on computers as constant. She feels that although a little time on the computers is appropriate, she would prefer to see them reading books. Interestingly, however, she says that the most popular computer applications are reading activities, such as Curious George Does the Alphabet and Mom and Me. When asked what age group spends the most time on the computer, Children's Librarian D says that younger children tend to use the computer most often because it is the first thing they encounter when entering the library and the children's section.

Moreover, she claims to have mixed feelings about this age group using the computer so often. She thinks that younger children need to be aware of computers and how to use them, since many of them do not have computers at home. Further, she acknowledges that they enjoy using the computer. On the other hand, she feels that the computer might be more appropriate for school age children, especially if it had a greater number of applications.

She is particularly interested in the idea of creating a permanent room for computers, suitable for homework help and online research. When asked to describe the purpose of computers in the children's section, Children's Librarian D answers in ideal terms, emphasizing that the computer should act as an educational and informational resource, rather than as a recreational opportunity only. She suggests that computers should enhance research and reading skills, as well as help children explore areas of interest. She feels that the computer in the children's section complements the mission and goals of children's services at Library D, which include "providing a wide range of programmes and services to supplement the schools, curriculum, [and promoting] literacy, appreciation of cultural and artistic diversity, environmental awareness, creative expression, and life-long learning." Children's Librarian D admits to having mixed impressions about the use of computers in the children's section. She reiterates the need for increased staff, more space for leisure reading, and child-friendly shelving, over OPACs and computers with internet access for the children's section.

COMPUTERS

The number of non-OPAC computers designated specifically for children in the children's sections of Libraries A, B, C, and D varies from zero to six. Most of these computers, however, are similar in age, ranging from two to three years old. Three out of four children's librarians felt that the children's section would benefit from having more computers, while only one expressed a need for newer computers.

Children's Librarian B, with six computers in the children's section, insisted that at this time, her staff needed computers more than her patrons. All four libraries distinguish between computers intended for children versus computers intended for adults, although they do not necessarily prohibit adults from using computers in the children's section. Library C stands out for not making computers available in the children's section. This distinction, however, is the result of limited physical space, rather than a philosophical choice. Moreover, all four children's librarians mentioned space issues when discussing inclusion of computers in the children's section.

In addition, they reported placing computers near the children's or adults' information desk. Likewise, they suggested that placement of computers contributed to use significantly. At Libraries A and D, where the computers are or were located at the entrance into the children's section, both children's librarians described active computer use.

Indeed, they alluded to the almost magnetic effect of computers on young children in particular. Libraries A, B, C, and D differ in the amount and variety of software available on computers in the children's section. Library A offers word processing and educational prog-rammes/games; Library B offers internet access only; Library C offers internet access primarily, as well as word processing and some educational programmes/games; and Library D offers educational CD-ROMs only. Children's Librarians A and B suggested that children might enjoy having a greater selection of games to choose from, but neither felt that more software was necessary.

Children's Librarian D wanted more CD-ROMs related to reading, but was particularly interested in developing a homework center for more research-oriented computer use. For the most part, Children's Librarians A, B, C, and D agreed that most of the software available in the children's section is age-appropriate and appealing to their audience, although each librarian gave at least one anecdotal example of inappropriate use of computers. For instance, Children's Librarian A highlighted a game about dinosaurs intended for older children, which appeals to younger children who are unable to use it successfully.

Similarly, both Children's Librarians B and C noted observing older children engaged in questionable internet activities, such as using chat rooms in an inappropriate manner or printing out explicit song lyrics. In terms of money allocation for technology, all four librarians demonstrated little knowledge concerning budge-ting for computers in the children's section. Children's Librarian A suggested that she and Library A's director would decide on the amount of money she could spend on computers; Children's Librarian B explained that the children's section's budget for computers was determined by the Computer Operations department; and Children's Librarian D said that her county library system established the amount of money designated for computers.

Clearly, allocation of money for computer services varies, especially in a year of budget cuts and crises. Interestingly, children's Librarian A called attention to a unique concern for children's librarians regarding staff training and new technology. While acknowledging that Library A "could come up with some money" for staff training on computers, she suggested that most "workshops offered by the state library usually have to do with online reference questions and NC Live." Seemingly, little training exists for the computer interactions children's librarians are most likely to observe, monitor, and guide in the children's section.

STAFF

The children's sections of Libraries A, B, C, and D employ a range of full-time, part-time, professionally trained, and non-professionally trained staff. Library B's children's section supports the largest staff, with two full-time librarians, two part-time librarians, one full-time library assistant, two part-time library assistants, and floaters, while Library A's children's section supports the second largest staff, with three full-time librarians and two part-time librarians. Both Libraries C and D employ only one full-time librarian and one part-time library assistant in their children's sections.

While staff numbers certainly reflect the size of each library's children's section, they also affect the quality of computer services these libraries are able to offer. It is not surprising that Libraries A and B not only provide more computers, but also report high levels of computer use among their patrons. Despite variation in staff numbers, however, all four children's librarians consistently expressed a desire for more staff, especially for assistance with programming. Children's Librarian C, in particular, explained that until Library C has a children's information desk, the inclusion of computers in the children's section will not be possible. It is noteworthy that all four children's librarians to participate in this study feel that they are understaffed to meet the demands of the children's section. While three out of four children's librarians described monitoring computers to be a constant staff responsibility, few viewed it as an overwhelmingly demanding task. Despite feeling understaffed, when asked if they spent a dispropor-tionate amount of time monitoring computer use two out of four children's librarians disagreed.

In fact, most of the time staff spends monitoring computer use appears to be related to procedure. For example, Library B, which uses an automated sign-in procedure, demands a markedly smaller portion of children's staff's time. Indeed, Children's Librarian B reported spending only ten per cent of her day addressing computer-related issues. This finding indicates that a combination of offering more computers, more staff, and automated sign-in reduces staff involvement in monitoring computer use dramatically.

PROCEDURES

Libraries A, B, C, and D utilize a variety of procedures for using computers in the children's section. Both Libraries A and C use a manual sign-in procedure, in which patrons sign their names and other pertinent information to a list in order to use the computers. Library B uses an automated sign-in procedure, in which patrons enter their library card numbers to gain access to computers. Library D operates on a first come, first serve basis, allowing patrons to use the children's computer any time it is available. Library D's internet access computers, however, involve a manual sign-in procedure. All four children's librarians report that these procedures work fairly well, with patrons following the rules properly, although Library B's procedure stands out as the most problem-free. While Children's Librarians A, C, and D must devote a significant part of their time to monitoring procedure, Library B's children's staff's involvement with computer procedure is notably hands-off.

Accordingly, Children's Librarians A, C, and D suggest that their procedures could be improved, although they also express some hesitancy about changing current practices. These findings demonstrate a need for improved procedure for computer use in the children's section, but a reluctance to depart from the status quo. Most libraries require patrons to be a certain age to use computers independently. Library A insists that children nine years old and younger be supervised by an adult while using the computer. Because Library B's computers are filtered, children of any age may use the computers independently. Library C requires patrons to be eighteen years old or older, or have signed parental consent, to use their internet access computers without supervision.

Library D allows children of all ages to use the computer located in the children's section, since this computer is not connected to the internet, but uses educational CD-ROMs only. They require children to be twelve years old or older, or have signed parental consent, to use their internet access computers independently. Children's Librarians A, B, C, and D unanimo-usly support these age requirements for a variety of reasons.

For example, Children's Librarian D speaks to both safety and legality issues related to the internet, noting that there is a lot of information on the internet that children "don't need to get into." Similarly, Children's Librarian A points out that younger children often do not have the manual dexterity or the maturity to operate computers without adult help. All four children's librarians demonstrate both a keen sensitivity and a vigilant awareness about children's safe and acceptable use of computers. In turn, Libraries A, B, C, and D all have written policies dictating appropriate computer use. Library A's "Rules of Conduct for Children's Personal Computers" stipulates fifteen guidelines for using computers in the children's section. Library B's "Internet Use Statement" offers county and state statutes regarding internet use, and appears on both its website and its automated sign-in page.

Library C posts a county "Policies and Procedures: Computer Use Policy" sheet, which includes specific information about computer use by children. Library D requires parents with children twelve years old and under to read and sign its "Internet Use Guidelines." All of these policies are determined by library, county, and state authorities, and posted with computers and at sign-in stations. Indeed, it is evident that all four libraries take child protection and responsible computer use seriously.

PATRONS

Children's librarians A, B, C, and D estimate that children spend different amounts of time on the computer, ranging from thirty minutes to several hours. At Libraries A and C, however, computer use is limited to a certain length of time. For instance, at Library A, children may only stay on the computer for thirty minutes, unless no one else is waiting for a turn.

According to all four children's librarians, educational and recreational games are by far the most popular applications. Even on Library B's internet access computers, Children's Librarian B reports that children most frequently visit online game sites. At both Libraries A and D, reading games/programmes are especially well-liked by children. Three out of four children's librarians say that they would prefer to see their patrons spending their time engaged in activities other than using computers, such as reading books, doing research, and attending programmes.

In particular, Children's Librarians B, C, and D mention that they would like their patrons to show more interest in books and reading, or at least demonstrate an equal balance between time spent with computers and time spent with books. Interestingly, Children's Librarian A describes her young patrons as "big readers," so perhaps it is not surprising that she is unconcerned by the amount of time they spend on the computers. Children's Librarians A, B, C, and D observe different age groups using the computers most often. Children's Librarians A and D report that three to five year olds are their most enthusiastic computer users; Children's Librarian B reports that six to twelve year olds are her most enthusiastic computer users; and Children's Librarian C reports that children nine years old to the early teens are her most enthusiastic computer users.

Children's Librarian A speculates that preschoolers may appear to use the computer most often simply because they patronize the library most frequently. Similarly, Children's Librarian B has the impression that six to twelve year olds show more persistence on the computers than three to five year olds. It is interesting to note that computers are most popular among young children in the libraries with educational games/programmes and CD-ROMs, whereas they are most popular among older children in the libraries with internet access.

Although this distinction may be related to age requirements regarding internet use, it is possible that games are more appealing to younger children, while the internet is more appealing to older children. In addition, Children's Librarians A and B both claim not to have any preference for which age groups use the computers.

Children's Librarian C feels that younger children should spend more time with educational, reading-related games/programmes, while older children should spend less time on the computers in general. Children's Librarian D, on the other hand, believes that young children should have access to and experience with computers, but wishes that their interactions did not revolve around play alone. Overall, Children's Librarians A, B, C, and D feel mixed about which age groups should be spending the most and least amount of time on computers in the children's section.

ATTITUDES AND RESPONSES

When asked what they consider to be the purpose of having computers in the children's section, Children's Librarians A, B, C, and D offer a variety of thoughtful and compelling responses.

These purposes include providing access to children who do not have computers at home; attracting patrons to the library; offering resources in a variety of formats; promoting a love of reading and fostering the pursuit of knowledge; supplying timely and sometimes obscure information; enhancing research and reading skills; and helping children explore their areas of interest.

Interestingly, none of the children's librarians repeated the same potential reason for offering computer services in the children's section. This array of responses not only indicates the different ways children's librarians perceive computers, but also demonstrates the plethora of opportunities that computers can afford in the children's section of the public library.

Further, while three out of four children's librarians express some ambivalence about the fulfillment of these potential purposes, most appear to feel that computers are a positive addition to the children's section. Similarly, all four children's librarians believe that computers complement the mission and goals of children's services, which most often included inspiring children's excitement about reading and learning.

Finally, when Children's Librarians A, B, C, and D were asked to characterize their overall impressions of computer use in the children's section as positive or negative, three out of four claimed to feel positively. Children's Librarian D's impressions were mixed based on her opinion that computers should be used primarily for educational, rather than recreational purposes.

She acknowledged, however, the potential benefits of inclusion of computers in the children's section. Children's librarians' positive impressions act as a promising predictor of the future of computer services in the children's section of the public library. Indeed, these results reflect children's librarians' commitment to providing exemplary computer services to their patrons.

CONCLUSION

This study addresses many of the issues discussed in current literature about children and computers. First, it offers further anecdotal evidence of children's librarians' perceptions of computers. In particular, it shows that children's librarians are demonstrating increased comfort and enthusiasm for computers.

Although Children's Librarians A, B, C, and D observed some problems related to computer use, they are working to remedy these challenges. Further, they showed attention to the developmental needs and abilities of young children by implementing age and adult supervision requirements, as well as by creating thoughtful policies dictating computer use. Moreover, quality computers and software appeal to their patrons' educational and recreational needs.

In addition, all four children's librarians underscored the importance of providing computer access to children who do not have computers at home. Such actions affirm the suggestions of children's services experts. They speak to the concerns of authors who worry about the potentially negative effects of computer use on young children. Children's Librarians A, B, C, and D exhibited careful consideration, sensitivity, and responsibility to children regarding computer services in the children's sections of their libraries.

Specifically, the results of this study yield patterns and similarities that reveal the strengths and weaknesses of current practices in the children's section of the public library. Strengths include: availability of quality computers and software in the children's section; children's staff's level of interaction with computers; improved sign-in procedures for using computers;

clear and prominent policies guiding computer use; appropriate age requirements for computer use; and children's librarians' positive attitudes towards the inclusion of computers in the children's section.

Weaknesses include: children's librarians' involvement in budgeting for computers; lack of staff; outmoded sign-in procedures for computer use; inappropriate use of computers by children; and children's diminished interest in books and reading. Thus, this research offers several implications for future practice in the children's section of the public library. First, it is apparent that many libraries must address larger concerns, such as providing adequate space, child-appro-priate shelving, and a children's information desk, before incorporating computers into their children's sections. For those libraries that already include computer services in their children's sections, most require both more and newer computers to meet the demands of their patrons. Second, children's staff need better training on how to provide excellent computer services.

Computer training should focus on applications that children's librarians will encounter on the computers in the children's section, thus engendering confidence and enthusiasm. Third, children's librarians should have the opportunity to participate in developing a budget for computer services. Further, they should be involved in shaping all aspects of library policy that affect the children's section. Fourth, children's services in most public libraries require more staff.

Increased staff would benefit all parts of the children's section, including reference, reader's advisory, programming, and outreach, in addition to computer services. Fifth, procedures for computer use should be improved. Automated sign-in procedures appear to be most effective and efficient. Sixth, children and young adults require guidance when using the computers in the children's section of the public library.

While most libraries insist that young children be supervised by an adult, it would be helpful for older children to be reminded of what constitutes appropriate computer use. Lastly, the children's section of the public library must attempt to strike a compromise between computer services and other more traditional services, such as the promotion of recreational reading. The results of this study also reveal a number of tensions regarding computers in the children's section of the public library.

For instance, three out of four children's librarians claimed to need more computers. Yet based on current evidence, having more computers would result in the need for greater staff involvement monitoring their use, when children's librarians already report being understaffed. Moreover, several children's librarians expressed ambivalence about children's current interactions with computers. Perhaps it is necessary for children's librarians to address these concerns before introducing not only more computers, but also a greater variety of software or internet access.

At this crucial stage of growth and development, it is particularly important that children's librarians define children's services' role in offering computers. Implementing good procedures for computer use represents another step towards ensuring children's staff's increased satisfaction with computers. Also, while all four children's librarians felt that having computers in the children's section complements the mission and goals of children's services, most were anxious to see a better balance between computer use and reading.

In addition, they noted that games are by far the most popular computer activity in the children's section. It is unlikely that when children's librarians speak of promoting access and providing service, that they are referring to computer game use. For this reason, children's services must attempt to reconcile their conflicting attitudes towards informational, educational, and recreational computer use. In many ways, the tensions children's librarians face in introducing computers to the children's section reflect larger issues for children's services as a whole.

Some of these issues include appropriate adult supervision of children, the children's section's role as a place of education or recreation, and children's librarians' commit-ment to promoting reading. This study's findings also demonstrate the symbiotic relationship between computers, children's staff, procedures for computer use, patrons, and, in turn, children' staff's attitudes and responses to computers.

To be sure, placing computers in the children's section of the public library necessarily demands the time and consideration of children's librarians. Next, procedure functions as the vehicle for negotiating the level of interaction between computers and children's librarians in making this service accessible to children. Further, children's use of the computers demands the attention of children's staff.

Thus, children's librarians involvement with patrons, proce-dures, and computers shape their overall attitudes and responses to computers in the children's section. Indeed, children's librarians represent the frontline of children's services at the public library. For this reason, their perceptions of computers are of considerable significance. Children's librarians have enormous influence over the way in which computers are implemented, utilized, and promoted.

Because they act as a filter between the needs of children and the services the library provides, they are in an excellent position to gauge the degree to which computer use among their young patrons is successful, as well as to suggest ways in which it could be improved.

Although computer use in the children's section of the public library is on the rise, insufficient literature exists to document this phenomenon. By consulting children's librarians in North Carolina public libraries, this study not only reflects children's librarians' perceptions of computers, but also offers a portrait of computer services in the children's section of the public library today. In turn, these findings have the potential to shape future practices and to illuminate note-worthy tensions in the field of children's librarianship.

FUTURE RESEARCH

As with any research based on case studies, the results of this study reflect only a small sample of the target population of children's librarians in the public libraries of North Carolina. For this reason, interviewing a greater number of children's librarians would ensure more reliable and conclusive data.

Further, a national, rather than a regional, study might reveal significant trends in children's librarians' perceptions of computers. Current literature indicates a growing disparity in computer access between more affluent public libraries and their less fortunate counterparts, which could in turn affect children's librarians' attitudes and responses towards new technology. Also, employing a different research method, such as conducting telephone or mail surveys, would make it possible to reach a greater number of research participants, although results would surely provide less detail.

Another study might involve children more directly, through observation, interviews, or surveys. In some ways, by removing the children's librarian or intermediary from the equation, this kind of research would address issues, such as appropriateness, more explicitly. Another study might compare computer use in the children's section of the public library with the school media center.

Lastly, an additional approach to this area of research would address computer services geared towards adults. Such a study might utilize the insights of reference and reader's advisory librarians in the adult section of the public library. In addition, each category of research in this study could be its own focus in a future study. For instance, procedures for computer use in the children's section of the public library alone, offer many potential avenues of exploration. Research projects related to this topic could include a study of the effectiveness of manual versus automated sign-in or the examination of various acceptable use policies.

Similarly, research geared even more exclusively towards gathering children's librarians' perceptions of computers could prove useful to the field of children's librarianship. Attention to specific aspects of children's computer use, such as OPAC use, internet use, or educational game use might demonstrate whether the children's section is meeting the needs of its young patrons successfully. Finally, conducting follow-up interviews with this study's research participants could be valuable.

It would be interesting to chart levels of computer use over time, changing staff responsibilities with regard to computers in the children's section, revised procedures and policies related to computers, patterns of patron use, and ultimately, children's librarian's changing perceptions of computers. Also, it would be useful to gather more information about the children's librarians included in this study. Experience, level of training, and professional background could be related to their perceptions of computers.

For example, it is telling that the most recently graduated children's librarian involved in this study is also the most excited about computers in the children's section of the public library. Perhaps this distinction indicates that comfort with and enthusiasm for computers is, in part, related to age and experience with them. It is clear that the implementation, utilization, and promotion of computer services in the children's section of the public library is in a state of flux. As these services become a more integrated part of the public library, it is especially important that library and information science professionals document and respond to this phenomenon. Children's librarians should play a primary role in this process.

5

Online Cataloguing

INTRODUCTION

Online cataloguing, such as Dynix, has greatly enhanced the usability of catalogues, thanks to the rise of *MA*chine *R*eadable *C*ataloguing = MARC standards in the 1960s. Rules governing the creation of catalogue MARC records include not only formal cataloguing rul lges like AACR2 but also special rules specific to MARC, available from the Library of Congress and also OCLC.

MARC was originally used to automate the creation of physical catalogue cards; Now the MARC computer files are accessed directly in the search process.

OPACs have enhanced usability over traditional card formats because:

- The online catalogue does not need to be sorted statically; the user can choose author, title, keyword, or systematic order dynamically.
- Most online catalogues offer a search facility for any word of the title; the goal of the grammatic word order (provide an entry on the word that most users would look for) is reached even better.
- Many online catalogues allow links between several variants of an author name. So, authors can be found both under the original and the standardised name (if entered properly by the cataloguer).
- The elimination of paper cards has made the information more accessible to many people with disabilities, such as the visually impaired, wheelchair users, and those who suffer from mold allergies.

TYPES OF CATALOGUING

- *Original Cataloguing:* For MARC records, you input a new master record cataloged according to current cataloguing practices and AACR2. If different rules for descriptive cataloguing are used to create the record (other than rules based on or consistent with AACR2, AACR1, ALA 1949, ALA 1941, or ALA 1908), then code the 040-‡e field with the appropriate MARC coding from the *MARC Code Lists for Relators, Sources, Description Conventions*. If you are using your own descriptive conventions, enter your OCLC symbol in subfield ‡e. Enter subfield ‡e immediately after subfield ‡a. Dublin Core users apply various standards when creating Dublin Core records:

  - The Dublin Core Metadata Initiative provides guidance on commonly-adopted best practices in *Using Dublin Core.*
  - In the library community, the DCMI-Libraries Working Group publishes the *DC-Library Application Profile* (DC-Lib): library-application-profile/.
  - Groups of libraries develop their own specific practices based on more general standards.

- *Copy Cataloguing:* A machine-readable record exists. You modify the record for local use and create a copy of the record with your modifications.
- *Transcribing Cataloguing Copy:* You create a master record using an existing nonmachine-readable catalogue record. Usually, you transcribe pre-AACR2 records, but you may also transcribe AACR2 records. Again, some records are created by other standards.

LEVELS OF CATALOGUING

- *Full-level Cataloguing:* Records that meet the requirements of second-level description (AACR2, rule 1.0D2).
- *Core-level Cataloguing:* Records that meet the requirements of first-level description (AACR2, rule 1.0D1) and some of the requirements of second-level description (AACR2, rule 1.0D2).
- *Minimal-level Cataloguing:* Records that meet the requirements of first-level description (AACR2, rule 1.0D1).
- *Abbreviated-level Cataloguing:* Brief records that do not meet the requirements of Minimal-level cataloguing specifications (*ELvl* code 3).
- *Dublin Core:* All records created in Dublin Core (*ELvl* code 3).

ORIGINAL CATALOGUING AND COPY CATALOGUING

Entering ISBD Punctuation

The General International Standard Bibliographic Description (ISBD) prescribes punctuation between elements or areas of bibliographic description for current cataloguing (i.e., AACR2):

- Supply ISBD punctuation that occurs within variable fields. Enter punctuation and spaces between elements within a field as prescribed by AACR2.
- If punctuation separates data that occur in separate subfields, enter the punctuation at the end of the first subfield.
- Do not supply ISBD punctuation (space-dash-space) that occurs between variable fields, *e.g.*, between the 250 and 260 fields.
- Do not supply parentheses around transcribed series statements.

Space-dash-space

The OCLC catalogue card print programme supplies a space-dash-space (-) before the following fields:

- 250 Edition Statement
- 254 Musical Presentation Statement
- 255 Cartographic Mathematical Data
- 256 Computer File Characteristics
- 260 Publication, Distribution, Etc. (Imprint)
- 362 Dates of Publication and/or Volume Designation (First indicator value *0*)
- 4xx Series Statements (First 4xx field)

If the field that precedes one of the listed fields ends with final punctuation (.? !), the print programme supplies a space-dash-space (-). If the preceding field does not end with final punctuation, the print programme supplies period-space-dash-space (-).

Verifying Headings

You must use AACR2 or AACR2-compatible forms for all headings and uniform titles for current original cataloguing. Search the OCLC Authority File to verify forms of entry. Use current Library of Congress (LC) AACR2 or AACR2-compatible forms. If those forms are not in the OCLC Authority File, construct the heading or uniform title according to AACR2.

INCLUDING NON-ROMAN SCRIPTS

The OCLC provides the capability to include Arabic, Bengali, Chinese, Devanagari, Cyrillic, Greek, Hebrew, Japanese, Korean, Tamil, and Thai scripts in bibliographic records. Include these scripts in your current original cataloguing if you have the knowledge and expertise to do so.

ROMANIZED DATA

If you provide Romanized (Latin-script-equivalent) data, Romanization should follow guidelines in the ALA-LC Romanization Tables on the Library of Congress Web-site.

GENERAL MATERIAL DESIGNATIONS

Use General Material Designations (GMD) for current original cataloguing. GMDs are generic terms describing the medium of the item. OCLC defines subfield ‡h (Medium) in field 245 (Title Statement) for GMD information. Enter GMDs in lowercase letters enclosed in brackets. Example: ‡h [electronic resource].

GMDs and Library of Congress Rule Interpretations

Library of Congress Rule Interpretations (LCRIs), rule 1.1C, lists GMDs and provides standards for use. The LC applies rule 1.1C for only certain types of materials. LCRI 21.29 limits the use of GMDs to the title area only. Follow LC practice except: If one of the following GMDs is applicable, it is mandatory for I-level, Core-level, and K-level records in field 245 subfield ‡h.

Dublin Core users apply different codes:

- ‡h [art original]
- ‡h [microscope slides]
- ‡h [art reproduction]
- ‡h [model]
- ‡h [chart]
- ‡h [motion picture]
- ‡h [diorama]
- ‡h [picture]
- ‡h [electronic resource]
- ‡h [realia]
- ‡h [filmstrip]
- ‡h [slide]
- ‡h [flash card]
- ‡h [sound recording]
- ‡h [game]
- ‡h [technical drawing]
- ‡h [graphic]
- ‡h [toy]
- ‡h [kit]
- ‡h [transparency]
- ‡h [microform]
- ‡h [videorecording]

TRANSCRIBING PRE-AACR2 COPY

Master Record

When you create a master record from a non-machine-readable record (often a paper record), you are transcribing cataloguing copy. Usually, the cataloguing copy is pre-AACR2. The National Union Catalogue, for example, has such records. Guidelines in this part apply to all pre-AACR2 cataloguing copy whether part of a retrospective conversion project, reclassifi-cation project or part of normal acquisition and cataloguing workflow.

LATEST ENTRY CATALOGUING

Verifying name, Subject, Uniform Title Headings

Use AACR2 (or AACR2-compatible) forms for all name and uniform title headings (including the name and uniform title portions of name and name/ uniform title subject headings) for retrospective cataloguing, even if the transcribed record is pre-AACR2. You must search the OCLC Authority File to verify forms of entry. If the forms of name and uniform title entries are not in the OCLC Authority File, OCLC encourages you to construct the heading or uniform title according to AACR2, but you are not required to do so.

If the subject headings are not in the OCLC Authority File, OCLC encourages you to construct the subject heading according to the *Subject Headings Manual* (formerly called the *Subject Cataloguing Manual*), but you are not required to do so. For entries in other 6xx fields, use the appropriate thesaurus. If the topical subject heading is not derived from a standard thesaurus but is compatible with the form of headings from that thesaurus and it has value to institutions other than yours, use either field 650 or field 651 with 2nd indicator 4.

Many pre-AACR2 headings for personal names, corporate bodies, etc., are similar to corresponding AACR2 forms. However, some pre-AACR2 headings will never have corresponding AACR2 forms. Often, these headings include obsolete form subheadings. Their inclusion in WorldCat and in local catalogues usually results in split files of headings for similar materials because of different practices under AACR2 and older rules.

Examples include:

- 100 1 Francesco d'Assisi, ‡c Saint. ‡k Legend ‡p Fioretti. ‡l English. ‡f 1959.
- 110 2 Jews. ‡k Liturgy and ritual. ‡g Tunis.
- 130 0 Arthur, King ‡k (Romances, etc.).

OCLC encourages you to construct the heading or uniform title according to AACR2, but you are not required to do so. Change the heading or delete the heading in favour of an appropriate subject or genre heading. If a heading appearing on retrospective cataloguing copy was incorrectly constructed under pre-AACR2, revise that heading to a valid pre-AACR2 or AACR2 form.

SERIES HEADINGS

- Fields 400, 410 and 411 Series Statement/Added Entry headings are obsolete as described in MARC 21. OCLC has invalidated and removed fields 400, 410 and 411. Enter such series statements as they appear in the retrospective cataloguing copy in field 490, correcting any obvious errors, and supply the series tracing in the appropriate 8xx field.
- OCLC encourages you to construct an AACR2 form for the series but you are not required to do so. The form in the 4xx field should be compatible with the rules used for description. Trace the AACR2 form in an 8xx field.
- If the name portion of a name/title series entry is verifiable online, enter the name portion to match the form in the name authority record.

USING GMDS (MEDIA QUALIFIERS)

General Material Designators are generic terms describing the medium of the item. Prior to AACR2, GMDs were known as media qualifiers. GMDs have also been called medium designators. Use subfield ‡h (Medium) for GMDs only in field 245 (Title Statement). Use only the current form of the appropriate GMD. Do not capitalize the first letter of the GMD. Enclose the GMD in brackets.

MAIN ENTRY, ADDED ENTRY

If the AACR2 form cannot be verified online and a single surname appears without a forename and is instead followed by a long dash, do not enter the long dash. Enter "Dezauche,- as "Dezauche,". If an asterisk precedes an added entry to indicate that the personal name has been revised, do not enter the asterisk.

TITLE STATEMENT

- If the title portion has underlining, do not enter the underlining.
- Enter the same number of ellipses as appear on the LC copy.
- If ellipses occur within data, enter a space before and after the ellipses.
- If the ellipses are followed by a mark of punctuation (. , : ; ! ?), do not enter a space following ellipses.
- If two vertical parallel lines (| |) appear on the copy, enter space-slash-space (/) instead of these vertical lines. Such lines show that the title of a work is printed in verse or distinguish two editions or versions of a rare book.
- If the title has superscript and subscript alphabetic characters, enter the characters as regular lowercase characters, except in formulas.

IMPRINT STATEMENT

- If the reprint statement has the appearance of a double imprint (*e.g.*, "Bonnae, Apud Henry and Cohen, 1856; Frankfurt/Main, Minerva, 1967"), separate the reprint statement from the imprint by a period. Enter the first (original) imprint as part of the preceding field (title or edition). Enter the reprint data in field 260 (Publication, Distribution, Etc.).
- In the following imprint, the place of publication appears to have a street address: "72-Souligne-sous-Ballon, l'auteur, 1968." But "72" is a postal code and "Souligne-sous-Ballon" is the name of the town. Enter both (as they appear on the card) as the place of publication.
- If a place name (*e.g.*, "Rio") is incomplete, enter the complete name with brackets around the data not appearing on LC copy (*e.g.*, "Rio [de Janeiro]").

- If two places of publication are separated by a conjunction (*and, und, u.*) or by a hyphen, enter a comma instead of the conjunction or hyphen and treat the two places as two separate places of publication.

GERMAN IMPRINT STATEMENTS

Separation of two place names by a hyphen usually (although not always) indicates that one place is located near a larger, better known place (*e.g.*, "Hamburg-Altona"). Treat such entries as a single place of publication. Two place names separated by "bei" or "b." (*e.g.*, "Ratingen b. Dusseldorf") constitute a single place. Treat two place names separated by *und* or *u.* as two separate places of publication.

COLLATION

Do not enter the statement *Cover title* in the collation. Enter *Cover title* in the first note field. When illustration information is given in the title paragraph or in a general note, but not in the collation, enter the collation as is. Do not add the illustration information to the collation. Do not enter illustration codes in the fixed field. If a statement of reprint is included, do not enter *reprint* in the 300 field. Use a 5xx note field for reprint information.

SERIES STATEMENTS

Some records have a "bound with" note in the series statement position and a series statement in the note position. Use the 4xx and/or 8xx fields for series statements and the 5xx fields for notes. Disregard the position on the card. Tag each field according to what it is rather than where it is.

LOCAL NOTES

Do not include copy-specific or institution-specific details (such as binding, imperfections, incompleteness or copy number) in the master record. If you want such notes to appear on cards or in OCLC-MARC records, include the notes in field 590 (Local Note).

- 590 L.C. copy imperfect: bibliography wanting.
- 590 L.C. has v.1, 3-5 only

Optionally, if the copy-specific or institution-specific details are of interest beyond the inputting library, enter them in a 500 field (General note) with subfield $5, Institution to which field applies.

TITLE TRACINGS

Follow local practice when entering the title added entry indicator. Some title tracings are inverted (*e.g.*, "Title: Retail Terms, A Manual of."). Use field 246 (Varying Form of Title) for such titles. LC copy for a work published in English but translated from a non-Roman language may have a phrase in the form "Russian title: [title in Cyrillic alphabet] (transliterated: [title in

Roman alphabet])" following the tracings. Do not enter these phrases and titles. They are not part of the tracings because they are not preceded by a Roman numeral.

Limited cataloguing records (identified by a double dagger after the card number) do not have series tracings. If you add series tracings, treat the resulting record as having been upgraded by your library. Enter your library's symbol in field 040 (Cataloguing Source) subfield ‡d (Modifying agency).

SUBJECT HEADINGS

- Enter only these subject headings: LC (including Library of Congress subject headings for children's literature), National Library of Medicine (NLM) and National Agricultural Library (NAL).
- Spell out in full, according to current LC practice, abbreviations that appear in older LC subject headings (*e.g.*, spell out "Bibl." as "Bibliography").
- Do not enter non-LC, non-NLM or non-NAL subject headings enclosed in brackets.
- Do not enter portions of subject headings enclosed in brackets.

If a portion of a subject heading is enclosed in sub-script parentheses, enter the data, but do not enter the parentheses.

FULL NAME NOTES (SECULAR NAME, NAME ORIGINALLY, ETC.)

Do not enter full name notes that appear in brackets between the tracings and the card number.

COPYRIGHT NUMBER

Do not enter copyright numbers that appear in the lower left corner below the LC legend.

CONTENT DESIGNATION

Use the following guidelines (New and Old) for tagging and entering data in subfields used for pre-AACR2 bibliographic data.

GUIDELINE 1–NEW CONTENT DESIGNATION

Use the new content designation when an old, corresponding content designation has been replaced.

Use the following guidelines:

- Enter an alternative title in subfield ‡a (Title) of field 245 (Title Statement).
  - 245 00 On the Little Big Horn; or, Custer's last stand
- Enter adjacent publisher statements (different publishers or agencies) in separate subfield ‡b's (Name of publisher, distributor, etc.) of field

260 (Publication, Distribution, Etc. [Imprint]). Use punctuation as a guide. If in doubt, use separate subfields.

- 260 Washington, ‡b Published for the Library of Congress by the Gertrude Clark Whittal Poetry and Literature Fund; ‡b [for sale by the Superintendent of Documents, U.S. Govt. Print. Off.] ‡c 1964.

- Enter printing dates in field 260 subfield ‡c (Date of publication, distribution, etc.) in pre-AACR2 records, regardless of whether the printing dates are enclosed in parentheses on the copy. Do not enter the parentheses.
  - *260 London:* ‡b J. Lane, ‡c 1902 (1907 printing)ã
  - *260 London*: ‡b J. Lane, ‡c 1902, 1907 printing.
- Enter accompanying material data in subfield ‡e (Accompanying material) of field 300 (Physical Description).
  - *300 6 v.*: ‡b ill., maps; ‡c 22 cm. ‡e and atlases (3 v.: ill.; 30 cm.)
  - 300 3 l., 100 p. ‡b illus. ‡c 25 cm. ‡e and portfolio (24 plates) 30 cm.
- Use subfield ‡v (Volume number/sequential designation) in field 490 (Series Statement).
  - 490 1 ACRL monographs, ‡v no.8
- Repeat subfields ‡a (Series statement) and ‡v for a subseries that follows the main series number (first subfield ‡v) in field 490.
  - 490 1 Biblioteca de arte hispanico; ‡v 8: ‡a Artes aplicades; ‡v 1

GUIDELINE 2–OLD CONTENT DESIGNATION

Use the old content designation when no new designation has been defined. For pre-AACR2 conference names entered under place (AACR2 form not verifiable online), use subfield ‡q (Name of meeting following jurisdiction name entry element) in x11 fields.

- 711 Hague. ‡q International Peace Conference, ‡n 2d, ‡d 1907.

Use the following guidelines to delimit short titles (field 245 subfield ‡a) in pre-ISBD records:

- If a title has a date or a range of dates, terminate the short title after the date.
  - 245 10 Disarmament and Soviet policy 1964-1968 ‡c by Thomas B.Larson.
- If a title has a colon as the first mark of punctuation, terminate the short title at the next logical break following the colon.
  - *245 10 Canada 2067:* Canada in the next century ‡c by John Smith.
- If a title has brackets, terminate the short title at the next logical break.
  - 245 10 Catalogue of musical instruments [in the] Victoria and Albert Museum ‡c [by] Raymond Russell.

SCORES

Use subfield ‡d (Plate or publisher number) for a plate or publisher number that is part of the imprint (field 260). In addition, enter the plate or publisher's number in a nonprinting field 028 (Publisher Number).

- 028 20 18315 ‡b Breitkopf and Härtel
- 260 Leipzig, ‡b Breitkopf and Härtel ‡c [1888 or 9] ‡d Pl. no.18315.

SOUND RECORDINGS

Use field 262 (Imprint Statement for Sound Recordings [Pre-AACR2]) for a pre-AACR2 imprint. Enter the publisher number in a nonprinting field 028.

- 028 00 SLT 43091 ‡b Telefunken
- 262 ‡b Telefunken ‡c SLT 43091. ‡d [1966]

If the retrospective copy consists of separate bibliographic records for each separately titled work, you are encouraged but not required to recatalog the item (AACR2, rule 6.1G) to describe the sound recording as a unit. (A record for a sound recording described as a unit may coexist with the records describing its separately titled works.)

AUDIOVISUAL MATERIALS

Use field 261 (Imprint Statement for Films [Pre-AACR2 Revised]) for pre-ISBD production and release information.

- 261 Archers Film Production, ‡f London, ‡d 1947. ‡b Released in the U.S. by Universal International Films, ‡d 1948.

MAPS

Use field 507 (Scale Note for Graphic Material) for a scale note:

- 507 Scale 1:500,000; ‡b 1 in. equals approx. 8 miles.

RECATALOGING

If you have retrospective copy and the item in hand, you may recatalog the item according to AACR2.

Use the following guidelines:

- The record must meet at least the K-level input standard.
- Use the OCLC Authority File to verify each heading. If an AACR2 or AACR2-compatible form is present, use that form. If no AACR2 or AACR2-compatible form is present, you must create an AACR2 form.
- If you are entering Library of Congress subject headings (6xx with second indicator value *0*), you must follow current LC cataloguing policy.

TRANSCRIBING AACR2 COPY

Because OCLC loads current LC and National Library of Medicine (NLM) cataloguing, you seldom transcribe printed AACR2 cataloguing. This part provides guidelines for such transcription in these rare cases.

LC OR NLM COPY

The legend *AACR2* in the lower right corner identifies current LC printed cataloguing. Transcribe the data exactly as shown on LC or NLM copy.

LC cataloguing

Enter *DLC* in field 040 subfield ‡a (Original cataloguing agency) and assign the code *b/*(National bibliographic agency) in *Srce*.

- ELvl: I
- Srce: b/
- 040 DLC ‡c XXX

NLM Cataloguing

Enter *NLM* in field 040 subfield ‡a and assign code *b/*(National bibliographic agency) in Srce.

- ELvl: I
- Srce: b/
- 040 NLM ‡c XXX

Supply other fixed-field elements and variable fields, indicators and subfield codes. Include the LC call number (field 050), the NLM call number (field 060) and the Dewey Decimal call number (field 082) if they appear on the LC or NLM copy. If you cannot transcribe the record exactly because of the limitations of the machine-readable record, modify the appropriate data. If you modify LC or NLM data, supply the appropriate MRec code.

MODIFICATIONS TO LC AND NLM COPY

If more than one MRec code applies, assign a code in the following order of preference: *s* (Shortened record), *r* (Record is completely romanized; corresponding LC manual record is in the original script), *o* (Record is completely romanized; corresponding LC manual record is also romanized). Enter your OCLC symbol in field 040 subfield ‡d to indicate that you have modified LC or NLM cataloguing:

- 040 DLC ‡c XXX ‡d XXX
- 040 NLM ‡c XXX ‡d XXX

Data Elements Defined in the MARC Formats but Not in AACR2

Some important data elements (*e.g.*, fixed-field *Lang* and field 041 [Language Code]) do not appear on printed LC or NLM cataloguing, but must be included in the record. Follow the I-level input standard for such data. Do not use a MRec code.

LC CATALOGUING IN PUBLICATION

You seldom transcribe AACR2 printed LC Cataloguing-in-Publication (CIP) because OCLC receives most CIP directly from LC. Contact OCLC if you have printed LC CIP which is not represented in WorldCat. Verify that LC has not used the LCCN appearing in CIP for cataloguing an earlier edition or different title. Do not add such records as LC cataloguing copy.

REPRODUCTIONS FROM LC COPY

You may use LC cataloguing for the original item to create a new record for a microform or photocopy reproduction. Treat the new record as your institution's original cataloguing. Use Srce code *d* and enter your OCLC symbol in field 040 subfield ‡a:

- Srce: d
- 040 XXX ‡c XXX

LIBRARY AND ARCHIVES CANADA COPY

To transcribe cataloguing (including Canadian CIP) from the Library and Archives Canada (NLC), treat the new record as your institution's original cataloguing. Use Srce code *d* and enter your OCLC symbol in field 040 subfield ‡a:

- Srce: d
- 040 XXX ‡c XXX

OTHER NATIONAL LIBRARIES

Treat current cataloguing records (including CIP) from other national libraries, such as the British Library and the National Library of Australia, as original cataloguing.

FULL, CORE, MINIMAL AND ABBREVIATED-LEVEL CATALOGUING

Historically, in cooperation with OCLC advisory groups, OCLC established input standards for entering bibliographic data into WorldCat. Unless noted otherwise, these standards conform to national standards. In addition, OCLC adopted the core-level standard that was defined in 1994 by the Cooperative Cataloguing Council (now known as the Programme for Cooperative Cataloguing (PCC)).

FULL-LEVEL CATALOGUING

Records that meet the requirements of second-level description (AACR2, rule 1.0D2). Correspondence between data in Full-level records and data required for second-level description is not exact. Input full records when possible.

CORE-LEVEL CATALOGUING

Records that meet at least the requirements of first-level description (AACR2, rule 1.0D1) and meet some requirements of second-level description (AACR2, rule 1.0D2). The core standard is a less-than-full standard, but is more inclusive than Minimal-level. The standard is optional. Use it as appropriate.

MINIMAL-LEVEL CATALOGUING

Records that meet the requirements of first-level description (AACR2, rule 1.0D1). Correspondence between data in Minimal-level records and data required for firstlevel description is not exact. Data required for online cataloguing may not be required by cataloguing rules. Input Minimal-level records as appropriate. Users may upgrade Minimal-level records.

ABBREVIATED-LEVEL CATALOGUING

Brief records that do not meet the requirements of Minimal-level cataloguing specifications. Because Abbreviated-level records may not meet Minimal-level standards, users with Full-level cataloguing authorization or higher can upgrade these records. Depending on the authorization level, users may upgrade to *K, I, 4* or *b/*.

ENCODING LEVEL

The code in ELvl identifies the standard to which a record conforms. In ELvl, use code *I* for Full-level, code *4* for Core-level, code *K* for Minimal-level, and code *3* for Abbreviated-level.

PROGRAMME FOR COOPERATIVE CATALOGUING

Various programmes (CONSER, BIBCO) support input of Core-level records.

Cooperative programme participants create Core-level records under the auspices of the Programme for Cooperative Cataloguing (PCC). Programme participants identify "Programme-created Core-level records" by entering *pcc* in field 042 (Authentication Code) and code *4* in ELvl. They may also create Fulllevel records (ELvl: blank) under the auspices of the Programme. They enter *pcc* in field 042.

Example of a Programme-created Core-level record:

- ELvl: 4
- Srce: c
- 040 System-supplied OCLC symbol.
- 042 pcc

Example of a Programme-created Full-level record:

- ELvl: b/
- Srce: c
- 040 System-supplied OCLC symbol.
- 042 pcc

Example of a Non-Programme created Core-level record:

- ELvl: 4
- Srce: d
- 040 System-supplied OCLC symbol.
- *[Omit field 042.]*

Programme participants must supply the applicable elements of the Core-level standard. They may supply additional elements, up to Full-level.

MINIMAL-LEVEL CATALOGUING

Input records according to the Minimal-level standard, as appropriate.

For example:

- Constraints on resources, collection development policies and cataloguing priority can also determine the kinds of materials receiving Minimal-level treatment
- Conversions of older cataloguing records that do not contain full bibliographic data
- Materials in foreign languages in which you lack expertise
- Materials such as theses and dissertations, pamphlets, exhibition catalogues, analytics, audiovisual materials, technical reports and locally produced publications of little interest outside the issuing institution

The Minimal-level standard has the following characteristics:

- Records must be identified as code *K* in ELvl
- Represents the minimum data necessary to identify an item. Minimal-level does not prohibit the addition of data that you think is necessary

LC and CONSER have defined standards for Minimal-level cataloguing. Those standards vary from K-level. If you are a member of such a cooperative project, use its standards.

6

Functions and Nature of Online Cataloguing

INTRODUCTION

During the past decade, the widespread adoption of the online catalogue has launched the library visibly into the computer age and has made the library a center stage for information access in academic institutions and in the communities served by the public library.

A whole generation of library users has traveled the path to computer and library literacy through the use of the online catalogue. Implementation of online library catalogues has given new impetus to programmes for user education, formal bibliographic instruction, and information desks, building, in the process, an infrastructure for electronic access to the resources of the library and the community. Within the profession, the online catalogue has led to a host of conference programmes, workshops, and professional discussion groups.

Not the least of these changes is the gradual redefinition of the 'catalogue.' Ten years ago, most librarians and library users would agree to a definition of the catalogue as displaying the bibliographic information for monographs and serial titles physically held in a specific library. Today, it would be harder to get agreement on the definition of a catalogue.

Present day online catalogues are beginning to provide access to abstracting and indexing databases, full text, and 'pass through' access to catalogues of material housed in physically diverse locations in different institutions. In addition to the simple find and display functions, online catalogues are providing printing, downloading, electronic mailing of results, requests for document delivery, and access to electronic full-text.

Notwithstanding the lack of clear definition of the online catalogue, large libraries now typically have online catalogues or are actively planning to install them. The effort and resources required for adoption are very substantial: choosing between numerous different systems; finding funding; installing and connecting terminals; connecting to local area networks and the Internet; training staff and users; harmonizing the online catalogue with other computerized systems; and so on.

Recent catalogue records were generally already in machine-readable form but the conversion or upgrading of older records has involved and continues to require a major effort. The widespread adoption of online catalogues is clearly a major advance in library service and yet, in another sense, there has been relatively little progress in the basic functionality of the online catalogue.

The searching functions of the best online catalogues of 1992 were not much better than the best online catalogues of ten years earlier. Online catalogues have evolved through 'generations,' a categorization proposed by Hildreth, to differentiate catalogues in terms of the sophistication of their search functions and user interface. A 'first generation' online catalogue allows searching in the same manner as a card catalogue, typically has one mode of interaction, limited help, and simple displays.

A 'second generation' catalogue supports, in addition, the searching of individual terms within the main entry, title, and subject headings, Boolean searches, two modes of interaction multiple display options, and help and error recovery facilities. The phrases 'third generation' and 'next generation' are used to describe the catalogues that do, or will in the future, include advanced functionality and broader access.

Over the last ten years, there has been a gradual development from first to second generation catalogues facilitated by the increasing awareness of the librarians and users of the potential of online access as well as by the rapid drop in costs of computing. Almost everything else around the online catalogue has changed more substantially: extensive installation of infrastructure; massive conversion of existing catalogue records to machine-readable form; the mounting of additional bibliographic databases in conjunction with catalogues or on CD-ROMS; and the mounting of full-text documents online. During the past ten years there has been a limited relationship between the users and the designers of online catalogues.

The origin of both the first and second generation online catalogues are deeply rooted in the card catalogue. We have often been constrained and our purposes determined, to an extent we often discount, by the types of technological advances currently available that happen to be more or less useful in the context of an online catalogue.

With the card catalogue as their frame of reference, most of us were not in any better position to provide meaningful input to the design process than the trailblazers who took the first steps. It turned out that online catalogues were easier and more rewarding to use than the card catalogue and users responded by expressing high levels of satisfaction with the online catalogue and using them more.

The online catalogue has brought with it relatively sophisticated tools for automatically gathering data on catalogue use. For example, transaction logs, combined with various other kinds of studies, provide a continuous flow of information on the strengths and weaknesses of online catalogues on the basis of patron usage. The information gleaned from these studies has been used to improve the catalogue and the library environment of the catalogue. Though most of these improvements, such as better help messages, new indexes for special functions, orientation programmes, glare-free locations for terminals, etc., have been small, the cumulative effect has been a gradual improvement of the catalogue and a rapidly broadening perception of its potential.

Although the state-of-the-art in functionality of online catalogues has evolved little, numerous constructive proposals have been made, increasingly by researchers interested in, but not responsible for, operational online catalogues. It is clear, however, from the research reviewed that users are experien-cing significant problems in making effective use of online catalogues in spite of expectations. When the users don't go away empty-handed, they may feel satisfied even though in reality they have received incomplete search results.

Because users may be unaware of what information they are missing, they have been slow to articulate these types of problems. This review examines problems with online catalogues, examines some actual and proposed solutions, and seeks to understand the changing position of the online catalogue. Although some of the solutions draw on other kinds of online bibliographic retrieval systems, our focus is on online catalogues, concentrating on recent literature, and is deliberately selective. From this analysis it is hoped to provide not only a convenient summary of recent developments, but also to contribute to the agenda for research, development, and design of future online catalogues.

The review is in five parts:

- The introduction defines the scope of the review and summarizes briefly the present situation;
- Difficulties encountered by users are then examined;
- Opinions and evidence concerning users are noted;
- Solutions for identified difficulties are examined; and, finally,
- Conclusions are drawn.

PROBLEMS

In this part identified problems of online catalogues are noted.

FORMULATING A SEARCH

Researchers have been observing users, conducting user surveys, and examining online catalogue trans-action logs to develop a picture of what is happening when users interact with the system. The results of these studies have been used to improve levels of search effectiveness. However, recent studies suggest that users continue to experience discoura-gingly low levels of search effectiveness using online catalogues. Larson conducted a transaction log study of the University of California's MELVYL online catalogue and concluded that subject searching had declined 2.15% per year over a 6-year period, while title keyword searching increased by a comparable amount.

He attributed the likely causes to the high incidence of search failure for subject searches and the problem of 'information overload' in successful subject searches as the size of database grows. In 1986, Shaw reported that novice searchers choose the wrong database, search several concepts in a single statement, and use unlimited truncation.

It has been widely observed that users do not base subject searches on known documents. Hildreth reports survey results indicating that 75% of users would be more likely to look up "any publication that may have information on a specific topic or subject area" rather than look up specific books they know about on the topic. People inevitably make mechanical errors using computers. Seaman found that 40% of user errors were due to incorrect author or title and 9% due to unsupported abbre-viations.

They also make spelling errors and have trouble with conjunctions, ellipsis, and missing or incorrect punctuation. A small, but significant, portion of search failures have been attributed to typographical and spelling errors (9.9%-15%) and system failure (9.7-18%), but an even larger proportion (29%) arise from the failure to match user terms with controlled vocabularies. Studies are showing that library users still do not find the use of Boolean operators intuitively obvious. Bellardo observed that searchers misuse logical operators. Peters found that 73.5% of Boolean AND searches fail while 84.8% of Boolean AND searches between two subject headings also fail.

In her recent study of online catalogue use, Ensor shows that there is still widespread lack of familiarity with Boolean operators. Ensor also found that computer 'literacy' affects the degree of facility with which users are using online catalogues. Peters found that remote users of online catalogues are more sophisticated in terms of search patterns than in-library users. For example, he found that 38% of remote users used right truncation while user-initiated truncation was almost non-existent among in-library users.

Users still make errors of basic strategy. Very early on, researchers noticed that catalogue users were failing to develop successful search strategies. A decade ago, searching on broad single terms that trigger large, unmanageable retrievals and missing obvious synonyms that could increase results of small retrievals were common user errors. In fact, most subject queries used "whatever popped into the searcher's mind".

The situation has not improved much a decade later. In a transaction log study of academic library use, Hunter found that subject searching was used most frequently, but least successfully. In addition to typographical errors and using uncontrolled vocabulary, she attributed this failure to a misunderstanding of how to use the system. Bates made the important observation that searchers fail to consider the inverse relationship between recall and precision in searching, *i.e.*, that expanding a search to find additional relevant records will also increase the number of non-relevant records and refining a search to exclude non-relevant records will also exclude some relevant ones.

The other side of the coin is search failure. Searches, even in large databases, frequently retrieve sets that are either null (*i.e.*, empty or 'zero-hit') or perceived by the user as too small. Ten years ago, between 23% to 45% of searches were reported as resulting in null sets. This problem has not changed significantly. Markey found that 34% of subject keyword searches retrieve no records and 53% of subject keyword searches retrieve only one relevant citation.

Peters reported a 40% zero-hit rate for searches of an online university catalogue. Hunter came to the daunting conclusion that 58% of searches fail. Of course, not all zero-hit searches are search failures. It is possible that in fact no relevant record in the database matches the search query. Perhaps the user was seeking to confirm the absence of a citation.

However, researchers examining zero-hit searches are demonstrating how minor changes in search statements succeed in retrieving the type and quantity of records desired (Berger, personal communication). For example, if a searcher queries a database indexed with Library of Congress Subject Headings (LCSH), a subject word search on 'Vietnam War' will fail where a subject word search on 'Vietnamese Conflict' will succeed.

An experienced searcher might find this by searching submitting a title word search on 'Vietnam War', look at the subject headings and discover that the material on this topic is in fact entered under 'Vietnamese Conflict'. This example reveals the effect of not implementing LCSH cross-references in MELVYL, but it is also characteristic of how LCSH terminology can differ from natural language that people really use.

Another example of this type of failure is the perfectly reasonable subject search on 'Bayesian statistics' which retrieves no records, because LCSH uses 'Bayesian statistical decision theory' for this subject category and provides no cross-reference. If these variant phrases were linked, the user would retrieve records on these topics. As these examples clearly demonstrate, zero-hit search results do not necessarily reflect a lack of records in the database. Several researchers have reported that users have difficulty using subject headings.

MODIFYING SEARCHES

Not only do library users have difficulty formulating searches, they also fail to modify them effectively. System features currently available on most online catalogue systems for dealing with problematic search results include truncation, Boolean operators, and date, language, and location limits. But users rarely use advanced features even when they are available. Harter reported that only half of searchers use these system features, usually the 'limit' command or a change of output format. Shenouda found that most changes are related to the deletion and addition of terms and facets. Even many experienced users do not use all system capabilities. Are users unaware of the existence of advanced features?

Are the advanced features too difficult, too complicated, or too much trouble to use? That library users rarely base subsequent searches on previous results seems to be a characteristic pattern. Tolle and Hah found that 15% of users quit immediately after receiving an error message. Both problems are perhaps due to incomplete understanding of how the database is structured. No satisfactory solution has yet been developed to cope effectively with null and 'too small' sets.

Novices generally accept null sets unquestioningly. Not only do searchers accept defeat rather quickly when confronted with a zero-hit result, they also flounder when rewarded with a few worthwhile records and want more like them. Ercegovac reported 46% of users having difficulty increasing results when too little is retrieved. More records on the search topic may very well exist in the database, but the necessary link that would lead to their successful retrieval has not been made, either on the part of the searcher or the system.

To compound the problem, indexing techniques and retrieval methods that work well with small and medium-sized catalogues tend to fall short and fail when catalogues become large. An increasing problem is the retrieval of excessively large numbers of records. Factors related to large retrievals include size of the database, keyword indexing, and use of the Boolean OR. Physical limitations of the display screen and inadequate search assistance compound the large retrieval problem, especially for untrained users.

When the retrieved set is large, users must decide whether to continue displaying more records, whether to reformulate the search query, and at what point to discontinue the search. Early studies showed users retrieving large sets 22%-53% of the time and 26% of users experiencing problems reducing the result when too much was retrieved. Repeated negative experiences with large retrieved sets without adequate online tools to cope with them continue to discourage users from using online catalogues. Kantor found that the number of positive and negative reinforcements affects when users stop. As the size of the database increases, legitimate types of searches tend increasingly to retrieve large, unwieldy sets.

Even though Bates observed in 1984 that a 30-hit response is considered an optimal search by many searchers, the reality is more often than not 'information overload'. The average subject search by a skilled user in MELVYL in 1987 was yielding over 181 records. A decade ago, Bates observed that users typically responded to searches that retrieved one hundred or more citations by either walking away from the terminal or displaying all of the citations. Larson found that the average number of records retrieved by searchers in a large online catalogue was 77.5, but users only displayed 9.1 records.

In 1992 MELVYL users were still finding many more records than they were willing to display, retrieving an average of 100 records, but only displaying about 15 records per search. With a large system like MELVYL, with 7 million records in its catalogue database, it has also been necessary during times of peak usage to implement a policy of blocking resource-intensive searches that typically return very large sets. Such searches would normally be considered reasonable in smaller databases. How can methods for modifying a search query be conveyed to users when search results are too large? As of 1992, online search aids provide little strategic help for higher-level problem-solving tasks involved in selecting, evaluating and modifying queries.

HANDLING RETRIEVED SETS

Having retrieved a set of records, what next? A search on a large database that presents the user with an unmanageably large retrieved set is only accomplishing part of the task. What assistance is available to help the user cope with a large set of records and make decisions about it? How can the user satisfactorily determine if any records in the set are likely to be relevant and where they are within the large set? How can a view of the set be presented so that the user can make reasonably informed decisions about how to proceed?

How can the user quickly obtain a summary of features that characterize the set and identify subsets likely to be of interest? Are there functions that can be applied that will sort and display views of the entire set from various perspectives, *e.g.*, language, publication date, location, subject headings, title words? Does the average user have, and know about, the tools to reduce the set size in an appropriate, helpful way?

Short of moving on to a new or modified search, the user ordinarily has only one option: to display screen after screen of records that have been sorted into alphabetical order of main entry, a tradition carried over from the card catalogue. There may be alternative forms of display for individual records, but, as of 1992, responses to a query on PACS-L indicated that few options were available and that it was still rare for an online catalogue to allow the user to choose any other ordering or to provide any tools for understanding anything about the retrieved records other than how many there are. It is, therefore, not surprising that users look at a limited number of items and select a few.

SYSTEM DEFICIENCIES

In spite of the afore-mentioned problems, online catalogues are still proving to be remarkably useful and popular. It is, therefore, fortunate that libraries can benefit from the continuing, dramatic improvements in the power and cost-effectiveness of computing, networks, and data storage. Unfortunately, increased speed, memory, and disk space are not enough to cope adequately with the problem of providing effective access to large numbers of records. Searching is computationally intensive.

Second generation online catalogues consume substantially greater computing resources than those of the first generation because of the need to support keyword indexes, keyword truncation, and Boolean combinations. This results in system slowdowns. In 1989, Farley reported that about 10% of searches on the University of California MELVYL system were resulting in large retrievals that took 60 or more seconds to report back findings.

There is also an emerging need to provide high speed downloading of records. This requirement was not expected a decade ago when the need was to support terminals at relatively low speed, but is now implicit in the expectation that high speed networks will be used to search and download results from remote catalogues.

DATA DEFICIENCIES

Data deficiencies affect the quality of search results. Close examination of any large bibliographic database reveals errors in the data. When searching is extended to non-indexed fields, the error rate will probably rise. This will present significant problems when more fields become searchable. Ballard and Lifshin have commented on the need to eliminate spelling errors in bibliographic databases. Large database size is an inhibiting factor in tracking down duplicate records. Software designed to analyse retrieved sets will also prove useful in identifying deficient data. The recent achievement of OCLC in correcting up to 30,000 records a day should be an inspiration to all.

TOPICAL ACCESS AND SYSTEM VOCABULARIES

The present review makes no attempt to duplicate Larson's review of subject searching in online catalogues in volume 15 of Advances in Librarianship to which reference should be made. In general, users have trouble expressing questions in subject terms and matching terms to information systems. Bates found that there is only a 10% to 20% likelihood that two people will use the same term for a concept.

Peters and Kurth found that 58% of search sessions begin with terms not used in the system's controlled vocabulary. Several researchers have reported that users have difficulty using LCSH for subject searching. In 1983, Markey found subject searchers did not consult LCSH even when it was easily available. Bellardo noted the failure to use controlled vocabulary. Even when users do attempt to base searches on LCSH, they are confronted with a formidably complicated maze of relationships.

Although modifications have been made, the loose structure of LCSH does not fit well into the typical thesaurus organization with highly structured broad, narrow, and related terms. Not only does this present problems in searching, but it also interferes with the presentation of retrieved sets to the user in a coherent fashion. LCSH phrase headings and inverted syntax disrupt the logical sequencing of subject heading subdivisions. Not surprisingly, Butkovich concluded that users do not understand the organization and structure of LCSH.

Hancock-Beaulieu argues that online catalogue systems at present do not offer any opportunity for a contextual approach to searching. There are no tools for negotiation or experimentation that the user can call upon to further define queries. She also believes that browsing system indexes is of limited value and that alphabetical listings of LCSH do not offer an overview of related subjects. In addition, there is the problem that browsing records ordered by class number fails to convey the structure of the classification scheme to the user.

She points out that combining pre-coordinate subject headings (LCSH) with post-coordinate keyword indexing can cause confusion. Larson reported that title word searches are being increasingly favoured over subject searches and Frost found that, as in a card catalogue, faculty do mostly known-item searches. One explanation for this is that faculty do not search for books in their own field by subject because they are already familiar with the books and authors they are investigating. However, this suggests that users are not basing their searches on the indexing system offered by the system.

USERS

WHAT DO LIBRARY USERS WANT

Unquestionably, online catalogues are enjoying high use, and perceived success in service leads to demands for more services.

Librarians are becoming familiar with requests that the online catalogue be extended to provide access to records for articles held in the library as well as records for books and, indeed, to the texts themselves. Gradually, many of these additional functions are being put in place. Meanwhile, several comments have been made about the features users want in an online catalogue.

Bates found that searchers want a sense of control over the search, to know what is going on during the search, and what information is being included and rejected and why. Crawford thinks that it is important to users to feel in control, but understanding all the mechanics involved is not critical. Ensor has found that about two-thirds of library catalogue users tend to look at a long list of results rather than take some action to narrow it.

She attributes this to two reasons:

- Users have difficulty learning and remembering appropriate actions to take to narrow a search; and
- Users want to maintain control over the whole process.

In her study of keyword and Boolean use in a university online catalogue, Ensor found that users do use Boolean operators when a search retrieves too much or too little, but faculty and graduate students find Boolean operators easier to learn than undergraduates. Interestingly, she also found that undergraduates use keyword searching more than either graduate students or faculty.

Sixty per-cent of all users felt that keyword searching is easy to learn, but this was affected by possession or lack of computer experience. Recent literature includes several comments concerning users' preferences. Ercegovac states that 45% of users want to see related terms. But online catalogues do very little to support this. Forty-two per cent want to search tables of contents or back-of-book indexes and 24% want to search title words. Fox and Harman say searchers prefer document-ranked retrieval, *i.e.*, with documents individually ranked according to an estimate of the probability of being relevant, to other methods.

Saracevic and others found that precision was associated with high satisfaction. This points to a need on the part of the users for additional points of access and more options to organize result sets that will allow them to judge relevance. As for how many records are wanted, a 30-record response is widely considered a typical optimal result, and professional searchers view 50 to 70 references as optimal. Kinnucan found satisfaction relatively unaffected by retrieval set size but sensitive to precision, though less so as retrieved set size increased.

WHAT DO EXPERIENCED SEARCHERS DO

There is good reason to examine what experienced searchers do. What works for experienced searchers could form the basis for redesign of the system to make the strategies adopted by experts more accessible to novice searchers. Experienced searchers tend to adopt stereotyped sequences of tactics which could be embedded, more or less, in the interface. Providing for 'strategic commands' that would trigger such a pattern of tactics might empower the novice as well as provide an appreciated labour-saving amenity for the expert.

Fidel has studied that informal, highly intuitive methods used by experienced searchers to select 'search keys' and how they can be formalized in a decision tree and incorporated into knowledge base of an expert system. Harris observed that experienced searchers view large sets as intermediary sets, *i.e.*, as a basis for a more refined, secondary search. Successful searchers tend to view large sets as being presented with a wider range of choices rather than feeling overwhelmed by information overload.

Hancock noted that searchers who consciously adopt a broad search formulation strategy are more successful than those who take an exact matching approach. Starting with more general terms to gain an overview of the domains they cover can often give a searcher a better idea of how to phrase a narrower search. If novices and successful searchers start their searches in much the same way, does the difference lie more in how they view and continue the search process? If so, how is that 'broad view' conveyed? Katzer sees user interaction with the system as a process of enhancing and refining the original query. In all cases, support for providing tools for analysing retrieved sets is indicated.

MODELS

Inevitably any but the most sophisticated design will be based on a set of assumptions concerning the expected users. Similarly, any but the most trivial usage depends on a set of expectations by the user concerning system behaviour. Ordinarily, 'cognitive model' is used to denote the system's assumptions concerning the user and 'conceptual model' to denote the user's assumptions concerning the system. People do not operate like machines, and some researchers have pointed out that people do not approach problems in a linear, logical fashion.

They have memory limitations and tend to organize information idiosyncratically. Several authors have urged that the development of cognitive models of how users process information ought to lead to the design of better systems. We still need to look at how people process information when solving problems. Belkin has urged the importance of discovering users' goals, tasks and behaviours.

This has led to attempts to base system design on a conceptual organization of knowledge and human information processing limits. One approach has been to study information-seeking activity at the catalogue and at the shelves as an interrelated process. An-other problem with developing concise models of users is that data from user studies is more often qualitative or impressionistic than quantitative. Although Bellardo did not find searching performance to be related to cognitive or personality traits, there have been several studies that found observable differences among groups. Horne found that solvers and non-solvers use different self-questioning strategies.

Harter reports that re-searchers in the 'hard' scientific and technological disciplines tend to share a common paradigm and agree more on terms than researchers in 'soft' literary and sociological disciplines. This makes agreement on terminology outside of narrowly specified domains much more difficult. For more on user models, see Ellis who analysed the search behaviour of academic social scientists in terms of six types of procedure: starting, chaining, browsing, differentiating, monitoring and extracting. Dickson concluded that gaps in users' conceptual models were a significant source of errors and several writers have urged the use of metaphor, maps, or models to orient users by providing a conceptual map of the system.

Mental models are effective for complex tasks according to Borgman, who has argued that conceptual training is superior to procedural training, at least for complex tasks. Brown suggested helping the user develop a search strategy using an outline metaphor. Using a flowchart to create a conceptual map of the search is one way to convey mental models of systems and teach users conceptual models. A flowchart model would include six basic steps: initiation, selection, exploration, formulation, collection, and presentation.

Researchers are more successful when they think in categorical terms and concluded that users who have difficulty lack a model of information flow, knowledge of the bibliographic chain, knowledge of relationships between subjects, and an under-standing of knowledge creation. Borgman observed that front ends tend more to ease mechanical rather than conceptual problems of use. Library activists made the interesting observation that people who learn to use a complex device without instruction modify their theories with experience, but these changes may be based on limited evidence and can instead reinforce incorrect understanding.

Reviewing the literature on what users want, how experts search, and, especially, cognitive and conceptual models, suggests that it makes little sense to study online catalogues in isolation from other retrieval systems. In the next part, we take a look at some solutions that have implemented or proposed.

SOLUTIONS

FORMULATING A SEARCH

Retrieval Techniques

The current state-of-the art of operational online catalogues is solidly based on the retrieval of sets of records and basic Boolean operations. This is in marked contrast to a quite separate thirty-year tradition in information retrieval experimentation which is almost as solidly based on probabilistic retrieval models and that rank each document by an estimated probability of relevance to each query.

Predictably, the dominance of Boolean techniques in online catalogues has been challenged. Exact-match Boolean retrieval systems show major performance and user deficiencies and partial match techniques and ranking of retrieval output to be more useful than Boolean logic. Prabha has observed that the limitations of keyword indexing and Boolean logic become more pronounced as databases get larger.

Boolean techniques are widely used but are generally unsatisfactory, that all retrieval techniques perform better for some queries than for others, and that experimental techniques perform better than Boolean techniques, but these have not been implemented on any large scale. Fortunately, experimental prototypes, such as Larson's Cheshire are becoming available. At the same time, standard Boolean systems are based on unweighted binary values: to retrieve, every record must have the specified attributes and all other, unspecified attributes are deemed irrelevant. Standard Boolean systems can be considered relatively undeveloped given the possibilities for weighted search terms and for supporting conditional search modifiers that can be invoked heuristically.

As Buchanan noted, Boolean systems can be used for creating and ranking small subsets. For example, sorting by date in reverse chronological order can provide a very useful ranking. There has been little systematic comparison done and since probabilistic systems and existing Boolean systems both have the potential to be refined considerably, there is much work to be done in this area.

Search Aids and Interfaces

The use of search profiles and searcher profiles has been examined by several writers. Interfaces can be designed to support searching in order of defined priorities. The OASIS front end to MELVYL supports a repeating FEWER command for progressive retrieved set reduction that invokes stored statements of users preferences. Researchers have examined different information retrieval models that integrate user profiles into the system. SAFIR is an expert system that offers information on search strategies based on information already known about the user and the domain.

One challenging area for research and development is the design of systems that can help searchers formulate a search strategy. Slack points out that most failed searches could be turned into successful ones with minimal guidance by such techniques as limiting searches by date or identifying several relevant records to find subject headings used by the system. It has been suggested that users be offered a variety of tools that they can adapt, mix, and match.

Library activists suggest that systems automatically determine the best search approach based on characteristics of search queries. Such an approach would take into account the number of words in the query and extent to which queries match the controlled vocabulary. Belkin suggest providing online maps, tables of contents, and the capability to browse by genre. Navigation has been suggested as a key concept crucial to building successful systems that empower the user. Among other recommendations, that menus and help screens should provide enough information to teach a person to navigate through the system. A prototype intermediary system called Knowledge-based Intermediary System for Information Retrieval (KISIR) has been under development in Finland since 1986. In the KISIR system, users can request information about the search at any point in the session.

The type of information KISIR provides includes:

- Current context;
- Status of the search; and
- Instructions on how to do the next step.

Current context is indicated by displaying defaults and other parameters in effect. Search status tells the user the stage they have reached in the process and suggest possible next steps. It also offers an option of saving displayed records in either a separate file or marked inside a general session history file. There seems to be general agreement that simple functions like automatic spelling and search statement format correction should be implemented. At first glance, spell-checkers seem simple to implement but the existence of multiple languages poses problems immediately. Although the CITE system was using error-correction techniques and expert system spelling correction systems could identify phonological and sequential errors in the early 1980s, these features have not yet to be widely implemented in online catalogues and researchers are still reporting the need for automatic spelling and search statement format correction.

Although interface design is out of the scope of this review, work relevant to this review includes looking at functional components of browsing, offering novel graphical interfaces that offer with direct manipulation approaches to query formulation, using forms-type interfaces and weighing the completeness of information against number of screens needed for display. Berger has discussed the need to allow the user to configure a number of elements in the interface, such as modifying the interface appearance, location of windows icons, and buttons. Researchers argues against low-density displays: "The more relevant information within the eye span the better". For a recent review of interface research see Shaw. Online catalogues are generally hierarchically structured. Searches can be prog-ressively narrowed, but branching is generally unsupported. This means that one typically backs out of one search before entering a new search.

Moving sideways or using one feature of a record to browse other records sharing the same feature is not usually an option. Hickey and Prabha have suggested browsing records and access to more fields, and Larson recommended the browsing functionality associated with hypertext. Dynix offers a 'related works' option and BLCMP offers 'titles on this subject' option.

Improved Use of Data

Because of the complexity involved in dealing with subject access, the use of non-topical attributes for searching and, especially, for search modification, may be an effective and easier first step. Searchers typically have basic preferences concerning such non-topical attributes such as date, language, and location. Furthermore, the values of such attributes are relatively easy to manipulate in Boolean systems. Harter discussed the use of identifying such non-subject search parameters as document type, date of publication, language, author, and corporate source. Databases are often organized by document type, making database selection crucial to search success. But this is not always clear to the user. Rubens has proposed actively soliciting the user for information on format, date, intellectual level, and subject. Researchers found that although personal name-matching techniques have been developed, they are being applied to databases where no significant name authority work has been done.

There is also considerable scope for improved use of topical data. Most systems offer a very limited subject searching approach. This is usually offered in the form of exact LCSH with implicit right truncation and, in second generation catalogues, keyword searching of terms derived from LCSH, but more should be offered.

One option is to use more of the existing data. For example the classification numbers present in catalogue records could be used to extend or modify the subject headings to help the searcher make relevance judgments. The keyword matching in the personal name and subject heading fields would increase both precision and recall.

A second option is to make more sophisticated use of existing data, using, for example, probabilistic ranking techniques. Cheshire, an experimental online catalogue developed by Larson at the University of California, Berkeley, uses a classification clustering approach. For each *Library of Congress Classification* (LCC) number, the title and subject keywords of all documents assigned to it are used to increase the number of terms associated with each individual bibliographic record. Micco proposes a term weighting scheme in which weights are based on the MARC tags the term is drawn from: the first 6xx field gets highest weight because it represents aboutness.

The lowest ranking goes to natural language keywords from titles, notes, tables of contents. She also suggests extracting and displaying in scrolling windows the x, y, and z subfields containing modifiers of the LCSH. Connell also recommends searching the subdivisions of LCSH. The use of surface matching of stems and syntactic phrase types to generate a hierarchical display of phrases showing equivalence, hierarchical, and associative relation-ships.

This category could include almost any non-standard matching algorithm, such as, for example, *Latent Semantic Indexing* (LSI) which accepts keywords in any order and returns hits with an index of relevance. One development of great promise is 'entry vocabulary' capability whereby whatever words the searcher uses are converted automatically to the system vocabulary terms with a high probability of corresponding to what the searcher wants.

A simple approach is to use the existing indexes or cross-references of the system vocabulary, possibly enriched with additional cross-references to anticipate use of non-standard terms. A more advanced approach is to use statistical relation-ships between, say, title words and assigned LCSH. The inferred system vocabulary terms can be presented to the searcher for adoption or rejection.

The Cheshire online catalogue provides a working example, deriving, from whatever combination of terms the searcher may enter, a ranked listing of the LC classification numbers most likely to denote what the searcher is seeking. Buckland nominated the development of entry vocabularies as the most promising single innovation for online catalogues.

A third promising line of development is to use additional resources beyond the standard catalogue record to improve or modify searches. Bibliographies are an obvious source. Providing access, online, to dictionaries or thesauri could be helpful to the searcher in modifying or extending topical queries. As networked information resources grow, there is also a need for directories of online library catalogues, file archives, online journals, and information servers.

Another suggestion is to give the user more help in finding the most significant literature, the 'classics' in a field. 'Classics' could be based on citedness, identification by subject experts, or other indicators. A fourth option is to use the 'nearest neighbour' technique: Never mind what the specific heading is, what other record resemble this one most closely when all features are compared? Blair noted that one of the simplest, but infrequently used, approaches is to begin with a highly useful document. Using a closest match search strategy along with a dynamic feedback to the user for search refinement.

Modifying a Search

Mechanisms for Modifying Searches

Successful modification of a search depends heavily on the user's assessment of what has happened in response to a query and ideas about what the best next steps would be. How can the system assist with these two tasks? There is no reason why the system's response should not be automatic. Functionality that would provide the prompt analysis of retrieved sets, although generally a precondition for search modification, has received little attention until recently. There has been more attention to built-in support for automatic search modifications by the system.

Researchers reviewed user studies and reported that systems should provide such recovery mechanisms as:

- Searching first word of author name followed by the first letter of the second word (ie., truncated);
- Searching unmatched terms in the appropriate index;
- Displaying alphabetically adjacent terms;
- Passing unmatched terms (other than author names) against a spell checker; and
- Forcing users into a help routine after one or more identifiable errors.

Bates suggests monitoring searches at the tactics and strategy levels rather than at the moves level. When there seems to be a need for other terms or the wrong terms seem to have been used, particular tactics should be available to the user as options. When there is a need to revise terms, a different set of tactics could be applied.

Search Expansion

Two fundamental strategies for dealing with zero or too few hits are to widen the scope of the search and process the search against all reasonable information sources. Standard practices are to relax Boolean ANDs and to use the Boolean OR to add broader, narrower, and related terms, including synonyms and variant spellings. Other techniques include using LCSH to enhance access, using LCC for subject retrieval, using both DDC and LCSH, adopting strategies to use LCC, and using LCC for term clustering and ranking has identified a number of tactical responses for query expansion: neighbour, trace, parallel, fix, super, relate, and vary. Connell suggests manipulating the grammar of LCSH and providing access to fields not usually searched.

Search Reduction

Approaches to dealing with excessive retrieval center around Boolean operations that limit both topical and non-topical parameters. When applicable, Henry recommended reducing ORed terms. Markey thought the user should be prompted to limit his or her search when retrieved sets exceeded 20 records. Bates has distinguished a variety of descriptively-named search tactics.

Harter proposed moving truncation characters to the right and limiting the search to a specific subject area by a classification code as effective methods of reducing large retrieved set sizes. Fidel suggested restricting fields, tightening proximity, limiting by language, or limiting by type of literature to deal with large sets. Morris recommended intersecting with another concept; adding narrower terms; applying more stringent proximity; limiting to one or fewer fields; using NOT and AND NOT; and limiting by language, document type, year, and first few items.

Prabha also supports the traditional approach of managing large retrievals by extending the use of restrictors such as language, format, and date of publication, but she has also suggested using library classification schemes as a limiting feature. Lesk pointed out the benefits of exploring uses of *Library of Congress Classification* (LCC) to deal with 'too many hits'. As Prabha has pointed out, there is much to be learned about the incidence of large retrievals, measures for evaluating retrieval performance, evaluating existing search features for increasing retrieval precision, and using additional data for managing large retrievals. The problem of excessively large retrieved sets does not arise with systems that rank documents, one simply accepts as many as one wishes. Similarly the problem could be reduced in Boolean systems if they included built-in mechanisms for creating subsets and ranking them.

HANDLING RETRIEVED SETS

The analysis of retrieved sets to examine the characteristics of what has been retrieved can provide an important basis for search modification decisions. Retrieved set analysis can also be used for database analysis, identifying erroneous data, and collection analysis. Hickey and Prabha suggest making tools available online that summarize large retrieved sets. These summaries could be presented in the form of tables, pie charts, and bar charts. Several writers have suggested trying new, more compact, approaches to managing browse displays. The size of LCSH displays could be reduced by suppressing the display of geographic and chronological subfield headings.

An important new function is now being added to online catalogues for retrieved set analysis. The European Space Agency's Information Retrieval Service (ESA-IRS) offers a command called 'zoom'. For any retrieved set, zoom provides a frequency analysis of the values for a number of attributes that can be specified by the user. Among the options ESA-IRS provides are arrangements by dates, authors, corporate sources, words, classification codes, molecular formulae, and titles.One good use of a 'zoom' command is to identify the most frequent subject headings in a set, perhaps a set initially defined by use of title keywords. Similar capabilities have been included in CITE, RUBIKON at Roskilde University Library in Denmark, and OASIS at Berkeley. In OASIS the 'summarize' command summarizes subject headings or holding libraries. Norway's national online catalogue, BIBSYS, offers sorting on the author, title, author and title, publication and issue fields. The publication and issue fields can be sorted in either ascending or descending order.

SYSTEM IMPROVEMENTS

Fortunately, recent advances in computer technology have made accelerated speeds, massive disk storage capabilities, and expanded memory capacity available at rapidly dropping costs. How-ever, the improvements in hardware are so substantial that new designs are indicated, such as, for example, a shift from traditional line-by-line displays to bit-mapped images and graphical user interfaces.

The increasing affordability of more powerful personal computers and workstations facilitates moving some of the processing to the user's desk top both for the experimental prototyping of enhanced systems and also for routine use. There is a growing recognition that the 'intelligence' necessary for aiding the searcher could and, perhaps, should reside in a front-end system. Post-processing tools can help users refine searches and browse records more easily. Other specific recommendations include adopting a multi-tasking interface that allows users to download bibliographies while carrying out other searches and providing online catalogues with more user-friendly and adaptive X-Windows graphical interfaces.

DATA IMPROVEMENT

Enhanced hardware, software, and searching techniques are still liable to be hampered by deficiencies in the data. Errors and variant forms create the additional problem of duplicate records, often separating records for different copies of the same title. These records need to be consolidated. The OCLC Duplicate Detection Project uses matching algorithms that look for duplicates resulting from typographical errors and cataloguing differences. Hickey initiated several techniques for comparing records, of which the 'matching trigrams' technique proved to be the most effective.

Another form of improvement is to make records more complete, adding optional fields and/or additional fields. This could include enriched subject vocabulary, standard non-roman scripts, more cross-reference structure for variant forms of names and subject headings and enhanced use of the LCSH Subject Authority File. Cataloguing rules, subject headings, classifications, and data format rules change over time. Card catalogues tended to receive rather minimal retros-pective modification to bring older records into line with newer practices.

With databases both the need and the means for maintaining standards change over time. The rapid trend towards mounting multiple databases implies the need for support for searching across databases. Since databases overlap in coverage, problems arise in identifying which records are variant representations of the same work and, more generally, linking works of similar nature across databases.

TOPICAL ACCESS AND SYSTEM VOCABULARIES

There are problems and opportunities that arise in the process of moving from the searcher's terms to the catalog's terms. Micco suggests guiding the user to select the best search strategy by mapping user's terms to the controlled vocabularies in the database. Bates recommends the provision of a super thesaurus with a large entry vocabulary that includes colloquial terms and spelling variants.

Warner advocates showing the user how language is mapped in the system by organizing both natural language and controlled vocabulary into a single display. The online catalogues that force users through a thesaurus lead to more satisfaction with search results than catalogues that do not. Gomez report that user success is improved when the number of terms indexed is increased.

However, larger retrieved sets are also a likely consequence. Many suggestions have been made to wrestle with the deeply-entrenched LCSH. Lester recommends modifying user input to match LCSH. Markey-Drabenstott and Vizine-Goetz report that exact matches with LCSH are usually queries for topical subjects, but queries with combinations of topical subjects and names rarely match LCSH.

The incorporating subject terms from the *Dewey Decimal Classification* (DDC) and other library classifications into online catalogues would enhance subject access and provide additional subject searching strategies. Possible solutions to the semantic problem include a semantic network approach for generating synonyms and related terms and a classification knowledge-base that could store the semantic components for each LC class or subject heading with which the user would form a query by selecting relevant facets.

Additional problems arise when the catalogue provides access through multiple vocabularies or several foreign languages, as is often the case in European systems. Mandel describes several strategies online catalogues are now using to provide access to multiple vocabularies: segregated files, mixed vocabularies, integrated vocabularies, and front-end navigation.

EXPERIMENTAL SYSTEMS

A development that deserves special note is the increasing viability of experimental prototypes. It used to be that only those responsible for operational catalogues were in a position to develop them, but now the prevalence of powerful, yet relatively inexpensive, workstations, reduced data storage costs, and increasingly available datasets enable anyone with sufficient expertise to experiment and develop a functioning experimental online catalogue.

Further, remote access to a wide variety of databases over the Internet offers the opportunity for widespread testing. In this way new techniques can be tried, tested, evaluated, and, perhaps, adopted and developed by others. Experimental systems are beginning to use natural language techniques developed by artificial intelligence researchers.

A good example of a promising experimental system is the Cheshire system developed by Larson. For nearly thirty years the advantages of probabilistic retrieval techniques have been advocated. Yet it was not until the Cheshire system was developed on a unix workstation at Berkeley with very little funding, using the MARC records of a nearby library, that one could actually use a probabilistic online catalogue with probabilistic document ranking. Another good example is the Okapi system, developed initially at the Polytechnic of Central London and later at the City University, London.

Okapi has been used for numerous interesting studies over the years. Okapi currently develops a query by selecting the best terms from a list of the original query terms as well as terms from records judged relevant by the user. The OASIS system, also developed at Berkeley, takes low-cost prototyping one stage further. OASIS, running on a unix workstation acts as a front-end to the massive MELVYL online catalogue of the University of California.

Ordinarily operating as a terminal connected to MELVYL, additional functionality can be supported through the pre-processing of new commands and new retrieval results can be achieved through the post-processing of records downloaded from MELVYL. The result is, in effect, a prototyping of enhanced MELVYL functionality using the MELVYL database and achieved without any interference with MELVYL software or service. Although there are limits to what can be done this way, the OASIS system has been successful in developing strategic searches and performing useful retrieved set analysis.

As search and retrieve protocols are adopted, any workstation could, in principle, develop and demonstrate enhancements to any online catalogue supporting a standard protocol. In Norway, BIBSYS provides access to a 5 million-record database with searching on 33 different fields. BIBSYS also handles e-mail search requests and offers a choice of eight output formats. Records can also be downloaded with FTP or Kermit.

Users have a choice of either a simple menu-driven or a command-driven search. In Finland, KISIR provides several browsers, including thesaurus-dictionary browsers, retrieval system description browsers, and database description browsers. As the online catalogue becomes less and less isolated from other retrieval activities, so less catalogue-like systems become of potential interest.

Also, as the role of libraries expands to include many of the resources provided by the online environment, many new forms of information are falling within the domain of the online catalogue. Full-text resources, for example, commonly have little or no human indexing and bring with them a whole new set of problems for both users and the catalogues. Second generation online catalogue techniques, particularly Boolean keyword searching, perform poorly, for many reasons, when applied to full-text documents.

Indexing and retrieval techniques new to the catalogue world will be needed. Fortunately there is much interesting research and experimentation going on outside of libraries. The Information Visualizer is a project at the Xerox *Palo Alto Research Center* (PARC) where researchers are experimenting with visualizing large amounts of data. The Information Visualizer uses colour and interactive real-time three-dimensional animation to depict complex aspects of in-formation.

Information is represented as 3D objects. The user is given the sense of moving around the objects to view them from different perspectives. Thinking Machines Inc. has designed a group of applications that work together to locate and retrieve documents. Known as the *Wide Area Information Server* (WAIS), WAIS accepts queries in natural language and translates them into key words that are used for a search. A query is entered in the user's own words which can then be sent out across the Internet, accessing the wide variety of servers and databases now available.

Thinking Machines Corporation is collaborating with Apple, Dow Jones and KPMG Peat Marwick to simplify information retrieval from personal files, corporate records and remote databases. The aim of the project is to develop approaches to the problems presented by the overwhelming surplus of electronic data now confronting large organizations.

The long-range goal is to develop technology for a scalable system that will allow users to access a variety of data sources, including large commercial databases, through a common interface. The WAIS system is based on the client server model consists of server software distributed by Thinking Machines and an open protocol for transmitting queries and responses.

Thinking Machines has also undertaken a project with Columbia University's Law School. Project Janus is implementing a full-text retrieval system that deals with both text and graphics. This means including full-text documents such as the United Nations library human rights collection.

Online versions of the legal texts like the Maastricht Treaty and the Rio Conference on the Environment are receiving high usage, with the North American Free Trade Agreement getting 200-250 hits per day. The project is aimed at alleviating storage problems in libraries, making fragile items accessible, and providing access to information increasingly only available in electronic form. The system will include user-friendly interfaces, better search methods, and the ability to make scattered databases appear to be a single one database.

Keyword searches will be replaced by natural language queries, allowing users to search an unknown domain in their own words. The search strategy uses weighting and focuses on uncommon words to direct the search. Portions of full-text documents can be used to form new queries and find more documents on the topic selected. The library is also planning to work with publishers to load copyrighted text onto their system.

Apple's Advanced Technology Group has used WAIS to create Rosebud, a personally customizable electronic newspaper based on the metaphor of reporters and news-papers. Basically an Internet search and text-filtering programme, Rosebud enables users to create a personal news-paper daily from wire-service reports, arrange documents by priority for action or reading, or locate specific items of correspondence. Rosebud finds information with user-defined keyword lists and provides a statistical content analysis.

Aimed at non-expert information users, Rose-bud searches numerous remote databases and presents its findings in a newspaper-like format, prioritizing documents according to user preferences. A commercially-available object-oriented information system called Topic uses a knowledge-based approach based on the idea of concept retrieval which uses hierarchically arranged 'topics' to search for entire concepts instead of words or phrases.

Topic uses typical Boolean retrieval techniques, but allows the user to create topics with rules about relationships to more specific topics. Topic handles data from databases as diverse as news wires, intelligence reporting services and electronic mail. AT&T Bell Laboratories is prototyping. The RightPages electronic library, the first phase of a plan to create an electronic analog of the traditional library environment.

The RightPages library alerts users to incoming scientific and technical journal articles that correspond to their interest profiles. It also allows them to view pages of the articles, browse other articles in the database and order printed copies. The United States *Defence Advanced Research Projects Agency* (DARPA) has specified research on three methods of intelligent document-retrieval for investigation under its Tipster intelligent document-retrieval project.

Keyword searching limitations and inaccurate queries present serious problems for searching documents. DARPA has is focusing on context vectors, conceptual graphs and inference networks as 'the most promising technologies' for detecting and retrieving desired documents. Context vectors automatically summarize and compare the meaning of portions of text. Conceptual graphs perform pattern-matching to detect the relationships between concepts in multiple bodies of text.

Inference networks are used to detect larger patterns in texts using statistical information retrieval and natural language processing techniques. The Sloan School of Management at MIT is engaged in a research project called Information Lens, which focuses on ways to handle large quantities of on-line messages. Information Lens is based on the concept of 'intelligent assistants' used in artificial intelligence applications and graphical user interface design. The intelligent assistant in Information Lens can sort, prioritize, and seek out incoming messages.

General Electric Research and Development Center is working on a system called Scisor that can handle large input and output of information. Scisor uses artificial intelligence, natural language, and database management to collect relevant financial data from the Dow Jones wire services. To do this, Scisor locates key words and 'reads' them before deciding to keep or discard them. Scisor is able to process news items at the rate of about six stories per minute. The system has also been used to obtain information from other subject areas. Scisor uses information retrieval techniques such as word-based text search and lexical analysis

In addition, special mention should be made of several other experimental 'environments' or test beds being developed for experimental techniques such as:

- I3R,
- CODER, and
- FERRET.

CONCLUSIONS

We conclude that, although more popular than the card catalogue, the actual effectiveness of online catalogue is lower than has been assumed. Where a searcher's terms coincide with the system's terms and when the searcher has a specific, definable target in mind, all may be well. But when these conditions do not hold, all is not well. First and second generation catalogues are quite well defined.

What of the third generation? It should add the following:

- Provide an entry vocabulary capability to lead from users' terms to the system's terms
- Prompt the user at any time in a situationally sensitive manner
- Have a well developed tool-kit for retrieved set analysis
- Support 'nearest neighbour' searching–Find more like this one!–and, perhaps through 'zoom' commands, allow the searcher to browse across the database using any one or more attributes of a record
- Offer document ranking or a mechanism for converting any retrieved set into small, ranked subsets

More generally, the future catalogue should blend harmo-niously with other retrieval tools, with the sources to which it provides access, and with the user's personal working environment. Using it should, in itself, be a learning experience. How this functionality will be provided is less clear, but there are numerous options to be explored. In the preparation of this review we concentrated on identified problems in the use of the online catalogue and on actual proposals for its improvement.

At the same time it became increasingly clear that deeper, more fundamental developments were afoot:

- In the last few years the online catalogue situation has been dominated by the effort of adoption and imple-mentation. There has been gradual movement from first to second generation catalogues despite the substantially greater storage and computing resources required and numerous smaller refinements. These have typically included options to search by call number and limiting searches by date of publication, by language, and/or by library in a union catalogue. In brief, progress has been more a matter of widespread adoption of existing functionality than of advancing the state of the art. But if the state-of-the-art does not appear to have advanced much in the past several years, there are reasons to expect major changes in the future.
- Although it has always been accepted that the catalogue is the key to the library, it has, in many ways, been determined by the needs of cataloguing and technical services. However, since cataloguing was in practice limited to the edition of the monograph and the title of the periodical, the extent of bibliographic access was in reality quite limited. This situation is changing radically. Other database files are being mounted alongside the catalogue and, increasingly, links are being made from the records in these bibliographies to the library's holding records. This can be seen either as a redefinition of the catalogue or as a return to an earlier era when analytical entries could be afforded. Either way, a significant and popular enhancement of bibliographic access results. Another of the major new growth areas for library catalogues is the linking of the

catalogue record to the address of full-text in electronic form, allowing, in principle, a smoother transition from record to text than with paper documents. Further, as all forms of media are increasingly stored online in digital form, the distinctions between the media become less significant, promising an increasingly unified approach to multiple media. In addition, as ever increasing numbers of electronic journals, books and texts become available, online catalogues will take on many of the functions of document delivery by enabling the user to inspect, to download, or to request document delivery - all from the catalogue terminal. But as more and more of these resources become available, how will they be indexed? A conventional catalogue record may enable one to identify and locate a text, but is of little benefit thereafter in finding material within the text. As the role of libraries expand to include access to many of the resources provided by the online environment, many new forms of information are falling within the domain of the online catalogue, for example, non-bibliographic records of community information and referral and *'campus-wide information services'* (CWIS). These expanded frontiers bring new challenges. These additional resources, which may have little or no human indexing, bring with them a whole new set of problems for both users and the catalogues. Some significant extension in our view of the catalogue and of cataloguing practice would appear inevitable following such convergence. Libraries and other organizations that manage large amounts of information have a great need for increased capacity to deal with the steadily increasing flow of electronic information from a wide variety of sources. Yet this increase is also contributing to the rapid growth in the number, size and complexity of databases. Much of the original search and display software was not designed for such large size and complexity.

- Catalogues are becoming less isolated. Librarians and library users are reaching beyond the online catalogue and venturing out onto the Internet. Comparison of catalogues has become much easier now that a few hundred online catalogues are accessible over the Internet and 'pass-through' connections are making access to multiple online catalogues routinely available to library users. Electronic bulletin boards such as PACS-L greatly enhance the possibilities for discussion and for the rapid dissemination of information and facilitating discussion.
- After years dominated by implementation, experience in using the systems provides a basis for considering what enhancements are needed. Tools are increasingly available for more evidence-based analysis. In particular, the analysis of transaction logs provides a diagnostic tool not

available with card catalogues. The literature has, hitherto, often been impressionistic. It need not stay that way. In effect, we have a new window on the user.

- Experimental prototypes are increasingly feasible. The increasing power of low-cost work-stations, decreasing mass storage costs, and the growing availability of large sets of records for experimental purposes makes online catalogue experimentation possible for many more people than before. Technology permits greater flexibility and standardized network protocols are making access to a wide variety of information resources increasingly feasible.

We are now at an exciting juncture. There has been a change in the way that online catalogues are perceived. The initial concern was to connect the online catalogue to the library's technical services system. Now there is interest in relating the online catalogue to online resources everywhere.

On-line catalogues are now evolving into much more than automated card catalogues for a single library's collection. They are changing how library users interact with the library services. If these interpretations are correct, then examination of the difficulties currently encountered in online catalogues and of proposals for improvement become very timely as the online catalogue shifts from being the end-product of technical services to being the framework for bibliographic access.

7

Electronic Resource Management in Libraries

WIRELESS LOCAL AREA NETWORKS

The WLAN market is exploding, with reported yearly growth figures of 300 per cent. WLAN systems are a technology that can provide very high data rate applications and individual links (*e.g.*, in company campus areas, conference centers, airports and in libraries) and represents an attractive way of setting up computers networks in environments where cable installation is expensive or not feasible. LANs and mobile computing, have recalling the attention of equipment manufactures.

This shows their high potential and justifies the big attention paid to WLAN by equipment manufacturers. Whereas in the early beginning of WLANs several proprietary products existed, nowadays they are mostly conforming to the Institute of Electrical and Electronics Engineering (IEEE) 802.11b (also known as Wi-Fi) standard. It operates in the unlicensed 2.4-GHz band at 11 Mbps and it is currently extended to reach 54 Mbps. A description of the MAC can be found in.

WLAN STANDARDS

802.11A

A physical layer standard in the 5 GHz radio band. It specifies eight available radio channels (in some countries, 12 channels are permitted). The maximum link rate is 54 Mbps per channel; maximum actual user data throughput is approximately half of that, and the throughput is shared by all users of the same radio channel. The data rate decreases as the distance between the user and the radio access point increases.

802.11B

This is a physical layer standard in the 2.4 GHz radio band. It specifies three available radio channels. Maximum link rate is 11 Mbps per channel, but maximum user throughput will be approximately half of this because the throughput is shared by all users of the same radio channel. The data rate decreases as the distance between the user and the radio access point increases.

802.11D

This standard is supplementary to the Media Access Control (MAC) layer in 802.11 to promote worldwide use of 802.11 WLANs. It will allow access points to communicate information on the permissible radio channels with acceptable power levels for user devices. The 802.11 standards cannot legally operate in some countries; the purpose of 11d is to add features and restrictions to allow WLANs to operate within the rules of these countries.

802.11E

This standard is supplementary to the MAC layer to provide QOS support for LAN applications. It will apply to 802.11 physical standards a, b, and g. The purpose is to provide classes of service with managed levels of QOS for data, voice, and video applications.

802.11F

This is a "recommended practice" document that aims to achieve radio access point interoperability within a multivendor WLAN network. The standard defines the registration of access points within a network and the interchange of information between access points when a user is handed over from one access point to another.

802.11G

This is a physical layer standard for WLANs in the 2.4 GHz and 5 GHz radio band. It specifies three available radio channels. The maximum link rate is 54 Mbps per channel whereas 11b has 11 Mbps. The 802.11g standard uses orthogonal frequency-division multiplexing (OFDM) modulation but, for backward compatibility with 11b, it also supports complementary code-keying (CCK) modulation and, as an option for faster link rates, allows packet binary convolution coding (PBCC) modulation

802.11H

This standard is supplementary to the MAC layer to comply with European regulations for 5 GHz WLANs. European radio regulations for the 5 GHz band require products to have transmission power control (TPC) and dynamic frequency selection (DFS). TPC limits the transmitted power to the minimum needed to reach the farthest user. DFS selects the radio channel at the access point to minimize interference with other systems, particularly radar.

802.11I

It will apply to 802.11 physical standards a, b, and g. It provides an alternative to Wired Equivalent Privacy (WEP) with new encryption methods and authentication procedures. IEEE 802.1X forms a key part of 802.11i

WIRELESS NETWORK CONFIGURATIONS

There are two kinds of wireless networks:

1. An ad-hoc or peer-to-peer wireless network consists of a number of computers each equipped with a wireless networking interface card. Each computer can communicate directly with all of the other wireless enabled computers. They can share files and printers this way, but may not be able to access wired LAN resources, unless one of the computers acts as a bridge to the wired LAN using special software. This is called "bridging". Each computer with a wireless interface can communicate directly with all of the others.
2. A wireless network can also use an access point, or base station. In this type of network the access point acts like a hub, providing connectivity for the wireless computers. It can connect (or "bridge") the wireless LAN to a wired LAN, allowing wireless computer access to LAN resources, such as file servers or existing Internet Connectivity.

There are two types of access points:

1. Dedicated hardware access points (HAP) such as Lucent's Wave LAN, Apple's Airport Base Station or Web Gear's Aviator PRO.
2. Software Access Points which run on a computer equipped with a wireless network interface card as used in an ad-hoc or peer-to-peer wireless network. The Vicomsoft Internet Gateway suites are software routers that can be used as a basic Software Access Point, and include features not commonly found in hardware solutions, such as Direct PPPoE support and extensive configuration flexibility, but may not offer the full range of wireless features defined in the 802.11 standard. With appropriate networking software support, users on the wireless LAN can share files and printers located on the wired LAN and vice versa.

APPLICATIONS OF WIRELESS LANS

When computers were first built, only large universities and corporations could afford them. Today we may find 3 or 4 personal computers in our neighbour's house. Wireless LANs have taken a similar path, first used by large enterprises, and now available to us all at affordable prices. As a technology, wirelesses LANs have enjoyed a very fast adoption rate due to the many advantages they offer to a variety of situations. As suggested, discuss some of the most common and appropriate uses of wireless LANs.

ACCESS ROLE

Wireless LANs are deployed in an access layer role, meaning that they are used as an entry point into a wired network. In the past, access has been defined as dial-up, ADSL, cable, cellular, Ethernet, Token Ring, Frame Relay, ATM, etc. Wireless is simply another method for users to access the network.

Wireless LANs are Data-Link layer networks like all of the access methods just listed. Due to a lack of speed and resiliency, wireless networks are not typically implemented in Distribution or Core roles in networks. Of course, in small networks, there may be no differentiation between the Core, Distribution, or Access layers of the network.

The Core layer of a network should be very fast and very stable, able to handle a tremendous amount of traffic with little difficulty and experience no down time. The Distribution layer of a network should be fast, flexible, and reliable. Wireless LANs do not typically meet these requirements for an enterprise solution. Wireless LANs offer a specific solution to a difficult problem: mobility.

Without a doubt, wireless LANs solve a host of problems for corporations and home users alike, but all of these problems point to the need for freedom from data cabling. Cellular solutions have been available for quite some time, offering users the ability to roam while staying connected, at slow speeds and very high prices. Wireless LANs offer the same flexibility without the disadvantages. Wireless LANs are fast, inexpensive, and they can be located almost anywhere. When considering wireless LANs for use in network, keep in mind that using them for their intended purpose will provide the best results.

Administrators implementing wireless LANs in a Core or Distribution role should understand exactly what performance to expect before implementing them in this fashion to avoid having to remove them later. The only distribution role in a network that is definitely appropriate for wireless LANs is that of building-to-building bridging. In this scenario, wireless *could* be considered as playing a distribution role; however, it will always depend on how the wireless bridging segments are used in the network.

NETWORK EXTENSION

Wireless networks can serve as an extension to a wired network. There may be cases where extending the network would require installing additional cabling that is cost prohibitive. You may discover that hiring cable installers and electricians to build out a new section of office space for the network is going to cost tens of thousands of Rupees. Or in the case of a large warehouse, the distances may be too great to use Category 5 (Cat5) cable for the Ethernet network.

Fibre might have to be installed, requiring an even greater investment of time and resources. Installing fibre might involve upgrades to existing edge switches. Wireless LANs can be easily implemented to provide seamless connectivity to remote areas within a building. Because little wiring is necessary to install a wireless LAN, the costs of hiring installers and purchasing Ethernet cable might be completely eliminated.

BUILDING-TO-BUILDING CONNECTIVITY

In a campus environment or an environment with as few as two adjacent buildings, there may be a need to have the network users in each of the different buildings have direct access to the same computer network. In the past, this type of access and connectivity would be accomplished by running cables underground from one building to another or by renting expensive leased-lines from a local telephone company.

Using wireless LAN technology, equipment can be installed easily and quickly to allow two or more buildings to be part of the same network without the expense of leased lines or the need to dig up the ground between buildings. With the proper wireless antennas, any number of buildings can be linked together on the same network. Certainly there are limitations to using wireless LAN technology, as there are in any data-connectivity solution, but the flexibility, speed, and cost-savings that wireless LANs introduce to the network administrator make them indispensable.

There are two different types of building-to-building connectivity. The first is called point-to-point (PTP), and the second is called point-to-multipoint (PTMP). Point-to-point links are wireless connections between only two buildings. PTP connections almost always use semi-directional or highly-directional antennas at each end of the link. Point-to-multipoint links are wireless connections between three or more buildings, typically implemented in a hub-n-spoke fashion, where one building is the central focus point of the network.

This central building would have the core network, Internet connectivity, and the server farm. Point-to-multipoint links between buildings typically use omni-directional antennas in the central "hub" building and semi-directional antennas on each of the outlying "spoke" buildings. There are many ways to implement these two basic types of connectivity.

LAST MILE DATA DELIVERY

Wireless Internet Service Providers (WISPs) are now taking advantage of recent advancements in wireless technology to offer last mile data delivery service to their customers. "Last mile" refers to the communication infrastructure wired or wireless that exists between the central office of the telecommunications company or Cable Company and the end user. Currently the BSNL and cable companies own their last mile infrastructure, but with the broadening interest in wireless technology, WISPs are now creating their own wireless last mile delivery service.

MOBILITY

As an access layer solution, wireless LANs cannot replace wired LANs in terms of data rates (100BT at 100Mbps versus IEEE 802.11a at 54Mbps). What wireless LANs do offer is an increase in mobility as the trade off for speed and quality of service. For example, a parcel delivery company uses wireless technology to update parcel tracking data immediately upon the arrival of the delivery vehicle. As the driver parks at the dock, the driver's computer has already logged onto the network and transferred the day's delivery data to the central network. In warehousing facilities, wireless networks are used to track the storage locations and disposition of products.

This data is then synchronised in the central computer for the purchasing and shipping departments. Handheld wireless scanners are becoming commonplace in organisations with employees that move around within their facility processing orders and inventory. In each of these cases, wireless networks have created the ability to transfer data without requiring the time and manpower to input the data manually at a wired terminal.

Wireless connectivity has also eliminated the need for such user devices to be connected using wires that would otherwise get in the way of the users. Some of the newest wireless technology allows users to *roam,* or move physically from one area of wireless coverage to another without losing connectivity, just as a mobile telephone customer is able to roam between cellular coverage areas.

In larger organisations, where wireless coverage spans large areas, roaming capability has significantly increased the productivity of these organisations, simply because users remain connected to the network away from their main workstations.

SMALL OFFICE-HOME OFFICE

As an IT professional, one may have more than one computer at the home. And if you do, these computers are most likely networked together so you can share files, a printer, or a broadband connection. This type of configuration is also utilised by many businesses that have only a few employees.

These businesses have the need for the sharing of information between users and a single Internet connection for efficiency and greater productivity. For these applications – small office-home office, or SOHO – a wireless LAN is a very simple and effective solution. The alternative of course is running wires throughout the office to interconnect all of the workstations.

Many small offices are not outfitted with pre-installed Ethernet ports, and only a very small number of houses are wired for Ethernet networks. Trying to retrofit these places with Cat5 cabling usually results in creating unsightly holes in the walls and ceilings. With a wireless LAN, users can be interconnected easily and neatly.

MOBILE OFFICES

Mobile offices or classrooms allow users to pack up their computer equipment quickly and move to another location. Due to overcrowded classrooms, many schools now use mobile classrooms. These classrooms usually consist of large, movable trailers that are used while more permanent structures are built. In order to extend the computer network to these temporary buildings, aerial or underground cabling would have to be installed at great expense. Wireless LAN connections from the main school building to the mobile classrooms allow for flexible configurations at a fraction of the cost of alternative cabling. Temporary office spaces also benefit from being networked with wireless LANs. As companies grow, they often find themselves with a shortage of office space, and need to move some workers to a nearby location, such as an adjacent office or an office on another floor of the same building.

Installing Cat5 or fibre cabling for these short periods of time is not cost-effective, and usually the owners of the building do not allow for the installed cables to be removed. With a wireless network, the network components can be packed up and moved to the next location quickly and easily. Wireless LANs are well suited to these types of environments.

Hospitals and other health care facilities benefit greatly from wireless LANs. Some valuable uses of wireless LANs within these facilities include doctors using wireless PDAs to connect to the networks and mobile diagnostic carts that nurses can move from room to room to connect to the patient and the network. Wireless networks allow doctors and nurses to perform their jobs more efficiently using these new devices and associated software.

Industrial facilities, such as warehouses and manufacturing facilities, utilise wireless networks in various ways. A good example of an industrial wireless LAN application is shipping companies whose trucks pull into the dock and automatically connect to the wireless network. This type of networking allows the shipping company to become automated and more efficient in handling the uploading of data onto the central servers.

CONCLUSION

The purpose of this thesis has been to describe and discuss the wireless technology in accessing information in the hope that libraries and librarians will benefit from using this technology. This thesis will help us in understanding the capabilities of WLAN. The evolution of wireless technology has perceived as a powerful tool for getting fast information which will become universal in the near future.

The goals of libraries are to provide information to their users. But the way users receive that information is changing. By integrating more effective delivery tools with current university infrastructure, libraries can help to attract more students and faculty to access information from inside or outside the library, 24 × 7 days a week. WLAN and its applications provide this extension possible to make "Library without Walls".

8

Guidelines for E-Reference Library Services

INTRODUCTION

The Due to the tremendous growth and continuous development of technology, the role of library becomes more responsive in making the users techno-savvy. Technological developments have affected not only the formats and sources of the information, but also how and where to provide library services. Libraries and their resources have partially moved to the virtual world of the Internet. As a result, library users can access the resources from outside the physical library.

In an effort to reach users accessing the library via their computers, many libraries and library consortia are extending their services to include virtual reference. Technology now allows users to submit their queries to the library at any time from any place in the world. Web Based Services, Digital Library Services, Internet Library Services and Electronic Library Services are terms with similar meanings.

As more libraries move towards providing services in a digital environment, the improved access to remote library collections is making the use of electronic information resources more realistic and more attractive. Traditional online services had transformed themselves into internet-based online services using web-based technologies. From traditional online services to today, four generations of information retrieval tools have passed that assist users in searching the World Wide Web.

The first generation of information retrieval tools was designed for use with bibliographic databases. The first generation provided access to references to the end documents rather than to the documents themselves, and indexing and searching were thus applied to document surrogates, such as titles or abstracts. These tools require considerable human efforts to collect, arrange, code, and annotate the various resources. A primary benefit of the first generation of tools is providing users with easy browsing capabilities.

The second generation of tools attempts to collect and index resources as an automated function. Automatic collection and indexing reduces the amount of human effort. The ability to search through massive amounts of information and locate the desired information for the user is the primary benefit of the second generation of tools. The third generation deals with World Wide Web Meta search engines, such as Harvester and Meta crawler. The fourth generation involves new ideas such as search agent technology currently being developed to search for information on the web. Web-based search engines are as a means of finding relevant pages on the Internet. Different search engines, directory, meta-search engines, gateways, subject portals, electronic journals and on line databases each type could be used in a different way, from simple keyword searching up to peer reviewed web sites.

WHAT IS WEB BASED LIBRARY SERVICE

A digital Library service manages and develops electronic services, the library web sites and library staff. It can be defined broadly as 'an information access service in which users ask questions via electronic means, *e.g.*, e-mail or web forms'.

WHY WEB BASED LIBRARY SERVICE

Library service on the internet requires many of the same qualities as traditional references: accuracy, promptness, courtesy, an understanding of the information need. It provides users with the convenience of accessing information in their own time, saving them traveling cost and time and new options for answering reference questions. The provision of these services is not constrained by the traditional opening hours but can be offered on a 24-hour, seven-days-a-week basis known as 24/7. And while there may be a disadvantage in not having a face-to face encounter, there are many advantages to this new medium and the greatest advantage is that many more users can be helped by using electronic library services. Advantages and disadvantages of electronic access over printed form access are showed in table.

Web based services are established due to the following reasons.

- Ensuring the needs of users and the accessible information sources are suitable matched at all times.
- Delivering those information sources to the user in a timely and appropriate fashion.
- Ensuring the information provided is high quality, accurate and appropriate.
- Assisting the user in interpreting the materials, if necessary.
- Promoting user awareness of new services and information sources as they develop.
- Providing users with individualised guidance and support as they build their information search and application skills.

DIFFERENT RESOURCES FOR WEB BASED LIBRARY SERVICES

Today, users may have access a variety of textual information resources. There are different kinds of webbased reference resources and services for accessing information from libraries such as OPAC, Gateways, Portals, Subject Portals, Electronic Journals, Online Databases, Subject Directories and Search Engines.

These resources overlap considerably in the type of information they cover, and sometimes it is difficult to distinguish between some of them. A library should have a good collection of these resources like selected Web links, subscription resources, and library materials in well-organised pages for serving better services to their users. Many libraries and organisations are providing digital reference service through collaborative services. Existing library consortia are adding digital reference to current shared services, and networks of libraries. Some regional library consortia are offering member libraries the opportunity to share reference questions with each other using the Internet and other technologies.

OPAC

OPAS's - On Line Public Access Catalogues, form an important part of many digital library's collections. It allows users to search for the bibliographic records contained within a library's collections. Now days, some OPAC also provide access to electronic resources and databases, in addition to the traditional bibliographic records.

GATEWAYS

A gateway is defined as a facility that allows easier access to network based resources in a given subject area. Gateways provide a simple search facility and a much-enhanced service through a resource database and indexes, which can be searched through a web based interface. Information provided by gateways is catalogued by hand. Gateways cover a wide range of subjects, through some areas, such as music and religious studies, currently lack subject gateways.

Some well-known gateways are as follows:

- Internet Public Library (IPL),
- Bulletin Board for Libraries (BUBL),
- National Information Services and Systems (NISS),

PORTALS

In the library community, portals may be defined as an amalgamation of services to the users where the amalgamation is achieved through seamless integration of existing services by using binding agents such as customisation and authentication services, search protocols such as Z39.50, loan protocols such as ISO10161, and e-commerce. The result is a personalised service which allows the individual to access the rich content of both print-based and electronic systems. Portals are either commercial or free web facilities that offer information services to a specific audience. The facilities include web search to communication to e-mail to news, etc.

There are three kinds of portals; Consumer (or horizontal), Vertical and Enterprise.

1. Consumer portals are aimed at consumer audiences and offer free e-mail, games, chat, etc. Examples are Yahoo!, MSN and AOL.
2. Vertical portals, target a specified audience, such as a particular industry, and offer many of the consumer portal features. Example includes VerticalNet.
3. Enterprise portals on the other hand are similar to consumer portals, but they are offered only to corporations or similar organisations. Examples include Epicentric and Corporate Yahoo! These portals can be best understood as electronic pathfinders for users, pulling together in one place in a web site selected links to subjects or interest-oriented resources located on the WWW.

SUBJECT PORTALS

Web Search Engines had been developed initially by computer scientists, by borrowing techniques from information retrieval search such as best match searching and relevance ranking.

Information professional are increasing bringing their skills to help organise the growing wealth of Internet resources. A good example of their influence is the development of subject-specific web search engines known as subject portals, where evaluation of material covered is a major concern.

Two prime UK subject portals are SOSIG Social Science Information Gateway, covering social science resources and OMNI Organising medical networked information covering medical resources. Subject portal sites can be very helpful, but they should be used with care.

Users should bear the following points in their mind:

- The aim of the subject portal is to list and review the most important sites on the web relevant to that subject. The sites are usually constantly peer-reviewed to ensure that the site is relevant and up to date.
- New sites are appearing all the time. Relying on a subject portal site to find everything users require may mean that they miss an important site that has recently appeared and has not yet been reviewed by the producers of the particular subject portal.
- A subject portal is a one stop shop for information on the topic it covers. Users don't have to carry out extensive Internet searches in order to find the information require. They can simply go to the required subject portal site.
- Subject portals save users having to have long lists of bookmarks (saved addresses of web pages), which are often, cumbersome and time consuming to arrange and keep up to date. However, if users

do prefer to use bookmarks they can arrange them in an order to suit the way they work and not have an order forced on them by the subject portal.

- A subject portal site is only as good as the reviewers who peer-review the site listed. The reviewers need to have a policy of keeping the portal sites up to date and of constantly reviewing the sites they list, to make sure that they are still relevant and still contain good, timely information.
- A subject portal may be available to everyone who needs to use it to only certain groups of users. A good portal should be publicly available to anyone who needs it.

ELECTRONIC JOURNALS

Electronic journals form a large part of the collection of a library for providing web based services. Today many journals are available electronically - some are full text and some contain only bibliographic information with abstract. Major advantage of electronic journals is that they are constantly updated and easy to access but disadvantage is that breaching of copyright law is very easy.

They are available as bitmaps, PostScript, PDF, ASCII, SGML and HTML. Library services may be delivering to users on CDRom, through e-mail or through web. Some international societies and associations have developed their own digital libraries through which users can get access to all their publications. Services are available to the members of society or associations through subscription.

ONLINE DATABASES

These are large collections of machine-readable data that are maintained by commercial agencies and are accessed through communication lines. Many libraries subscribe to them for easy access and use of current information.

The disadvantage is that only bibliographic data is presented and not full text. The information cannot be accessed when the system is down for any reason. Examples Ei Compendex, SciFinder Scholar, Web of Science, Current Contents, etc.

SEARCH ENGINES

Search Engines are huge databases of web page files that have been assembled automatically by machines where as the subject directories are human-compiled and maintained. Search engine indexes every page of a web site and subject directories linked only homepages.

Search Engine is the popular term for an information retrieval (IR) system. A search engine is computer software that searches a collection of electronic materials to retrieve citations, documents, or information that matches or answers a user's query. The retrieved materials may be text documents, facts that have been extracted from text, images, or sounds. A query is a question phrased so that it can be interpreted properly by search engine.

Depending on the type of software, it may be a collection of commands, a statement in either full or partial sentences, one or more keywords, or in the case of non-text searching, an image or sequence of sounds to be matched.

SUBJECT DIRECTORIES

Subject directories differ from search engines in that search engines are populated by robots that finds and index sites whereas humans making editorial decisions that populate subject directories. Subject directories are basically index home pages of sites and can be classified as general, academic, commercial or portal.

Among the well known subject directories are the Argus Clearinghouse and Yahoo. Strengths include relevance, effectiveness and relative high quality of content. Weaknesses are that they lack depth in their coverage of the subjects.

NEW WEB BASED LIBRARY SERVICES

VIRTUAL LIBRARY TOURS

Web sites of libraries provides virtual library guide to the physical facilities including collections, services and infrastructure available in the library. The combination of library maps and floor plans, library departments and photographic views are used for the tour. Virtual library tours are also using new technologies such as QuickTime movies etc and are beginning to replace image maps on main campus Web sites.

ASK-A-LIBRARIAN

Ask-A-Librarian services are Internet-based question and answer service that connects users with individuals who possess specialised subject knowledge and skill in conducting precision searches. Most "Ask-a-Librarians" services have a web-based question submission form or an e-mail address or both. Users are invited to submit their queries by using web forms or through e-mail. Once a query is read by a service, it is assigned to an individual expert for answering.

An expert responds to the query with factual information and or a list of information resources. The response is either sent to the user's e-mail account or is posted on the web so that the user can access it after a certain period of time. Many services have informative web sites that include archives of questions and answers and a set of FAQs. Users are usually encouraged to browse archives and FAQs before submitting a question in case sufficient information already exists.

REAL TIME SERVICES

A new and exciting method of digital reference service that libraries are attempting to provide more and more now is live reference. These are real-time, interactive reference services in which the users can talk to a real, live reference librarian at any time, from anywhere in the world. User and librarian can interact using chat technologies, and unlike with e-mail reference the librarian can perform a reference interview of sorts by asking the users to elaborate or clarify if needed before proceeding to answer the question. The librarian can perform Internet searches and push web sites onto the user's browser, and can receive immediate feedback from the users as to whether their question have been answered to satisfaction.

BULLETIN BOARDS

A bulletin board is an electronic communications forum that hosts posted messages and articles connected to a common subject or theme or interest. It allows users to call in and either leaves or retrieves messages. The messages may be directed to all users of the bulletin board or only to particular users. But all messages can be read by all users.

Several libraries are using bulletin boards for their web-based library services. The bulletin board system is also used as an interactive interface to invite suggestions on activities and services of a library. It can also be used as an interface to distribute library services.

WEB-BASED USER EDUCATION

Web guides and teaching tools are found everywhere on the Web because they are easily updated, accessed, and printed on demand. The web-based user education provides a high degree of interactivity and flexibility to the users. The library web sites can use web-based user education for imparting training to users in teaching the basic library skills along with glossary of library terms, using Library OPAC, locating books, magazines, biographical data and other library materials, understanding how to navigate the libraries web site and how to select the most relevant database, instructions for searching CD ROM and guidance in locating web-based databases and other electronic resources and instructions on subject searching training, using Boolean operators and searching internet resources through search engines.

WEB FORMS

Library web sites have some web forms for suggestions and comments on the Library Services. Different types of Web Forms are available on web that may be an Indent form for acquiring some publications, interlibrary loan request form for document delivery, Ask-a-Librarian forms, on line reservation form or user survey form, etc.

INDIAN SCENARIO

The Indian libraries also have realised to give web based services to users and they have recognised that working together can accomplish for more than they can do individually. Many Indian libraries in India are not geared up for accessing e-journals due to various reasons including user ignorance, infrastructure and initial funds.

The library and information networks in India were initiated in early eighties. The growth during this period can be linked to some of the policies that Government of India pursued. Some institutions like CSIR, ISRO, DRDO, DAE, ICAR, SIRNET, NICNET, NISSAT, INFLIBNET, MHRD and IIM libraries are actively working continuously to improve the present situation.

They spend annually a huge amount of money towards library acquisition, especially towards journals, e-journals and e-databases. Some initiative include, Indian Institute of Management for accessing bibliographic databases, CSIR laboratories for Science Direct, FORSA for accessing Astronomy and Astrophysics journals, Hyderabad Knowledge park members of J-gate, INFLIBNET (UGC–INFONET) initiative for full text and databases like BIOSIS and CAS and INDEST for a host of full text sources and few bibliographic databases for the benefit of IITs, IISc, NITs and Engineering colleges.

In India, library consortia are emerging as one of the important service to users. The Indian consortiums will help the library to provide better services to the users by investing meagre amount. To expand the access for more number of e-journals, e-books and other resources, we have to develop the digital library infrastructure as a platform for e-learning.

THE FUTURE OF WEB BASED SERVICES

Library Web services will continue to spread out, offering more full-text electronic journals and indexes that do not now include full text will begin to do so, or link to external resources. Bibliographic access to full-text periodicals either through cataloging, databases, or vendors will be in improved form. There will be more Web forms for user feedback, and perhaps a virtual librarian who interacts in real time chat or video conferencing. More Document delivery services to distance education or users and Savings on Interlibrary Loan and user convenience are incentives. Information resources through creative consortia purchasing will be popular. A well-developed user education modules or tutorials, especially to support independent exploration of library and Web resources.

WEB PUBLISHING: GETTING STARTED

WEB PUBLISHING

The Oracle's Hyperion® Data Relationship Management Web Publishing module provides an auxiliary means of accessing Data Relationship Management system functionality.

This application provides the following capabilities through a Web browser interface:

- Viewing hierarchies and node properties.
- Running exports.
- Printing hierarchy trees.
- Searching for nodes in a given hierarchy.

Data Relationship Management Web Publishing connects to the Data Relationship Management application server, but operates in a read-only mode. Various requests can be made using HTTP to either retrieve information or execute a command such as running exports or reloading from the database. Web Publishing can be run on its own server or hosted on the Data Relationship Management multi-tier Web Server or the primary application server.

SYSTEM REQUIREMENTS

The following topics describe the Data Relationship Management Web Publishing system requirements for the Web server and the client computers.

Web Server Requirements:

- Windows 2000 Server or Windows Server 2003.
- Internet Information Services (IIS) version 5 or later.
- Microsoft Data Access Components (MDAC) 2.7 or later (required only for MS SQL.)

Client Computer Requirements:

- Windows 2000 or later (ME, 2000, XP, Server 2003)
- Internet Explorer version 5 or later.

INSTALLING, CONFIGURING, AND UNINSTALLING

PRE-INSTALLATION TASKS

The following topics describe tasks that must be performed before you can install and use Data Relationship Management Web Publishing.

System Administrator Tasks

Your Data Relationship Management system administrator must complete the following tasks before you can install and use Data Relationship Management Web Publishing:

- Ensure that the Data Relationship Management system Release 9.3 is currently installed and operational.
- Create a new Data Relationship Management user name specifically for accessing Data Relationship Management Web Publishing (for example: mdm_Web). Assign the desired access rights to the user.
- Since the engine needs access to all paths that might be used for exports, provide a list of these paths to the network administrator. The system preference WebExDir controls the directory root for file storage location on the Web Publishing server.

- Configure the appropriate Data Relationship Management system preferences related to Data Relationship Management Web Publishing.

Network Administrator Tasks

Your network administrator must complete the following tasks before you can install and use Data Relationship Management Web Publishing:

- Create a new network user/application id that the Engine can use to login to the system. This id should have full access rights (including file creation) to any network shares that are designated for Data Relationship Management exports.
- Verify that IE browser policies allow for the use of digitally-signed ActiveX controls. While most Data Relationship Management Web Publishing implementations provide for browser access, some may be used strictly for automating exports. Configuring the browser can be skipped if interactive access is not desired.

General Tasks

In addition to system administrator and network administrator tasks described in the preceding topics, the following tasks must be performed before you can install and use Data Relationship Management Web Publishing:

- You must manually uninstall prior versions of Data Relationship Management Web Publishing before installing Data Relationship Management Web Publishing Release 9.3.
- Ensure that the intended host machine(s) meet or exceed the minimum system requirements defined in this document.
- Ensure that the user performing the installation has administrative rights to the Web server machine.
- Ensure that the Data Relationship Management Web Publishing release package is available.

INSTALLING DATA RELATIONSHIP MANAGEMENT WEB PUBLISHING

To install Data Relationship Management Web Publishing:

- Do one of these tasks:
  - If you have a Data Relationship Management Web Publishing CD or DVD, insert the CD or DVD into your CD or DVD drive.
  - If you downloaded the Data Relationship Management Web Publishing software from the Download Center:
    a. Navigate to the directory where you downloaded the installation programme.
    b. Select File > Run or Start > Run and enter Drive:\Folder \mdm_web_pub_server_setup.exe, where *Drive* and *Folder* are the installation programme location.

- Review the Welcome box and click Next.
- Read the license agreement, select I AGREE and click Next.
- From Web Publishing Installation Options, do one of the following:
  - Click Next if the computer where you are installing Data Relationship Management Web Publishing is also a Data Relationship Management Web server.
  - Select Ntier Director if Data Relationship Management Web Publishing is being added to a computer that is not a Data Relationship Management Web server or if it is a standalone server, and click Next.
- Click Next to accept the default installation directory, or click Change to select another directory, and click Next.
- Do one of the following:
  - If you are installing Ntier Director, continue with the next step.
  - If you are not installing Ntier Director, continue with step 8.
- Enter the machine name or IP address of the Data Relationship Management primary application server and click Next.
- From Windows COM+ Logon, enter a user name and password for a user who has rights to perform the following actions and click Next:
  - Edit registry settings
  - Read and write to the local file system
  - Launch processes
  - Run as a service
- Click Install.
- Optional: After installation completes, you can select Launch Data Relationship Management Web Publishing Console.
- Click Finish.

MANUALLY CONFIGURING DATA RELATIONSHIP MANAGEMENT WEB PUBLISHING

Configuration must be completed for the following:

- Data Relationship Management Web Publishing Service
- IIS Virtual Directory/Pool Configuration
- Data Relationship Management Web Publishing Engine
- When installing on a stand-alone server: COM+ Director and Process Manager Proxy Components

Configuring Data Relationship Management Web Publishing Service

To configure the service:

- Select Start > Programmes > Administrative Tools > Services.
- Select the Hyperion Data Relationship Management Web Publishing service.

- Right-click the service and select Properties.
- On the General tab, ensure that Startup Type is set to Automatic.
- On the Log On tab, select This Account.
- Enter a username and password for a Windows administrative user..
- Click OK.
- Close the Services dialog box.

Configuring Internet Information Services

For IIS 5.0:

- Select Start > Programmes > Administrative Tools > Internet Services Manager (or Internet Information Services (IIS) Manager).
- Expand to the default Web site.
- Select the mdm_web virtual directory.
- Right-click and select Properties.
- On the Virtual Directory tab, verify the following:
  - The Local Path is pointing to the Data Relationship Management Web directory.
  - The Read option is selected.
  - Execute Permissions is set to Scripts and Executables.
  - The Application Protection is set to High (Isolated). Selecting this option enables you to unload the mdm_web application without restarting IIS.
- On the Directory Security tab, enable and configure anonymous access.
- Click OK.
- Click OK.
- Close the IIS Manager.

For IIS 6.0 or later:

- Select Start > Programmes > Administrative Tools > Internet Services Manager (or Internet Information Services (IIS) Manager).
- Expand to the default Web site.
- Select the mdm_web virtual directory.
- Right-click and select Properties.
- On the Virtual Directory tab, verify the following:
  - The Local Path is pointing to the Data Relationship Management Web directory.
  - The Read option is selected.
  - Execute Permissions is set to Scripts and Executables.
  - Application Pool is WebPool. This setting enables you to unload the mdm_web application without restarting IIS.
- Click OK.
- Select the Web Service Extensions node and select Active Server Pages from the list of Web Service Extensions on the right.

- Verify that the Status column displays the status Allowed.
- Create a new Web service extension named mdm_web_pub_gateway that points to mdm_web_pub_gateway.dll and is set to Allowed.
- Close the IIS Manager.

Verifying System Access

To verify system access:

- At the prompt, select to install the mdm_web_client ActiveX control: This digitally signed control is safe to install. If you are not prompted to install the component, then it may be necessary to adjust the current browser settings to allow download and installation of ActiveX controls.
- Click OK: The Data Relationship Management Web Client page is displayed. No data (versions or hierarchies) is displayed until the service is started at the end of the installation/configuration/ startup process.

Configuring Data Relationship Management Web Publishing Engine

To configure the Web Publishing Engine:

- Select Start > Administrative Tools > Component Services.
- Expand the Component Services node to the DCOM Config folder.
- In the DCOM Config folder, select the mdm_Web_Pub_Engine object, right-click and select Properties.
- For Windows 2000 only: From a command line prompt, type: dcomcnfg.
  - In the list of applications, select the mdm_Web_Pub_Engine object and click Properties.
  - On the General tab, set Authentication Level to None.
- On the Identity tab, select This User and enter the same user and password that were configured for the Data Relationship Management Web Publishing Service.
- On the Security tab, under Launch and Activation Permissions, select Customise and click Edit.
- Add the user that is configured for IIS anonymous access to the mdm_web virtual directory.
- Allow Local Activation for this user.
- Repeat this process for the Access Permissions section, by selecting Customise > Edit, and adding the same user and enabling the Local Access permission.
- Click OK to close the Properties dialog box.

Configuring Director

If you install on a stand-alone server where Director does not already exist, you must configure the COM+ Director component.

To configure the COM+ Director component:

- Select Start > Programmes > Administrative Tools > Component Services.
- Drill down and select the Director component.
- Right-click and select Properties.
- On the Security tab, verify that Enforce Access Checks for this Application is not selected.
- On the Identity tab, verify that the appropriate user is setup and then close the Properties dialog box.
- Drill down to the Components folder of Director.
- Select all components by pressing CTRL-A, then right-click and select Properties.
- Verify that Enable Object Pooling is selected on the Activation tab and then close the Properties dialog box.
- Close the Component Services window.

Configuring Process Manager

If you install on a stand-alone server where Process Manager does not already exist, you must configure the COM+ Process Manager Proxy component.

To configure the COM+ Process Manager Proxy component:

- Select Start > Programmes > Administrative Tools > Component Services.
- Drill down and select the Process Manager component.
- Right-click the component and select Properties.
- On the Activation tab, verify that the remote server is correct.
- Close the Component Services window.

USING THE DATA RELATIONSHIP MANAGEMENT WEB PUBLISHING CONSOLE

The Data Relationship Management Web Publishing Console is designed to allow configuration, control and monitoring of the Web Publishing system. The Server Monitor Page allows the Web Publishing Service to be controlled (Start, Stop, Restart, Force Shutdown) and displays the current status of the service.

In addition there are three tabs for further information:

- System Status.
- Event Log.
- Web Server.

The System Status tab shows some basic operating system information as well as information on COM+ and DCOM (Out of Process) applications. Currently Web Publishing does not use any COM+ so this section is blank. The Event Log tab filters the application event log to show events for the Web

Publishing module. Clicking on an event in the top panel shows the detail for the event in the lower panel. Events shown are filtered to include only events after the console was started.

To see historical events you can check the Show History and click Refresh. Clear resets the filter time to the current date and time. The Web Server tab provides two browser views to validate access to the Web Server system. The first panel displays the test HTML in the mdm_web virtual directory and validates access to the virtual directory for Web Publishing.

The second view tests the Web Publishing Gateway to perform the List Versions command. If the system is up and running, the list of versions available for Web Publishing is displayed. When stopping and starting services such as IIS, you may need to refresh these views. To refresh, right-click on the view and select Refresh.

You can set the Data Relationship Management username and password for the Web Publishing module on the Configuration page. This user is the Data Relationship Management user that the Web Publishing engine uses to retrieve the data for display on the Web client. Limiting access to this user allows the Web Publishing to be restricted. It is important that the user specified for Web Publishing be exempt from session timeout.

Thus, the system preference IdleTimeExcludeUsers should be set to include the name of the user for Web Publishing. If this user is not excluded from session timeout, then the Web Publishing service needs to be restarted each time the user session expires.

CONFIGURING DATA RELATIONSHIP MANAGEMENT WEB CLIENT

Data Relationship Management Web provides a specific set of frequently-used Data Relationship Management functionality in a Web browser. This document assumes that the user is already familiar with the overall Data Relationship Management system, including its terminology and feature set. The appearance and behaviour of Data Relationship Management Web Publishing can be configured using both System Preferences and embedded parameters.

ELECTRONIC THESES AND DISSERTATIONS FOR INDIAN UNIVERSITIES: A FRAMEWORK

Even though the electronic publishing and writing offer demanding environment in academic scholarship, the theses and dissertations are still written and published in print and archived in shelves in university libraries where the vast majority gather dust, read by perhaps one or two interested researchers who access them in print with lot of difficulty, often for a fee and most are never consulted at all. Digital libraries of electronic theses and dissertations (ETDs) offer an alternative to this waste of valuable academic scholarship and offer researchers and University Libraries in India opportunities to explore the possibilities electronic publishing trend in academic sector. The emergence of UGC Infonet, the aspiring and dream project of University Grants Commission, which also aims at Content Creation by Indian Academic Sector, will definitely boost this idea.

UGC-INFONET

As technology is becoming a driving force in the contemporary education systems, University Grant Commission has launched an ambitious programme to bring about a qualitative change in the academic infrastructure, especially for higher education. Under this initiative UGC is modernising the University Campuses with State-of-the-art campus wide networks and setting up its own nationwide communication network named UGC-Infonet. UGC-Infonet will be a boon to the higher education systems in several ways to facilitate spread of quality education all over the country.

This will function as a tool to distribute education material and journals to the remotest of areas and a resource centre for researchers and scholars for tapping the most up-to-date information. As a main feature of UGC Infonet, a data center with large server capacity is being set up, where content of common interest can be maintained. Each University will have the option of hosting their web site, digital content like ETDs and the E-journals subscribed through INFLIBNET Consortia.

THESES AND DISSERTATIONS IN INDIA

Indian universities play a major role in generation and dissemination of knowledge by conducting research works and producing Ph D theses as a unique genre of information sources. Every year, nearly 8000- 10000 Ph Ds are awarding in India. The purpose of the thesis is to provide an experience in scholarship, which will be of enduring value to the student in understanding how new knowledge is acquired and communicated within the chosen field. These works contain valuable content, including focused literature reviews and details on research, which are not generally made available elsewhere.

At present there are some lacunas in publication, control and access theses information in India, and some attempts have been made to address them. At the moment, most unpublished theses are hard to get hold of, as they are filed only in the university library where the student has worked. The Indian thesis literature is beset with many problems like Lack of Systematic acquisition, Lack of Access, Uncertain publication practice, Enormous Growth in the number of theses, etc.

In western countries, these problems were addressed already and serious attempts have been made to solve them. In North America, less than 5 per cent of all accepted dissertations and masters' theses are initially conceived of and executed as electronic documents.

BENEFITS OF ETD

- Broader exposure of university research through greater accessibility;
- Opportunities to use new forms of creative scholarship through use of interactive elements, multimedia, hyperlinks, etc.;
- Ability to have a hyperlink to the thesis/dissertation on homepages and electronic CVs;
- Professional development experience for research students as they learn the basic skills of scholarly publishing in an electronic format;
- Conservation of paper, library storage space and of library staff time;
- Theses and dissertations more immediately accessible: publication occurs near point of submission rather than three to four months later; and
- The option to have theses or dissertations accessible to any potential reader every day at any time.

ELECTRONIC THESES AND DISSERTATIONS FOR YOUR UNIVERSITY

Format to Create ETD

PDF stands for *Portable Document Format:* Adobe Systems developed the PDF standard and provides the premiere package for creating and manipulating PDF files, Adobe Acrobat. The process of converting to PDF takes instructions that would ordinarily be sent to a specific printer and prepares them to be viewed or printed on any computer with the free Acrobat Reader installed. Postscript is a standard language developed by Adobe Systems, which is used to send instructions to postscript compatible printers.

These instructions describe the contents of all text and graphics to be printed, and where on the page each piece of content is to be printed. Ordinarily, these instructions are transferred to a Postscript printer, which interprets them, creates a printed copy based on the instructions, and then discards the instructions.Other file types for image files can be.gif.jpeg, or.tif; for video files.mov.mpg, or.avi; and for audio files.aif.midi.snd.wav, or as CD-DA, CD-ROM/XA, or MPEG-2.

Facilities Required

Researchers need to create their original thesis using a word processor, such as Microsoft Word or WordPerfect and once it is done, then it can be converted to a PDF file, which will retain the original document format (for the purpose of future editing). Conversion into a PDF file is a straightforward process. Libraries and Campus labs have to be equipped with Windows based computers set up to convert theses and dissertations written in Microsoft Word to Adobe Acrobat format. This application will allow us to convert the word processing document to PDF format as well as create bookmarks. Researchers must submit the document on disk, CD, or Zip drive; the conversion machines are not attached to the network. Library staff can provide assistance with using the software to convert files, but cannot assist with document preparation.

SOFTWARE TO MANAGE ETDS

D-Space is a groundbreaking digital library system that captures, stores, indexes, preserves and redistributes the intellectual output of a university's research faculty in digital formats. The future of Etheses and of archiving and searching in general depends on institutions being able to deliver top quality services, with a high degree of interoperability. This means, among other things, that systems must continue to be developed and they must be able to handle many different types of digital object.

It is believed that DSpace will fulfill these requirements to a higher degree and will continue to improve in this way in the future. As an open source system, DSpace is now freely available to other institutions to run as-is, or to modify and extend as they require to meet local needs. From the outset, HP and MIT designed the system to be run by institutions other than MIT, and to support federation among its adopters, in both the technical and the social sense. INFLIBNET believes that it is our responsibility to lead the charge for a realistic assessment of how we can head off an otherwise inevitable loss of academic resources.

Awareness building in Open Archives and Institutional Repositories in Indian academic Institutions will be the main focus of INFLIBNET in coming future. For long-term preservation of our knowledge base and cultures, we have to find out an economical way to save digital content for future generations. Institutions in India started using variety of open source archiving solutions like Green Stone, E-Print, DSpace etc since 2000. After experimenting all popular solutions, INFLIBNET decided to opt DSpace for its Institutional Repository and archive its publications, conference proceedings, lecture notes, etc.

The capability of Dspace to handle multilingual content, even at Metadata level using globally accepted UNICODE standard was the important issue for selecting this solution, especially a country like India with its mullti-lingual dilemma in digital content creation and storage. It has been installed in test-bed and experimented its capabilities and performance. After all sorts of testing required, Dspace was customised according to our requirements and it was installed on one of the WWW Server on Linux platform.

Then we have requested Corporation for National Research Initiatives (CNRI) site for providing *Persistent Identifiers (CNRI Handles)* which promotes interoperability among open archives through Open Archives Initiative Protocol for Metadata Harvesting (OAI-PMH). The Handle System® covers assignment, management, and resolution of these persistent identifiers and are compliant with the IETF's Uniform Resource Name (URN) specification.

ROLE OF THE FACULTY AND REVIEW PROCESS

Faculty will continue to be responsible for upholding the quality of the thesis or dissertation, whether that thesis or dissertation is submitted using electronic formats or through paper. The electronic format can facilitate communication among members of the dissertation committee and the student. Electronic distribution of drafts allows multiple readers to markup and comment within one copy of the work simultaneously, regardless of the readers' physical location, and to see others' comments.

It also allows the student to collate the comments of all readers within one document. For defence, some committees may require that students provide all members of the committee with a paper copy of the ETD before the defence; others may elect to read on-screen or to have committee members take individual responsibility for working from screen or paper they print out themselves.

Printed versions of the textual components of an ETD can always be made available to committee members at their request. If non-text elements of the ETD are part of the defence, the committee can consider the most effective way to ensure that all members of the committee have access to non-text elements during the defence. After the committee approves thesis or dissertation, it can be sent to a particular contact person in the library for processing, who will be responsible for processing ETDs by making sure that the file's formatting is correct, the links work, etc. Metadata of ETD can be created and made available for searching and accessing.

ISSUE OF COPYRIGHT

The copyright issue involves two components: Protecting the information/ work produced as part of the research programme; and Granting license to University or to any ETD Programme to make the work available for use. This also includes obtaining permission to use parts of the work that have already been published in other sources.

If the material we are quoting or reproducing does not fall under the general guidelines of "fair use" then as suggested, need to get written permission from the copyright owner. Since a dissertation or thesis is published for non-profit educational purposes, the author is permitted limited use of copyrighted material under the guidelines of "fair use." The purpose, amount, nature and effect of the work reproduced determine whether or not one must seek permission from the copyright owner. More information about copyright issues in general.

INDIAN INITIATIVES

As a bibliographical tool to know about theses of awarded Ph Ds, Association of Indian Universities started publishing of Doctoral Bibliographies in all subjects and Theses of the Month column through its weekly publication *University News*. In 1994, INFLIBNET hosted a regularly updated free online union database of Ph D theses submitted to Indian universities. At present it is freely available for searching at INFLIBNET web site and contains around 1,40,000 of unique bibliographical records covering all subjects and all universities.

Being the data supplied by the Universities themselves, it is considered as the only authoritative online-tool available to find-out the research out put of Indian Universities. Recently University of Mysore, in collaboration with NISSAT and Ford Foundation initiated a project called Vidyanithi to host individual full-text thesis from various universities who are willing to become a member of this project. Even though, this project tries to evolve as a national depository for Indian theses, but it is not compulsory for Universities to become a part of this project. All these efforts are, off course, helpful for researchers in locating theses, but in the case of access, still we need remedies.

IN THE END WE CAN SAY

Popularisation of ETDs and its full advantages for faculty, students, and researchers are the foremost attempt to be start of. Brochures, communications, web sites etc conveying this information need to be written, designed, published and disseminated to all affected by this far-reaching change. Workshops and training programmes for both students and faculty need to be developed that cover issues of copyright and choice of access, and that encourage research scholars to carefully consider the ethics of restricting their research from access by the national and international scholarly community. Well-equipped computer labs must be put in place to provide workstations, software, and technical support staff for students writing ETDs.

And standards need to be developed for the presentation of dissertation research—standards which facilitate the development of a useful and easily navigable digital collection of works, but which do not unnecessarily constrain the use of software and design considerations graduate students deem essential to their research. Careful consideration of these requirements and their full support will contribute substantially to making this transition smoothly. The potential ETDs have to transform graduate education in ways that benefit both students and the scholarly community depends upon it.

SEARCH TECHNIQUES FOR ACCESSING CD-ROM DATABASES

Due to the development of information technology, information is increasingly recorded in digital format and electronic databases which are continually becoming more complex, information storage and retrieval As the technology obsolete very fast, CD-ROM is also facing problems due to emergence of the DVD. In today's business, education, and government environments the amount of information, data and software being archived and distributed on CD-ROM and DVD-ROM media is overwhelming. For years the medium of choice for storing, archiving and distributing digital content has been the CD-ROM.

As capacity requirements of data intensive applications and databases grow, DVD-ROM, with a capacity potential over 13 times that of CD-ROM, is fast becoming the most popular medium. (CD-ROM media can store up to 700 MB of data). Single-sided, single layer DVD-ROM media can store up to 4.7 GB of data. Doublesided, single layer DVD-ROM media store up to 9.4 GB of data). DVD which is used primarily with movie/ video features will not affect the CD-ROM, but DVD-ROMs will be, which can carry information on both sides of the disc. DVD-ROM will replace the CD-ROM, but that it will take a few years.

As information is increasingly recorded in digital format and electronic databases are continually becoming more complex, information storage and retrieval processes have profoundly changed. Over the past decades three major migrations have occurred in library academic services: from printed resources to online electronic databases; from online databases to bibliographic and full-text CD-ROM databases; and from CD-ROM databases to online Internet access to bibliographic and full-text/full-image databases.

CD-ROM DATABASES

CD-ROM is abbreviation for 'Compact Disc-Read-Only Memory' a type of optical disk capable of storing large amounts of data up to 1GB, although the most common size is 650 MB (megabytes). The term 'database' has been used in the literature in two different connotations. In Computer Science this is referred to as a database management system. In this sense a database has a logically consistent structure in which records are actually linked.

In library and Information science, these are referred to as bibliographic or inventory in nature and comprise a collection of related logical records here a database is defined as an organised and generally unlinked set of machine, or it can be said, these databases are the electronic version of published literature traditionally appearing in printed form in various field.

Databases are produced by different agencies in a computer readable form, the contents of which are accessible in various ways according to requirements with the help of suitable software. Various agencies (governmental and non-governmental) are involved in developing databases by collecting information from varieties of sources and packaging the information in the form of databases.

Databases can be stored on CD-ROM, on the Internet, or on commercial sites that are accessible only if user's library has a subscription. CD-Rom in the library contains periodical indexes, abstracts, statistics, directories, and other complete texts. Some databases provide information that is primarily numeric, such as data from a recent government census and some contain information that is primarily textual. Database some time also called data bank.

USE CD-ROM DATABASES IN LIBRARIES

Access to Cd-Rom databases is fast, accurate and thorough. A clever search by a users may get them in seconds most of the information they need. In contrast, traditional print services may take months for same task, with still great deal of information left out. As a matter of fact, libraries can not possibly continue with the sluggish manual information service methods and hope to remain in business tomorrow.

Libraries can have economic access to information, space saving and users friendly Libraries and information centers used these databases in providing various library services as mentioned below

- Literature search services, current and retrospective literature searches
- Current awareness services in various forms including SDI
- Full text databases may be utilised for search services
- Document delivery services
- For producing digest trend reports, etc.
- Compilations of bibliographies
- Abstracting and Indexing Services

WHY WE DON'T WANT TO USE CD-ROM DATABASES

It is always beneficial to know about the pros and cons of any information so that one can proceed systematically.

- CD-ROM databases are not updated in time, some web journals or indexing services are available online even before their print editions roll out of the press. For example, Engineering Index on disc is updated quarterly, and Dissertation Abstracts on disc only once in a year.
- Retrieval from CD-ROM databases take seconds, as against online databases, which take only milliseconds, however complex the command search statement may be (of courses with higher bandwidth telecom pipes provided)
- If not acquired from a single producer, CD/DVD Rom databases require skills in using different search engines. Making menu-driven index searching or single keyword searching at command prompt may be easy to use in each system. But, users must make command, or Boolean searches, to get at exacter or less abstract hits. Sometimes users have been found key boarding DIALOG syntax instead of SPIRS one to search into MathSci Disc or PsycLIT from SilverPlatter, and vice versa. Both the search engines are so dissimilar in construct.

Again, generally, users keyboard a collection of key words at the command prompt. They are flummoxed to discover that one access engine parses the search statement with "or" operator between words, and the other with 'and' operator. The former results come in too many hits and the latter in too few. Therefore, all new uses require basic education in the techniques of bibliographic database searching.

- If adequate jukeboxes are not provided for permanent mounting of optical databases, it is a great hassle for users to switch from one disc to another for either a different file or part of the same file. By comparison, on online services, like DIALOG's the process is just a click away.

Yet another disadvantage of CD-ROM, they are vulnerable to damage by dust, fingerprints and scratches, etc. Therefore they need very careful handing. Libraries will have to make backup copy of each CDS disc to be kept in safe custody, so fresh copies can be made.

SEARCHING CD-ROM DATABASE

Conducting effective searches requires knowledge of a number of techniques. Users should not only have been an understanding of the nature, content and structure of the database, but also be familiar with the various option available in the search screen, the tools and techniques for searching, and the techniques and formats for display of the search output.

The search features commonly available are Keyword Search, Phrase Search, Boolean Search, Truncation, Index and/or Thesaurus Support, Proximity Search, Field-Specific Searches, Free-Text Search, Combing Search Sets and Search Refinement, Limiting or Range Search, Searching through the Retrieved Records and they may vary from one CD-ROM to another.

SELECTION OF DATABASES FOR COMPARISON

Four CD-ROM Databases have been selected for a discussion on the various search and retrieval features available, 'Ulrich's on disc', 'Books in Print' from the category of general or ready reference sources, 'Ei Compendex', 'LISA plus' are Bibliographic databases containing details of documents including abstracts and Emerald full-text database of journal articles.

Ulrich's on Disc

Ulrich's on Disc from R. R. Bowker provides the ability to search and browse the entire Ulrich's family of databases. They included nearly 250,000 titles from over 200 countries, Information on about 11,000 new titles per year, annotations for almost 90,000 titles, full text reviews from *Magazines for Libraries* and *Library Journal* for over 8,700 publications, indicators for over 21,000 refereed publications and complete names and addresses for 80,000 serials publishers and distributors. The main screen of Ulrich's is shown in figure.

EI COMPENDEX BIBLOGRAPHIC DATABASE

DIALOG OnDisc® Compendex, produced by (Ei) Engineering Information Inc., provides coverage of the world's significant engineering and technical literature. Subject coverage includes but is not limited to the various disciplines of engineering, applied physics, electronics and instrumentation, light and optical technologies, and other areas of significant technology.

Compendex contains references to and abstracts from journals, technical reports, books, proceedings and conference papers, and more. Author-prepared abstracts are used when available. Publications from around the world are indexed, including approximately 4,500 journals and 2,000 conference proceedings per year. Approximately 10 percent of the documents indexed are in a language other than English.

LIBRARY AND INFORMATION SCIENCE ABSTRACTS (LISA PLUS)

LISA plus is the world's best known resource for the coverage of ongoing research in all aspects of library and information studies. Over 245,000 abstracts keep user well informed about such topics as artificial intelligence, information and knowledge management, publishing and copyright, World Wide Web resources and much more since 1969. Lisa plus main screen is as figure

EMERALD FULL-TEXT DATABASE OF JOURNAL ARTICLES

Emerald is a full text database from MCB, covers more than 82 top journal across ten broad subject areas. It provides access to the full text of articles in PDF and HTML format published from 1994 to date. The subjects covered include Marketing, Human Resources, Quality Management, Information Management, Library and Information Services, Training and Education, General Management Property, Operations and Production Management, etc. Users can choose any subject and get a list of all the journals covered in that subject. First screen of Emerald is as figure

ACCESSING DIFFERENT DATABASES

Searching in Specific Field of Selected CD-ROM Databases

There are two forms of searching for information in CD-ROM databases – field-specific and free-text search. A user may know which field to search, or might like to restrict a given search to one or more fields. This is a field specific search. If the user are not sure of the field to be searched, they can conduct a free-text search, which means that the search is not restricted to any particular field.

While the free-text search is not universally available, field specific search is the simplest form of search, and CD-ROM databases offer various options to conduct searches on one or more specific fields. The simplest option is the form search, where the user can select a specific box for a particular field and can key in the search term/phrase. Which search field can be searched in a database depends on the content and structure of the database concerned, and there fore they differ from one database to another.

Ulrich's on Disc

Search fields are Abstracting and Indexing Service, Area Code, Circulation, CODEN Number, Country, Dewey Number, Document Availability, Electronic Vendor, ISSN, Keyword, Keyword In Title, LC Class, Media Type, Personnel Name, Price (US Dollar), Publication Code, Publisher, Special Features, Special Index, Status Code, Subjects, Title, US State/Zip, Year First Published. Search screen is shown by figure

Ei Compendex

Under option 'Search/Modify' search fields are Word/Phrase Index, EI Subject Headings, Author Name, Author Affiliation, Title Words, Journal Name, Conference Search Options (Conference Title, Conference Location, Conference Sponsor, Conference Year), Limit Options 'English…', Additional Search Options (Words/Phrases, EI Classification Codes, Major Subject Headings, Treatment Codes, Year of Publications, Language) different fields and Search results screen shown in figure

LISA Plus

Subject, Title, Abstract, Index Term Or Keyword, Author, Source, Title Database Name,, Keyword, Language, Publication Date, Author Affiliation, Country Of Research, Record Number, CODEN, CATNI name, ISSN, Thesaurus term

Boolen Search

Combine terms to make the search broader or narrower. How broad or narrow the search is depends on the search logic used to combine search terms. Three logical connectors, or Boolean operators, are used to define the relationship between search terms: "and", "or ", and "not". The Boolean operators may be used to join search terms within search fields in all search modes and to join search criteria between search fields in the Advanced and Expert search modes only. (Novice mode always uses a Boolean AND between search fields). Boolean searches can not be conducted in the 'browse index' mode of CD-ROM.-

Ulrich's on Disc

Operators are AND, OR, NOT/AND NOT and Options are, In the Form Search mode user can combine terms/phrases with Boolean operators in a chosen field box, or can type one term/phrase in each box and click on a

Boolean operator in the box next to the box next to the term on the right. In the search mode user have to type the Boolean operator to combine terms/ phares from the same or different fields. Ei Compendex: Operators are AND, OR, NOT and Options are: use these operators to combine search terms in the 'Modify Search Option'

LISA Plus

Operators are AND, OR, ANDNOT (not can also be used in free-text search mode) Options: In the Easy Search mode, user can combine terms/ phrases with Boolean operators in a chosen field box, or can type one term/ phrase in each box and click on a Boolean operators in the box next to the term on the right. In the Expert Search Mode, user has to type the Boolean operator to combine terms/phases from the same or different fields. No nesting is possible. Emerald: Operators are And or, not and Options enter theses operators in the search in the search as well as Advanced Search Mode

Truncation Search

Truncation of the three kinds of truncation (left, right and middle truncation), left truncation is not commonly available in CD-ROM databases. The symbols for truncation and their syntax and effect vary, and the user has to learn these to conduct an effective search.

Ulrich's on disc

Ulrich's on disc: * or $ substitute for any number of characters and can be used for right truncation only. '?' Substitutes for one character, can be used anywhere in a word, or user can use multiple '?'Symbols. LISA: Truncation is the substitution of a wildcard symbol for any portion of a word to retrieve a group of words. Most often, truncation is used to abbreviate a word — to trim a term back to its stem, or root word.

Truncating lets user search for word variants thereby broadening the search. The asterisk * is a multicharacter wildcard and the question mark ? is a single character wildcard. Wildcards are typically used at the end of a word but may be embedded within a word as well. Right and middle or internal truncation is allowed. Both the symbols can be used for right as well as middle truncation. User can enter the symbol as appropriate in the Easy Search as well as the Expert Search mode. Multiple ? can be used. Wildcards are typically used at the end of a word but may be embedded within a word as well. Avoid truncating words to less than five characters or user may retrieve unwanted results.

Index Search and Thesaurus Search

The indexes allow users to select the search terms/phrases from the term index, and a thesaurus allows users to consult a map of available terms to widen or narrow down a given search, as required. CD-ROM retrieval software provides index search facilities, ie users can select an index to browse and select from the index for searching. There may be an index file or a separate index for each searchable field so that the user can choose a field and then browse the corresponding index file. Index search facilities are more commonly available than thesaurus facilities. Thesauri are hierarchically structured. This means that they go from broad terms to narrower, more specific, terms.

Ulrich's on disc

User can choose a field from either the search or the From Search mode. In each case user can display and browse the corresponding index and select a term/phrase from the index.

Ei Compendex

In order to conduct a search, user need to choose an index: author, subject heading, keywords, etc, and then the corresponding index will be open for user to browse and to select the search term

LISA plus

The thesaurus may be accessed via the Browse window by clicking on the Index drop-down list and selecting Thesaurus Term; highlight the required term and click View Titles. In the Expert Search mode enter the thesaurus term in the Search Query Box, click on ok or press Enter. Press the 'View Brief' button to display the results of the search ie the thesaurus block. A thesaurus term can be selected to conduct a search in the database

Emerald

In the Advanced Search mode, user can choose one or more fields to search, and once users have entered a search term correspond to a field, they can click on the 'Thesaurus' button to get other words correspond to the search term.

Proximity Search

With a proximity search, user can specify the number of words allowed between the search terms. In a general sense, there is a correlation between the number of intervening words (the words creating the "distance" between search terms) and the topical relevance of users search results. The closer the distance between users search words, *e.g.*, 5 words, the more relevant but fewer the results may be.

Likewise, the wider the distance between the search words, *e.g.*, 20 words, the less relevant but larger the CD-ROM results may be. The type of proximity search operator to use depends upon whether user need search terms to be found in the same order as listed in the search statement (adjX) or found in the same or reverse order of what user originally specified (nearX).

RESULTS

After the comparison we come to know that all databases have almost same basic accessing techniques as keyword search, Phrase Search, Boolean Search, Truncation, Index and/or Thesaurus Support, Proximity Search, Field-Specific Searches, Free-Text Search, Combing Search Sets and Search Refinement, Limiting or Range Search, Searching through the Retrieved Records and they may vary from one CD-ROM to another with a slight variation as given below;

- Boolean searching is possible in all the CD-ROM database, through how it is carried out varies. Boolean searches cannot be conducted in the 'browse index' mode of a CD-ROM database for the obvious reason that only one term/phrase can be keyed in to display the corresponding portion of the index.
- None of the sample databases provides left-truncations facilities. The symbols for truncation vary from one database to another.
- Search refinement of a given search can be refined by adding or dropping one or more search terms or criteria, such as limiting the output to a given language, year of publication, price range, and so on.
- Some CD-ROM products have more than one search interface, for example, Ulrich's on disc, while others have on search interface giving options for both - simple, novice and other advanced/ expert search.
- Some retrieval system such as EI Compendex show the result instantly, while in others the user has to chose the view/display option, as in LISA plus
- Proximity search in CD-ROM databases allows users to conduct proximity searches in order to specify how closely the terms prescribed in a search expression.
- Two types of indexing practice are followed word index and phrase index.in the word index, each individual word in a field is indexed, while in the phrase index, a given phrase that may comprise several keyboard, is indexed. The user may need to check whether a field is a word- or phrase-indexed, by browsing through the index for the particular field, before entering a search term/phrase.
- CD-Rome databases do not usually provide facilities for ranking the search results according to relevance.

CONCLUSION

The standards for organising web-based resources are still in the early stages of development, and librarians are forced to utilise standards for print resources that were not designed for electronic resources. Additionally web-based information resources are volatile in the sense that may be moved from one site to another or may be removed altogether from web. Web-based library services will become more widespread and sophisticated as the web becomes common place throughout the world, and to be successful players in the E-world.

Libraries must continue to address the web design and implementation issues. As we actively transfer library services, our central purpose remain the same, to serve and teach users to find, evaluate, and use information effectively. The librarians should be expert to hold the hands of the users who are moving towards new communication paradigm a shift from face to face human contact to human machine interaction, from paper to electronic delivery, from text centered mode to multimedia and from physical presence to virtual presence.

Despite these changes in communication technology, the reference interview will remain at the heart of the reference transaction. To meet these challenges the librarians may play a leadership role in providing better Web Based library Services facilities to their current techno savvy users

9

Fundamentals of Network Security

INTRODUCTION

Digital Library systems are the computerized information storage and retrieval systems connected to computer networks and have maximum flexibility, durability, immunity, stability, scalability, accessibility and compatibility with other media at minimum cost, space and maintenance. Library network provides transmission of information dissemination of catalogues; abstract and full text formats as well as various basic functions of libraries like acquiring, digitizing and archiving of contents. The networking of library resources means that users or patrons can access the information from their desktops irrespective of their physical location. The library networks provides library without walls.

TRADITIONAL LIBRARY NETWORK MODEL

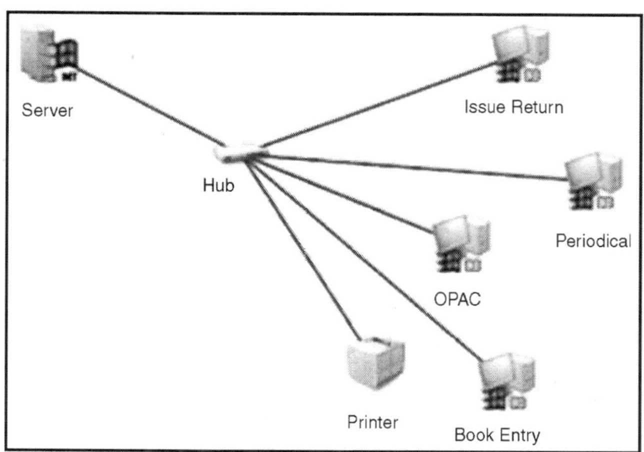

Fig. Traditional Library Network Setup with one Server and Four Client Machines

Traditional library network setup was established with Ethernet technology and fewer clients and server machines. Ethernet has become the most commonly used LAN (Local Area Network) technology worldwide. More than 85% of all installed network connections are using Ethernet technology, according to International Data Corporation. As a transport protocol, Ethernet operates at 10Mbps data transmission speed and Layers 1 and 2 of the 7-layer OSI networking model, delivering its data packets to any device connected to the network cable. This type of network have very limited infrastructure.

The hardware and software is used make library network it includes one server machine and 5 to 10 client machines connected to gather. The server is responsible for all library related activities and like storage and retrievals. The same server runs library management software like SOUL and provides resources to the clients. The other hardware requires is hub/switch, network interface card (NIC) etc. while software need is generally network client software and network card drives.

GENERAL NETWORK MODEL

Traditional library networks model operate at 10Mbps speed. At these speed libraries that use extremely large files such as transferring audiovisual contents to desktop, can experience long delays when sending such data across the network. This model uses the extended version of Ethernet called fast Ethernet, which is simply, an extension of existing Ethernet technology, running 10 times faster at 100 Mbps.

This setup model has two servers one for library applications and the other is for Internet access through remote location. These two servers provide information to switch, which is of 100Mbps. Both the server NIC are of 100Mbps, which is little, bit higher then the traditional network setup. The Windows NT server provides user authen-tication and library management services to the various clients connected to it. While Internet server provides Internet services with remote online libraries, and Internet services .

HIGH SPEED NETWORK MODEL

Traditional and general setup model operates at 10/100Mbps speed, while high speed network operates at gigabit 1000Mbps speed. Easy and straightforward migration to higher performance level without disruption, low cost of ownership including purchase and support cost and flexibility in network design are prime criteria for the high speed network model.

This model is 100 times faster than regular 10 Mbps Ethernet and 10 times faster than 100Mbps fast Ethernet. This also employs the same protocol, same frame format and same frame size as its predecessors like 100Mbps fast Ethernet. This model setup has three main server connected to central switch with 1000Mbps gigabit data transmission speed. All three-server has gigabit Ethernet card Installed. The high speed network switch has 1000Mbps network link and distributes network traffic to four hub/switch segments like Internet services, digital content reading room, audiovisual learning and finally library management. Out of four hub/switch segments three are working at 100Mbps speed with 100Mbps fast Ethernet cards installed on each desktop machines.

The hub connection has also 100Mbps link support. Transferring this high bandwidth intensive file on the shared Ethernet makes network busy or low so that this segment must of 1000Mbps. This high-speed network segment provides simultaneous access to all the clients with streaming audio and video without any hustle form network speed.

The high-speed performance is possible because the traffic is segmented. The NAS server has very large capacity storage with 1000Mpbs gigabit card installed on it. This server provides automatic storing and transfer of data on network with supporting domain server. IIS server provides Internet access and web services of any other digital library from Internet.

NETWORK SECURITY

The process of securing your library network begins with realizing what the library stands to lose if security is not pursued. Network security is not just "another thing to do." Its importance lies in protecting the library's network resources. Network resource means the equipment, software, and data that make up a networking system, including the user data that is shared over the network.

In terms of network communication, this includes the servers, workstations, hubs, switches, routers, firewalls, and telecommunications links that make up a network. In terms of usage, this includes shared printers, database systems, shared software, user accounts, the shared or user-specific files stored on a central server, and the keystrokes and form information that travel across the network.

IMPLEMENTING NETWORK SECURITY

We divide the realm of network security in libraries into seven main categories: physical security, password security, hardware security, server security, workstation security, perimeter security, and financial security These areas are expanded in the *Checklist* by separating out specific configuration issues related to web servers and general administrative issues related to budgeting, planning, and policy development.

There are many sections in the security checklist:

- General security.
- Physical security of computers and network equipment.
- Password security.
- Hardware security.
- Workstation security.
- Network server security.

- Network equipment security.
- Switch/Router/Hub security.
- Web server security.

LOCAL AREA NETWORK SECURITY

Securing any computer in a library must be achieved without any compromise to these three basic concepts: public service, user privacy and legal access. In an office or business environment, security is a matter of making sure those documents and transactions haven't been tampered with, corporate information is protected, personal employee information is kept private, and data is available when the business wants it to be.

Network and computer security in a library setting faces these same challenges and a few additional ones. The major local area network security points are: Password Security, Hardware Security, Workstation Security, LAN/Domain Server Security, and Network Equipment Security. As a librarian we have to protect these levels of security in the network.

PASSWORD SECURITY

The least expensive and most important aspect of network security is the use of appropriate passwords.

Password protection is inherent in various aspects of the network:

- Administrative access to server functions
- Workstation access to various files and services (such as the Internet)
- Administrative access to network hubs, switches, routers, and firewalls
- Access to administrative files, such as confidential personnel files or reports

Here are the checklist items related to password security:

- Develop written password policy and provide to all staff and patrons using specific user logons
- Develop written instructions in creating strong passwords and provide to all staff and patrons using specific user logons
- Document passwords for all network equipment, servers, and workstations
- Store password documentation in secure location known only by library director and one other person

HARDWARE SECURITY

Hardware security is a convenient category used to classify miscellaneous items related to your computer and network hardware. The first set of items relate to the BIOS (the Basic Input/Output System) of your servers and workstations. The BIOS is a well-known feature on all Intel/AMD PCcompatible servers and workstations. It performs basic tests of internal components to be sure they are working satisfac-torily. It also stores and manages the configuration of many of the parts inside the CPU case.

WORKSTATION SECURITY

Properly securing workstations is a very important part of the overall network security in a library. There are a large number of configuration issues to address when securing workstations. Using the Windows NT Workstation/2000 Professional operating system provides a better security foundation than does Windows 98. Those libraries using Windows 98 on public workstations are highly encouraged to install special software to secure many of the workstation functions:

- Configure NT Workstation/2000 Professional partitions with NTFS file systems.
- Windows NT/2000, unlike Windows 98, includes a feature known as file system security.

LAN/DOMAIN SERVER SECURITY

This paper assumes the use of Windows NT/2000 as the library's server operating system. In most small library local area networks, there will be one or two servers: a main server, usually a *domain controller* under Windows NT/2000, which verifies the logins of all users, and a file server used with the library automation system.

In some libraries, these two services are combined on one server. It is possible to operate in a very small environment with just Windows NT Workstation/2000 Professional-based computers and no server at all, but it is more difficult to maintain security in this environment. So this base level of security assumes the presence of at least one server.

The following items are needed to secure the local area network servers in the library:

- Configure all NT Server partitions with NTFS file systems.
- Configure separate operating system and data partitions (both NTFS).
- Mirror server drives (or implement RAID), if funding allows, for redundancy.
- Configure servers with private IP addresses (LAN-wide recommendation).
- Remove unnecessary services.
- Remove unnecessary files/programmes.
- Configure file system with proper file/folder access permissions.
- Restrict access to the Network Monitor Agent.
- Disable anonymous user logons.
- Disable caching of user logons.
- Configure account policy to restrict unauthorized logon attempts.

- Create logon-warning message (a warning against unauthorized logon or access and use of restricted resources).
- Create alternative Administrators group and restrict membership.
- Restrict privileges of default Administrators group
- Create alternative Administrator account (with new name) with full privileges.
- Disable default Administrator account.
- Configure auditing of Administrator account logon attempts (to track hacking attempts).
- Set a strong password for current administrator account.
- Use different passwords for domain/server accounts than for local workstation accounts, or use different account names.
- Restrict access permissions for the everyone group.
- Disable Guest account if enabled.
- Create appropriate user and group accounts (minimum of three groups: Patrons, Staff, and Administrators).
- Set appropriate group access permissions.
- Implement procedures for file backups according to backup plan.
- Restrict access to backup programme.
- Create and maintain current Emergency Repair Disks, and store in a controlled location.
- File all server component documentation (papers/manuals/disks) for use by service technicians.

NETWORK EQUIPMENT SECURITY

Network equipment refers to all the devices required to get data signals from one computer to another. Generally, these include hubs, switches, routers, and firewalls. Libraries should be purchasing network equipment that provides management capabilities.

This provides the possibility of remote management of the network even if the library does not contract for that service initially:

- Set appropriate network management protocol (SNMP) passwords/ community strings
- Record and secure any password settings created by staff or contractors

These two items minimize the risk of network equipment configurations being altered by unauthorized personnel. When the library hires a vendor to install and configure network equipment, be sure to document all passwords used to secure the equipment.

It is the library's responsibility to secure these passwords by documenting them and storing the documen-tation in a secure (preferably locked) location.

- Configure audit logs properly, if available
- Implement procedure for monitoring audit logs
- Schedule periodic installation of firmware updates
- Document equipment settings for future use in reconfiguring equipment
- File all network equipment documentation (papers/manuals/disks) for use by service technicians.

CONCLUSION

A Library network service is an assemblage of digital computing, storage and communication machinery together with the software needed to reproduce, emulate and extend the services provided by the conventional libraries. The analysis of depicted models indicates that scalability in the increasing processing capabilities of digital computing of workstations and servers providing services to the clients, larger and larger storage needs and effective management of storage and increasing requirements of network bandwidth and high speed data transfer are the prime issues of infor-mation technologies.

The library network once established is not secured from the administrators' point of view but must provide network security policy for servers, clients and other connectivity devices to provide satisfactory level of network security.

10

Cataloging Electronic Resources

INTRODUCTION

DEFINITION

AACR defines an electronic resource as material encoded for manipulation by a computerized device. This material may require the use of a peripheral directly connected to a computerized device or a connection to a computer network. Electronic resources that do not require the use of a computer, are not included in this definition.

For cataloguing purposes, electronic resources may be treated in one of two ways depending on whether access is direct (local) or remote (networked):

- Direct–a physical carrier can be described. This carrier, (*e.g.* disc/ disk, cassette, cartridge) must be inserted into a computerized device.
- Remote–no physical carrier can be handled. Remote access can only be provided by use of an input-output device.

CONTENT VERSUS CARRIER

Until 1997 electronic resources were coded for carrier and not content. In June 1997 MARBI (the committee that governs MARC changes) revised the definition of code "m" in the fixed field Type. Electronic resources are now cataloged and coded according to their content and not the carrier.

Type code "m" is now used only for the following general classes of electronic resources:

Computer software (including programmes, games, fonts):

- Numeric data
- Computer-oriented multimedia
- Online systems or services

Examples:

- Census data on CD-ROM or the Internet – Type "a" (book)
- Online maps – Type "e" (cartographic materials)
- Maps on floppy disks – Type "e" (cartographic materials)
- Most web pages – Type "a" (book)

- Multimedia encyclopedia on CD-ROM or online –Type "m" (electronic resource)
- Computer games online or on CD-ROM – Type "m" (electronic resource)

GUIDELINES FOR CODING ELECTRONIC RESOURCES IN LEADER/06

DOCUMENTATION

- *MARC 21 Concise Format for Bibliographic Data* defines the codes and conventions that identify data elements in MARC bibliographic records. It is updated on an annual basis.
- OCLC's *Cataloguing Electronic Resources: OCLC-MARC Coding Guidelines* assists catalogers creating biblio-graphic records for electronic resources and includes information on the proper coding of fixed fields, including Leader/06 (Type of record).
- *Guidelines for Distinguishing Cartographic Materials on Computer File Carriers from other Materials on Computer File Carriers* helps catalogers working with carto-graphic electronic resources to distinguish them from other types of electronic resources and to select the correct Leader/06 (Type of record) based on that distinction.
- *Relationship of Fields 006, 007, and 008* explains the general model adopted to indicate how repeti-tions of field 006 (Fixed-length data elements-Additional material characteristics) and a single field 008 (Fixed-length data elements-General information) coexist in bibliographic records, especially in relation to the values in Leader character positions 06 (Type of record) and 07 (Bibliographic level), and clarifies the relationship of field 007 (Physical description fixed field) to fields 006 and 008.
- *Use of fixed fields 006/007/008 and Leader codes in CONSER records* presents guidelines for coding in CONSER records.

PRINCIPLES AND GUIDELINES FOR CODING LEADER/06

An electronic resource is a manifestation of a work that requires the use of a computer for access. Peripheral devices attached to the computer (such as a CD-ROM drive) may also be required. The manifestation's carrier is accessed either directly (*e.g.*, via CD-ROM, etc.) or remotely (*e.g.*, via the Internet).

Items that do not require the use of a computer, such as audio CDs or movies on DVD-videodiscs, are excluded from this definition. The Leader/06 (Type of record) character position in the *MARC 21 Format for Bibliographic Data* contains a one-character alphabetic code that differentiates MARC records created for various types of content and materials. The definition of code "m" (computer file) in Leader/06 was revised in June 1997 as a result of *Proposal No. 97-3R*.

The new definition narrowed the choice of code "m" to the following types of electronic resources:

- Computer software (including programmes, games, fonts)
- Numeric data
- Computer-oriented multimedia
- Online systems or services

Code "m" is defined as follows in the MARC 21 Format for Bibliographic Data:

- *m-ComputerFile:* Code m indicates that the content of the record is for the following classes of electronic resources: computer software (including programmes, games, fonts), numeric data, computer-oriented multi-media, online systems or services. For these classes of materials, if there is a significant aspect that causes it to fall into another Leader/ 06 category, code for that significant aspect (*e.g.*, vector data that is cartographic is not coded as numeric but as cartographic). Other classes of electronic resources are coded for their most significant aspect (*e.g.* language material, graphic, cartographic material, sound, music, moving image). In case of doubt or if the most significant aspect cannot be determined, consider the item a computer file.

This revised definition stipulates that catalogers code electronic resources for the significant aspects of their content, as opposed to their carrier. The Leader/06 determines which 008 code (Fixed-length data elements-General information) is used and the appropriateness and validity of other fixed data elements in a record.

PRINCIPLES AND GUIDELINES FOR CODING FIELDS 006, 007 AND 008

The 008 field contains character positions that provide coded information about the record as a whole and about special bibliographic aspects of the item cataloged. This field is not repeatable.

Field 006 (Fixed-length data elements-Additional material characteristics) permits coding for additional aspects of an electronic resource (including any computer file aspects) if the 007 and 008 fields do not adequately describe it. Some cataloguing utilities and groups (such as CONSER) require the use of 006 fields under certain conditions.

Sample records in this document include 006 fields for those who may wish to use this field. Coding all of these positions involves making a series of decisions.

Consider the following when deciding what code values to select:

- What are the primary characteristics of the content of the resource (as opposed to the physical format or carrier)? Look at the definitions of the various Leader/06 codes. Is the content primarily language material, notated music, cartographic material, a computer file, a musical sound recording, etc.?

- Does the resource match the Leader/06 definition of a computer file? If so, "m" (for computer file) goes in Leader/06, and the 008 field is coded for computer files. Position 008/26 contains the code for the type of computer file described in the record.
- If Leader/06 is coded "a" (language material), is the resource a monograph or a continuing resource? This determines the code in Leader/07 (Bibliographic level), which in turn influences 008 field coding (Books or Continuing resources). For other material types, the Leader/06 code determines 008 coding.
- Does the cataloger wish to add a 006 field to record characteristics that cannot be coded in the 008 field? Some electronic resources might need more than one 006 field. For others, a 006 field may not really add any additional information and could be left out.
- Note that *Proposal No. 97-3R* specifies that a 007 field (Physical description fixed field) for electronic resources is mandatory regardless of the Leader/06 code value when the physical form of the resource is an electronic format in order to provide an explicit indication that the item is in an electronic format.
- Some combinations of 006, 007, and 008 fields may result in a certain amount of redundancy, in the sense that the same information about an electronic resource might appear in more than one of these fields. Catalogers must decide whether the infor-mation added as a result of recording additional characteristics of an item justifies the redundancy.

In case of doubt, or if the most significant characteristic cannot be determined, code the resource "m" in the Leader/06 position.

Coding for Different types of Electronic Resources

- Bibliographic database on the Internet
- Collection of databases on the Internet
- Textual continuing resource
- Textual continuing resource with search software
- Textual continuing resource received via e-mail
- Textual document
- Cartographic material
- Still images
- Notated music
- Census in textual form
- Database containing manipulable numeric data
- Computer operating system

- Computer software
- Computer game
- Internet search engine
- Web portal
- System or service on the Internet, such as an E-commerce site
- Web site with significant audio and video content
- Streaming video
- Streaming audio

Notes:

- The sample records are partial records.
- Some of the records have a Leader/07 with a value of "i" (for integrating resource). Bibliographic Level "i" for integrating resources was fully implemented in June 2006.
- Some of the 006 fields in the sample records do not necessarily provide much additional information but were added for illustrative purposes.

Bibliographic Database on the Internet

The record describes collections of bibliographic records retrieved via search software; the presence of such software does not change the content of the resource and does not mean that Leader/06 should be coded "m." The resource is primarily textual bibliographic data, so it is coded as language material. The type of computer file (006/09) is bibliographic data.

- *Example(s):*
  - The Library of Congress' online catalogue of bibliographic data.

Ldr/06	:	a [type of record: language material]
Ldr/07	:	m [bibliographic level: monograph]
007	:	[cr||||||||||||]
006/00	:	m [form of material: computer files/electronic resources]
006/09	:	e [type of computer file: bibliographic data]

Collection of Databases on the Internet

The record describes the system itself and not the content of individual databases. The type of computer file is online system or service.

- *Example(s):*
  - *MEDLINEplus,* a system of databases and data-banks on the Internet offered by the U.S. National Library of Medicine (NLM) and the National Institutes of Health (NIH).

Ldr/06	:	m [type of record: computer files/ electronic resources]
Ldr/07	:	m [bibliographic level: monograph]
007	:	cr#m||||||||||
008/26	:	j [type of computer file: online system or service]
245 00	:	$aMEDLINEplus $h [electronic resource]

Textual Continuing Resource

The resource is the equivalent of a print item, but in electronic form. The resource is coded as language material.

If a 006 field for computer files/electronic resources is added, the type of computer file (006/09) depends on the content of the resource.

- *Example(s):*
  - *MEDLINE*, a monthly periodical available in PDF format.

Ldr/06	:	a [type of record: language material]
Ldr/07	:	s [bibliographic level: serial]
006/00	:	m [form of material: computer files/electronic resources]
006/09	:	d [type of computer file: document]
007	:	cr#c||||||||||| [category of material: electronic resource specific material designation: remote]
008/21	:	# [type of continuing resource: periodical]
008/23	:	s [form of item (continuing resources): electronic]
245 10	:	$a NIH MedlinePlus $h [electronic resource]:$b the magazine.

Textual Continuing Resource with Search Software

The resource is the equivalent of a print item, but in electronic form. Search software is included.

The presence of such software and/or the location of the serial on the Internet does not necessarily change the content of the resource and does not mean that Leader/06 should be coded "m."

The resource is primarily textual data and is coded as language material. If a 006 field for computer files/electronic resources is added, the type of computer file (006/09) depends on the content of the resource.

- *Example(s):*
  - *MLA international bibliography*, a database of citations available on CD, cumulated quarterly.

Ldr/06	:	a [type of record: language material]
Ldr/07	:	s [bibliographic level: serial]
006/00	:	m [form of material: computer files/ electronic resources]
006/09	:	e [type of computer file: bibliographic data]
007	:	co#ugu||||||||| [category of material: electronic resource specific material designation: optical disc]
008/21	:	p [type of continuing resource: periodical]
008/23	:	s [form of item (continuing resources): electronic]
245 00	:	$a MLA international bibliography $h [electronic resource].

  - *Project Muse*, a service providing Internet access to a collection of over 110 journals from numerous scholarly publishers.

Ldr/06	:	a [type of record: language material]
Ldr/07	:	i [bibliographic level: integrating resource]
006/00	:	m [form of material: computer files/ electronic resources]
006/09	:	e [type of computer file: bibliographic data]
007	:	cr|||||||||||| [category of material: electronic resource specific material designation: remote access]
008/2	:	d [type of continuing resource: updating database]
008/23	:	s [form of item (continuing resources): electronic]
245 00	:	$a Project Muse $h [electronic resource]: $b scholarly journals online.

Textual Continuing Resource Received via E-mail

The resource is the equivalent of a print item but is received via e-mail from a news wire service. It is coded as language material. The type of computer file is document.

- *Example(s):*
  - *CNS daily brief,* a daily summary of appellate opinions.

Ldr/06	:	a [type of record: language material]
Ldr/07	:	s [bibliographic level: serial]
006/00	:	m [form of material: computer files/electronic resources]
006/09	:	d [type of computer file: document]
007	:	cr|||||||||||| [category of material: electronic resource specific material designation: remote access]
008/23	:	s [form of item (continuing resources): electronic]
245 00	:	$a CNS daily brief $h [electronic resource].

Textual Document

The resource is the equivalent of a print item, but in electronic form. It is coded as language material. If a 006 field for computer files/electronic resources is added, the type of computer file (006/09) depends on the content of the resource.

- *Example(s):*
  - William Blake's *The book of Urizen,* available on CD-ROM.

Ldr/06	:	a [type of record: language material]
Ldr/07	:	m [bibliographic level: monograph/item]
006/00	:	m [form of material: computer files/electronic resources]
006/09	:	d [type of computer file: document]
007	:	co#ug||||||||| [category of material: electronic resource specific material designation: optical disc]
008/23	:	s [form of item (books): electronic]
245 14	:	$a The book of Urizen $h [electronic resouce]: $b London, ca. 1818/ $c William Blake; commentary by Nicolas Barker.

Cartographic Material in Electronic Form

The resource is non-manuscript cartographic material in electronic form. It is coded as cartographic material. The type of computer file is representational.

- *Example(s):*
  - *Vector map level 0 (VMAP0),* vector-based geo-spatial data issued by the National Imagery and Mapping Agency on optical discs.

Ldr/06	:	e [type of record: cartographic material]
Ldr/07	:	m [bibliographic level: monograph/item]
006/00	:	m [form of material: computer files/ electronic resources]
006/09	:	[type of computer file: representational]
007	:	co#cg#|||||||| [category of material: electronic resource specific material designation: optical disc]
008/29	:	s [form of item (maps): electronic]
245 10	:	$a Vector map level 0 (VMAP0) $h [electronic resource]/ $c National Imagery and Mapping Agency.

Still Images

The resource is an electronic collection of graphic materials, such as drawings or photographic prints. Additional items, such as captions and other explanatory text or manuals, may be present, but the primary content is graphic and the resource is coded as graphic material. The type of computer file is representational.

- *Example(s):*
  - *Corel stock photo library,* a collection of photo-graphs on CD-ROM.

Ldr/06	:	k [type of record: two-dimensional non-projectable graphic]
Ldr/07	:	m [bibliographic level: monograph/item]
006/00	:	m [form of material: computer files/electronic resources]
006/09	:	c [type of computer file: representational]
007	:	co#cg#|||||||| [category of material: electronic resource specific material designation: optical disc]
008/29	:	s [form of item (visual materials): electronic]
245 04	:	$a The Corel stock photo library $h [electronic resource].

ArtServe, a collection of photographs of art and architec-ture available on the Internet.

Ldr/06	:	k [type of record: two-dimensional nonprojectable graphic]
Ldr/07	:	i [bibliographic level: integrating resource]
006/00	:	m [form of material: computer files/ electronic resources]
006/09	:	c [type of computer file: representational]

006/00 : s [form of material: continuing resource]
006/01 : k [frequency: continuously updated]
006/04 : w [type of continuing resource: updating Web site]
006/06 : s [form of item: electronic]
007 : khbo| [category of material: non-projected graphic] specific material designation: photoprint]
007 : cr|||||||||||| [category of material: electronic resource specific material designation: remote resource]
008/29 : s [form of item (visual materials): electronic]
245 00 : $a ArtServe $h [electronic resource].

Notated Music

The resource is an online collection of sheet music in electronic form. It is coded as notated music. The type of computer file is other.

- Example(s):
  - *Historic American sheet music,* a collection of sheet music on the Internet.

Ldr/06 : c [type of record: notated music]
Ldr/07 : m [bibliographic level: monograph/item]
006/00 : m [form of material: computer files/ electronic resources]
006/09 : z [type of computer file: other]
007 : cr|||||||||||| [category of material: electronic resource specific material designation: remote resource]
008/23 : s [form of item (music): electronic]
245 00 : $a Historic American sheet music, 1850-1920 $h [electronic:$b selected from the collections of Duke resource] University.

Census in Textual Form

The resource consists largely of numeric data, perhaps in tabular form, but is the electronic equivalent of a print item. It is coded as language material.

- Example(s):
  - *County business patterns (CD-ROM),* an annual series from the US Census Bureau that provides subnational economic data by industry.

Ldr/06 : a [type of record: language material]
Ldr/07 : s [bibliographic level: serial]
006/00 : m [form of material: computer files/ electronic resources]
006/09 : d [type of computer file: document]
007 : co#ug||||||||| [category of material: electronic resource specific material designation: optical disc]
008/23 : s [form of item (continuing resources): electronic]
245 00 : $a County business patterns $h [electronic resource].

Database Containing Manipulable Numeric Data

The resource consists largely of numeric data that can be manipulated. It is coded as a computer file. The type of computer file is numeric data.

- *Example(s):*
  - *Census 2000 redistricting data.*

Ldr/06 : m [type of record: computer file]
Ldr/07 : m [bibliographic level: monograph/item]
007 : co#ug||||||||| [category of material: electronic resource specific material designation: optical disc]
008/26 : a [type of computer file: numeric data]
245 10 : $a Census 2000 redistricting data (PL 94-171). $p Summary file$h [electronic resource]
: $b 2000 Census of population and housing.

Computer Operating System

The resource consists of an ordered set of instructions directing a computer to perform certain operations.

It is coded as a computer file in Leader/06 and the type of file is computer programme.

- *Example(s):*
  - *SuSE Linux 10.0,* available on optical disc.

Ldr/06 : m [type of record: computer file]
Ldr/07 : m [bibliographic level: monograph/item]
007 : co#cgu|||||||| [category of material: electronic resource specific materialdesignation: optical disc]
008/26 : b [type of computer file: computer programme]
245 00 : $a SuSE Linux 10.0 professional $h [electronic resource].

Computer Software

The resource consists of an ordered set of instructions directing a computer to perform certain operations.

It is coded as a computer file in Leader/06 and the type of file is computer programme.

- Example(s):
  - *Foxit,* a PDF document viewer and printer.

Ldr/06 : m [type of record: computer file]
Ldr/07 : m [bibliographic level: monograph/item]
007 : cz|||||||||||| [category of material: electronic resource specific material designation: other]
008/26 : b [type of computer file: computerprogramme]
245 00 : $a Foxit $h [electronic resource].

Universal currency converter, a continuously-updated software programme on the Internet.

Ldr/06	:	m [type of record: computer file]
Ldr/07	:	i [bibliographic level: integrating resource]
006/00	:	s [form of material: continuing resource]
006/01	:	k [frequency: continuously updated]
006/04	:	w [type of continuing resource: updating Web site]
006/06	:	s [form of item: electronic]
007	:	cr#||||||||||| [category of material:electronic resource specific material designation: remote access]
008/26	:	b [computer programme]
245 04	:	$a The universal currency converter $h [electronic resource].

Computer Game

The resource is a game that allows multi-user play online. The type of file is game.

- *Example(s):*
  - *World of warcraft,* a computer game.

Ldr/06	:	m [type of record: computer file]
Ldr/07	:	m [bibliographic level: monograph/item]
007	:	co#cga|||||||| [category of material: electronic resource specific material designation: optical disc]
008/26	:	g [type of computer file: game]
245 00	:	$a World of warcraft $h [electronic resource].

Internet Search Engine

The bibliographic record below describes the system itself, not the system's content. It is coded as a computer file. The type of file is computer programme.

006 fields may be added to bring out the "seriality" or any additional characteristics of the web site.

- *Example(s):*
  - *Google,* a web search engine that allows users to search the Internet for web sites, news, images and postings in Usenet discussion forums.

Ldr/06	:	m [type of record: computer file]
Ldr/07	:	i [bibliographic level: integrating resource]
006/00	:	s [form of material: continuing resource]
006/01	:	k [frequency: continuously updated]
006/04	:	w [type of continuing resource: updating Web site]
006/06	:	s [form of item: electronic]

007	:	cr||||||||||||| [category of material: electronic resource specific material designation: remote access]
008/26	:	b [type of computer file: computer programme]
245 00	:	$a Google $h [electronic resource].

Web Portal

The bibliographic record describes the system and its content. It is coded as a computer file. The type of file is combination. 006 fields may be added to bring out the "seriality" or any additional characteristics.

- *Example(s):*
  - *Yahoo!,* a web portal organized by subject, that also offers a variety of other features, including news, sports and weather updates, an e-mail service, business and shopping services, as well as a streaming audio and and video service.

Ldr/06	:	m [type of record: computer file]
Ldr/07	:	i [bibliographic level: integrating resource]
006/00	:	s [form of material: continuing resource]
006/01	:	k [frequency: continuously updated]
006/04	:	w [type of continuing resource: updating web site]
006/06	:	s [form of item: electronic]
007	:	cr||||||||||||| [category of material: electronic resource specific material designation: remote access]
008/26	:	m [type of computer file: combination]
245 00	:	$a Yahoo $h [electronic resource].

System or Service on the Internet (Includes E-Commerce Sites)

The resource has system-based user interaction that allows users to purchase various types of products or services. The bibliographic record describes the web site.

It is coded as a computer file. The type of file is online system or service. 006 fields may be added to bring out the "seriality" or any additional characteristics of the web site.

- *Example(s):*
  - *Travelocity,* an online travel reservation service that also offers various types of travel pack-ages.

Ldr/06	:	m [type of record: computer file]
Ldr/07	:	i [bibliographic level: integrating resource]
006/00	:	s [form of material: continuing resource]
006/01	:	k [frequency: continuously updated]
006/04	:	w [type of continuing resource: updating web site]
006/06	:	s [form of item: electronic]

007	:	cr											[category of material: electronic resource specific material designation: remote access]
008/26	:	j [type of computer file: online system or service]
245 00	:	$a Travelocity.com $h [electronic resource].

– *Amazon.com*, an online commerce site with browsing and search access to millions of items available for purchase.

Ldr/06	:	i [bibliographic level: integrating resource]
006/00	:	s [form of material: continuing resource]
006/01	:	k [frequency: continuously updated]
006/04	:	w [type of continuing resource: updating web site]
006/06	:	s [form of item: electronic]
007	:	cr											[category of material: electronic resource specific material designation: remote access]
008/26	:	j [type of computer file: online system or service]
245 10	:	$a Amazon.com $h [electronic resource].

Web Site with Significant Audio and Video Content

The resource consists of several types of materials, including audio and video. Leader/06 is coded as a computer file. The type of file is combination since there is no one significant aspect. 006 fields may be added to bring out the "seriality" or any additional characteristics.

- *Example(s):*
  - *CNN Web site*, a site that covers news, weather, and other subjects such as sports and enter-tainment. Includes text, still images, video and audio.

Ldr/06	:	m [type of record: computer file]
Ldr/07	:	i [bibliographic level: integrating resource]
006/00	:	s [form of material: continuing resource]
006/01	:	k [frequency: continuously updated]
006/04	:	w [type of continuing resource: updating web site]
006/06	:	s [form of item: electronic]
007	:	cr											[category of material: electronic resource specific material designation: remote access]
008/26	:	m [type of computer file: combination]
245 00	:	$a CNN.com $h [electronic resource].

Streaming Video

The resource is an electronic moving image. It is coded as a projected medium in Leader/06.

The type of computer file is combination, as there is audio as well as moving images.

- *Example(s):*
  - *Atoms and molecules,* an educational streaming video.

<table>
<tr><td>Ldr/06</td><td>:</td><td>g [type of record: projected medium]</td></tr>
<tr><td>Ldr/07</td><td>:</td><td>m [bibliographic level: monograph/item]</td></tr>
<tr><td>006/00</td><td>:</td><td>m [form of material: computer file]</td></tr>
<tr><td>006/09</td><td>:</td><td>m [type of computer file: combination]</td></tr>
<tr><td>007</td><td>:</td><td>vz#czazzu||||| [category of material: video recording specific material designation: other]</td></tr>
<tr><td>007</td><td>:</td><td>cr|||||||||||| [category of material: electronic resource specific material designation: remote access]</td></tr>
<tr><td>008/29</td><td>:</td><td>s [form of item (visual materials): electronic]</td></tr>
<tr><td>245 00</td><td>:</td><td>$a Atoms and molecules $h [electronic resource].</td></tr>
</table>

Streaming Audio

The resource is a collection of sound recordings in electronic format. It is coded as either a musical or non-musical sound recording, depending on the content. The type of computer file is sound.

- Example(s):
  - *Fogler Library Listening Center Online,* a collection of sound recordings.

<table>
<tr><td>Ldr/06</td><td>:</td><td>j [type of record: musical sound recording]</td></tr>
<tr><td>Ldr/07</td><td>:</td><td>c [bibliographic level: collection]</td></tr>
<tr><td>006/00</td><td>:</td><td>m [form of material: computer file]</td></tr>
<tr><td>006/09</td><td>:</td><td>h [type of computer file: sound]</td></tr>
<tr><td>007</td><td>:</td><td>sz|uunnnnnznud [category of material: sound recording specific material designation: other]</td></tr>
<tr><td>007</td><td>:</td><td>cr|||||||||||| [category of material: electronic resource specific material designation: remote access]</td></tr>
<tr><td>008/23</td><td>:</td><td>s [form of item (music): electronic]</td></tr>
<tr><td>245 00</td><td>:</td><td>$a Fogler Library Listening Center Online $h [electronic resource] Fogler Digital Library.</td></tr>
</table>

GUIDELINES FOR THE USE OF FIELD 856

Field 856 in the MARC 21 bibliographic, holdings, authority, classification, and community information formats is used for electronic location and access information to an electronic resource.The field may be used in a bibliographic or holdings record for a resource when it or a subset of it is available electronically.

In addition, it may be used to locate and access an electronic version of a non-electronic resource described in either the bibliographic record, a portion of the resource described, or a related electronic resource. Field 856 contains the following elements.

FIELD 856-ELECTRONIC LOCATION AND ACCESS (R)

Indicators:

First Indicator	Access method
#	No information provided
0	E-mail
1	FTP
2	Remote login (Telnet)
3	Dial-up
4	HTTP
7	Method specified in subfield $2

Second Indicator	Relationship
#	No information provided
0	Resource
1	Version of resource
2	Related resource
8	No display constant generated

Subfield Codes:

- *$a:* Host name (R)
- *$b:* Access number (R)
- *$c:* Compression information (R)
- *$d:* Path (R)
- *$f:* Electronic name (R)
- *$h:* Processor of request (NR)
- *$i:* Instruction (R)
- *$j:* Bits per second (NR)
- *$k:* Password (NR)
- *$l:* Logon (NR)
- *$m:* Contact for access assistance (R)
- *$n:* Name of location of host (NR)
- *$o:* Operating system (NR)
- *$p:* Port (NR)
- *$q:* Electronic format type (NR)
- *$r:* Settings (NR)
- *$s:* File size (R)
- *$t:* Terminal emulation (R)
- *$u:* Uniform Resource Identifier (R)
- *$v:* Hours access method available (R)
- *$w:* Record control number (R)
- *$x:* Nonpublic note (R)
- *$y:* Link text (R)
- *$z:* Public note (R)

- *$2:* Access method (NR)
- *$3:* Materials specified (NR)
- *$6:* Linkage (NR)
- *$8:* Field link and sequence number (R)

GENERAL INFORMATION

The data in field 856 may be a Uniform Resource Identifier (URI), which is recorded in subfield $u. The necessary locator information may also be parsed into separate defined subfields. Note that separate subfields for locator data was provided when this field was first established in 1993, but generally, these are seldom used.

An access method, or protocol used, is given as a value in the first indicator position (if the access method is e-mail, FTP, remote login (telnet), dial-up, or HTTP) or in subfield $2 (if the access method is anything else). The access method is the first element of a URL. The field may also include a Uniform Resource Name or URN [(*e.g.*, a DOI (Digital Object Identifier) or handle)].

Uniform Resource Identifier

For any access method, a Uniform Resource Identifier (URI) is generally recorded in subfield $u. Separate subfields may be used if it is desirable to display data in a particular way.

The most commonly used data elements in field 856 are as follows:

- 1st indicator = 4 for HTTP (earlier records may use blank)
- Subfield $u = [HTTP URL]
- Subfield $3: data specifying to what the URI refers, if applicable
- Subfield $z (Public note): data relating to the electronic location of the source that is adequate for public display

Required Subfields

A URI in subfield $u is required unless electronic location and access information is parsed into separate subfields, in which case no single subfield is required. When using this technique, the subfields used largely depends on the access method indicated in the first indicator or in subfield $2 (if first indicator = 7).

Encoding Non-MARC Characters

In February 1994, Proposal 93-10 defined additional characters in the MARC character set to both accommodate existing bibliographic needs and to align it with the ASCII and ANSEL character sets. Both the spacing underscore and the spacing tilde were added at the time because of the need in directory and file names for electronic resources. Many systems have implemented these characters.

For systems that have not implemented the spacing underscore and tilde, the following alternative characters may be used:

- Spacing underscore%5F
- Spacing tilde%7E

Since these characters are valid ASCII strings, the method allows for the functionality supported by Z39.50 clients and Web browsers which permit users to click on links to access resources represented by URLs. When the additions to the MARC 21 character set are implemented to support the encoding of the spacing characters, it will be possible to replace all instances of the%xx strings.

Multiple 856 Fields

There are many reasons to include multiple 856 fields in records.

The following are the most common:

- Location data elements vary (the URI in subfield $u or subfields $a, $b, $d, when used)
- Different access methods (*e.g.*, a document available through HTTP and from an FTP server)
- Different parts of the item are electronic, using subfield $3 to indicate the part (*e.g.*, table of contents accessible in one file and an abstract in another)
- Mirror sites (the same resource is made available at two different locations, often to facilitate access, perhaps internationally)
- Different formats/resolutions (*e.g.*, the ASCII version of an electronic journal vs. the Web home page for that journal; a thumbnail vs. archival copy of a digitized photograph)
- Related items, using subfield $3 and second indicator value to specify

Field 856 in Bibliographic or Holdings Records

Since field 856 is valid in both bibliographic and holdings records, institutions may favour recording it in the holdings record. It is intended to be an electronic equivalent to field 852 (Location), which contains information used to identify the holding organization and other detailed information required to locate a physical item in a collection. In early 1999, the Network Development and MARC Standards Office elicited opinions on whether it is desirable to use the field in bibliographic or holdings records. Responses received generally favoured recording the field in the holdings record where practical. However, for a variety of reasons, such as the wider exchange of bibliographic records, many institutions use the bibliographic record despite the benefits of using holdings records.

The following advantages of using holdings records have been expressed:

- Ownership to an electronic resource may vary by institution. Such access information belongs in local holdings.

- The holdings record is a means to bring together various versions.
- Use of a single record approach for the bibliographic item has been implemented widely. This practice makes it clearer to use holdings for the specific versions.
- Having a hot-linked 856 field in holdings forces users to think of it as holdings information, and to separate information about the universal bibliographic item.
- The "universal URL" that is for general access and any general information on access in note fields should be in the bibliographic record. Specific local access URLs should be in holdings (although this may result in unpredictability).
- Bibliographic field 856 might usefully be limited to links that do not apply to the entire bibliographic item (*e.g.*, finding aid, table of content, abstract).

In order to move towards this approach in the future, it will be necessary to persuade vendors to make the following changes to their ILS systems:

- Allow for hot links from holdings records
- Allow for the ability to do link checking from holdings records
- Provide indexing of holdings records
- Allow for the ability to export the fields from holdings, to be exchanged either as separate holdings records or embedded in an exported bibliographic record
- Provide for more logical displays of bibliographic/holdings information where necessary
- Allow for sequencing multiple holdings records

At this point, it is a local decision whether to use the field in bibliographic or holdings records.

SPECIFIC DATA ELEMENTS

First Indicator (Access Method)

The first indicator contains information about the access method to the resource and has values defined for E-mail, FTP, Remote login (Telnet), Dial-up, and HTTP. Access methods without defined values may contain a first indicator value 7 with the method indicated in subfield $2. Older records may contain value 7 and subfield $2 (with content http) if created before value 4 (HTTP) was defined.

The list of indicator values and the values used in subfield $2 is specified in the URL standard (RFC1738) and maintained by the Internet Assigned Numbers Authority (IANA). For those access methods that have an indicator value defined (ftp, telnet, electronic mail), the URI is included in subfield $u with the appropriate indicator value recorded, even though it is redundant with the first element of the URI.

Value # (blank) (No information provided) may be used if only a URN is recorded in subfield $u. If using a URI in subfield $u with one of the access methods that has a value defined in the first indicator, the access method may be repeated in subfield $2. Value 7 and subfield $2 is used for electronic access to host-specific file names (*i.e.*, files stored locally) with the access method, "file." This designation is also a defined URL scheme.

Second Indicator (Relationship)

A second indicator is provided to show the relationship between the information in field 856 and the resource described in the record. This may be used for the generation of a display constant or for ordering multiple 856 fields.

Suggested display constants for the indicator values are:

- # (blank): Electronic resource:
- *0:* Electronic resource:
- *1:* Electronic version:
- *2:* Related electronic resource:
- *8:* [no display constant generated]

Subfield $3 (Materials Specified)

Subfield $3 is used to specify to what portion or aspect of the resource the electronic location and access information applies.

Specific situations may be:

- A portion or subset of the item is electronic
  - *Example:* $3table of contents; $3v. 2-5; $3abstract; $3b&w copy negative
- A related electronic resource is being linked to the record
  - *Example:* $3author's self-portrait

Subfield $q (Electronic Format Type)

Subfield $q was originally defined as File transfer mode to include "binary" or "ascii". It was redefined in June 1997 as Electronic format type to accommodate an Internet Media Type (MIME type), such as text/html. Alternatively, textual information about the electronic format type may also be recorded.

Subfield $u (URI) Repeatability

Subfield $u may be repeated only if both a URN and a URL or more than one URN are recorded. Field 856 is repeated if more than one URL needs to be recorded. Some institutions may wish to record a persistent name (URN) as well as a resolvable HTTP URL in field 856.

Persistent Uniform Resource Locators (PURLs) at OCLC are intended to deal with the problem of changeable URLs. Functionally, a PURL is a URL, but it is intended to point to an intermediate resolution service. Its persistence depends upon the updating of a PURL database when the location of the resource changes. When recorded in field 856, it is intended to allow for persistence so that each record containing the URL need not be updated when the location changes.

Since the PURL is supposed to provide persistent access to the resource, it can be argued that there is no reason to retain a URL that might become invalid. However, this is an internal decision, and institutions that use PURLs should use subfield $x (Nonpublic note) for the original URL if they wish to retain it. This is an appropriate subfield, since it may not be desirable to display the URL to the public because it could cause confusion. The CONSER programme has, however, repeated subfield $u to include both the PURL and cooresponding URL in the past.

Subfield $y (Link Text)

Subfield $y contains link text which is used for display in place of the URL in subfield $u. Often URLs are difficult to read and most systems do not display them to the user. Since subfield $y was not approved until June 2000, there have been various practices in terms of systems using data in the field as link text. Some systems have used subfields $3 or $z in the past for this purpose. It is not clear how widespread the use of subfield $y is since its approval.

Subfield $z (Public Note)

Subfield $z may be used for any additional notes about the electronic resource at the specified location. Examples include subscription information or access restrictions.

Institutions have used subfield $z in various ways. Some have created a note for display repeating the URL in subfield $u. It would be preferable for systems to display subfield $u rather than have those preparing records to include information redundantly.

URIS IN OTHER FIELDS AND FORMATS

URLs in Fields other than Field 856

Several proposals resulted in the definition of a subfield $u (URI) in other fields.

These fields include:

- 505 (Formatted Contents Note)
- 508 (Creation/Production Credits Note)
- 511 (Participant or Performer Note)
- 514 (Data Quality Note)
- 520 (Summary, Etc.)
- 530 (Additional Physical Form Available Note)
- 538 (System Details Note)

- 555 (Cumulative Index/Finding Aids Note)
- 583 (Action Note)
- 670 (Source Data Found) *in the MARC 21 Format for Authority Data*
- 678 (Biographical or historical data) *in the MARC 21 Format for Authority Data*

As with field 856, subfield $u should be repeated only when both a URL and URN is recorded.

Field 856 in Other Formats

Field 856 is also defined in the authority, classification, and community information formats.

It may be used as follows:

- *Authority Format:* Field 856 was defined in June 1998. Guidelines will be needed from policy making bodies to further describe its use, especially in cooperative projects. The intent of Proposal No. 98-13 (Define Field 856 in the MARC 21 Authorities Format) was to provide electronic access to Web sites for organizations and other supplementary information within an authority record.
- *Classification Format:* Field 856 provides a link from a MARC classification record to a related electro-nic resource. This allows for accessing visual aids from an online database of MARC classification records.
- *Community Information Format:* Field 856 provides a link from a MARC community information record to community information available on the Web, *e.g.*, Web pages for organizations, events, services, etc.

LC USAGE

Field 856 has been used at the Library of Congress as follows. Records for resources that have been digitized (or otherwise made available electronically) as part of the National Digital Library Programme (American Memory) may contain field 856.

Generally, the field is added to the record for the original item, rather than a new record created (unless it consists of components that have been gathered together and only exist as an entity in electronic form). In some cases, LC has also recorded a handle, which is a URN. Older records may contain a URN in subfield $g (which is now obsolete).

LC uses local codes in subfield $q to indicate the different categories of a complex object. This is because digital reproductions created by the Library of Congress are not single files and thus, Internet media types recorded in subfield $q are not applicable.

For example, the reproduction of a book usually combines page images and text marked up in SGML.

MAJOR CHANGES INCLUDED

The following are major changes made to the August 1999 revision to create these (March 2003 revision) guidelines:

- Added a table of contents, along with making other struc-tural changes to enhance the document's readability.
- Updated the element list to include the changes made to the repeatability of subfield $u. Subfield $g was also deleted because it was made obsolete in 2000.
- Added and revised the repeatability guidelines for field 856 and subfield $u.
- Updated the "Encoding non-MARC characters" section to include implementation information for the spacing underscore and the spacing tilde.
- Added descriptions of subfields $q and $y to the "Specific Data Elements" section.
- Expanded the "URLs in fields other than field 856" section to include a complete list of bibliographic and authority fields that include subfield $u.
- Expanded and added examples to the "Field 856 in other formats" section.
- Expanded the "LC Usage" section to include updated information about how the Library of Congress uses field 856 in various projects.
- Deleted the "Attachment B: Subfield Use When Not Using $u (URL)" section.
- Updated the examples in the "Examples" section to match current usage of field 856.

CATALOGUING ELECTRONIC RESOURCES: OCLC-MARC CODING GUIDELINES

This document originally combined and superseded two older sets of OCLC guidelines for dealing with electronic resources: "Cataloguing Electronic Resources: OCLC-MARC Coding Guidelines," by Rich Greene, first published in February 1998; and "OCLC Guidelines on the Choice of Type and BLvl for Electronic Resources," by Jay Weitz, first published in March 1998. This consolidated document was originally prompted by the issuance in June 1999 of "Guidelines for Coding Electronic Resources in Leader/06" by the Library of Congress Network Development and MARC Standards Office.

Like the two superseded OCLC documents, this revised set of guidelines is intended to assist catalogers in creating records for electronic resources in WorldCat, the OCLC Online Union Catalogue. These guidelines pertain to OCLC-MARC tagging (that is, content designation). Cataloguing rules and manuals (such as AACR2) govern the content of records. You should implement these guidelines immediately.

In addition to LC's valuable June 1999 "Guidelines for Coding Electronic Resources in Leader/06", which should be consulted for helpful details, sources for further information include the following documents:

- *CONSER Cataloguing Manual*: Module 31—Remote ccess Electronic Serials (Online Serials)/CONSER.
- *Integrating Resources:* A Cataloguing Manual/Programme for Cooperative Cataloguing.
- Draft Interim Guidelines for Cataloguing Electronic Resources/ Library of Congress.
- Guidelines for Distinguishing Cartographic Materials on Computer File Carriers from Other Materials on Computer File Carriers/Library of Congress.
- Guidelines for the Use of Field 856/Prepared by the Library of Congress, Network Development and MARC Standards Office.
- *ISBD(ER):* International Standard Bibliographic Description for Electronic Resources/recommended by the ISBD(CF) Review Group. (Munchen: K.G. Saur, 1997).
- Use of fixed fields 006/007/008 and Leader codes in CONSER records/ Library of Congress.

All of these documents remain primary sources for guidance in the cataloguing of electronic resources. The recommendations made here are meant to be extensions of these documents, not replacements for them. Note that Nancy Olson's "Cataloguing Internet Resources: A Manual and Practical Guide, 2nd edition," formerly listed here, has been withdrawn because it is out of date. Remember that these guidelines affect mainly (although not exclusively) the choice of certain fixed field elements, particularly the Type of Record, Bibliographic Level, and Type of File codes. The descriptive rules in AACR2 for cataloguing electronic resources continue to apply, as do most other MARC coding decisions.

DEFINITION OF ELECTRONIC RESOURCE

According to AACR2, 2005 Update, an electronic resource is: "Material (data and/or programme(s)) encoded for manipulation by a computerized device. This material may require the use of a peripheral directly connected to a computerized device (*e.g.*, CD-ROM drive) or a connection to a computer network (*e.g.*, the Internet)." This definition does not include electronic resources that do not require the use of a computer, for example, music compact discs and videodiscs.

"TYPE OF RECORD" CODING (FIXED FIELD "TYPE")

The definition of Leader/06 ("Type of Record") code "m" (Computer file) was revised and greatly narrowed in June 1997 (LC Update No. 3 to *USMARC Format for Bibliographic Data*) to allow for the coding of electronic resources for the significant aspect of the content, rather than their physical form.

Code "m" is now used only for the following general classes of electronic resources:

- Computer software (including programmes, games, fonts)
- Numeric data
- Computer-oriented multimedia
- Online systems or services

For these classes of materials, if there is a significant aspect that causes it to fall into another Leader/06 ("Type of Record") category, code for that significant aspect (for instance, vector data that is cartographic is not coded as numeric but as cartographic). Other classes of electronic resources are coded for their most significant aspect (for instance, language material, graphic, cartographic material, sound, music, moving image).

In case of doubt or if the most significant aspect cannot be determined, consider the item a computer file. If the resource is essentially the equivalent of a print item but in electronic form, use the same Type code you would use for the print version.

FIELD 006

In records for electronic resources where the Type Code is not "m," OCLC mandates including the field 006 for the electronic aspects so that the "COM" search qualifier will continue to retrieve these materials. Remember to code the "File" value correctly, usually "d" for textual materials.

"TYPE" AND "FILE" CODING

In keeping with the current definition of Type code "m," OCLC is recommending the following choices of "Type" code and CF 006/09 and CF 008/26 "File" ("Type of Computer File") values for the following categories of electronic resources. Included below are resources accessible directly, such as on CD-ROMs or computer disks, and remotely, such as from Web sites and online files. In its definitions of certain values for the Computer File 008/26 ("File"), *MARC 21 Format for Bibliographic Data* clarifies coding for electronic resources that include search software. The presence of search software does not alter the basic intent of the resource and does not mean that the resource should be coded as software. If its primary purpose is, for instance, textual or bibliographic, it remains textual or bibliographic and is coded as such.

In the area of online systems and services, consider whether the system itself (for example, a library system providing an interface to several databases), or the content of the several constituent databases, is being cataloged. When cataloguing the system itself, use "Type" code "m" and "File" code "j".

"FORM OF ITEM" CODING

As part of the MARC 21 format changes implemented by OCLC in April 2000, a new code "s" was validated for the "Form of Item" fixed field, 008/23 and 006/06 in the Books, Serials, Mixed Materials, and Scores formats, and 008/29 and 006/12 in the Maps and Visual Materials formats. On 2002 December 1, the code "s" was also implemented in the "Form of Item" fixed field, 008/23 and 006/06 for the Sound Recordings format.

When cataloguing an electronic resource that includes a significant aspect in any of these bibliographic formats according to current definitions, use "Form of Item" code "s" in the fixed field "Form" and/or in the "Form element of any 006 fields for that aspect, as appropriate.

FIELD 007

According to LC's Draft Interim Guidelines for Cataloguing Electronic Resources, the computer file 007 is mandatory in any record representing an item whose carrier is a computer file. OCLC endorses this recommendation.

FIELD 856

Please be careful about the correct coding of the field 856 second indicator:

- "Blank" is used when no information is provided about the relationship of the electronic resource to the bibliographic item described in the record (for instance, use "blank" when the subfield $u contains a URI that is no longer accessible but there is another 856 with a currently accessible URI). Display constant: None.
- "0" is used when the electronic location in the field is for the same electronic resource described by the record as a whole. Display constant "Electronic resource:" may be generated.
- "1" is used when the electronic location in the field is for an electronic version of the resource described by the record (for instance, an electronic version when the record is for a nonelectronic version). Note that the Library of Congress uses code "1" in conjunction with subfield $3 to indicate the electronic location of tables of contents. Display constant "Electronic version:" may be generated.
- "2" is used when the electronic location in the field is for an electronic resource that is related to the bibliographic item described by the record. In this case, the item represented by the bibliographic record is not the electronic resource itself. Use subfield $3 to further characterize the relationship between the electronic item identified in field 856 and the item represented by the bibliographic record as a whole. The display constant *Related electronic resource*: may be provided. Limit this use to electronic resources that have a specific bibliographic relationship to the resource described in the body of the record. This would include links to such resources as a finding aid for an archival collection or the Web site of a musical group on

a bibliographic record for a sound recording. This would not, however, include Web sites that have merely a general subject relationship to the resource.

LCRI 9.7B, marked "LC Practice," deals with "Remote access electronic resources that are no longer available."

Because of OCLC's indexing needs and its electronic address checking software, however, we suggest leaving URIs in field 856 subfield $u and adding an appropriate subfield $z note under the following circumstances:

- URI no longer works at all, does not redirect to a more current URI.
- 856 4 $u [Dead URI] $z This electronic address not available when searched on [Date].
- URI redirects (either automatically or with a forwar-ding link) to a new URI.
- 856 4 $u [Redirected URI] $z This former electronic address redirects to current address when searched on [Date].

In both of these cases, change the 856 Second Indicator to blank.

Character	Hex Value	Note
Spacing underscore	%5F	Because the spacing Underscore may cause problems with MARC output users may prefer to continue entering it with the hex value %5F.
Spacing tilde	%7E	
Spacing grave	%60	
Spacing circumflex	%5E	
Vertical bar or pipe	%7C	Continue to use the hex value for this character.

In cases where multiple URIs may be appropriate, record them as follows:

- Record a PURL and its corresponding original URL (both of which resolve to the same resource) in separate subfields $u in the same 856 field.
- For most other instances of multiple URIs, record them in separate 856 fields.

When the following characters appear in URIs, you may now use the proper character or substitute the appropriate hex value.

GENERAL MATERIAL DESIGNATION

The General Material Designation (GMD) "[electronic resource]" will now be used for items that are coded as Type "m."

Also use the GMD "[electronic resource]" for all records that would include the computer file 006 according to the OCLC guidelines, regardless of the Type Code.

INTEGRATING RESOURCES

According to AACR2, 2005 Update, an integrating resource is: "A bibliographic resource that is added to or changed by means of updates that do not remain discrete and are integrated into the whole. Integrating resources can be finite or continuing. Examples of integrating resources include updating loose-leafs and updating Web sites."

Beginning immediately, follow these guidelines for integrating resources:

- Use the Continuing Resources (formerly Serials) workform when creating records for textual integra-ting resources. Continue to use the 006 field for Continuing Resources (formerly Serials) to create 006 fields for non-textual integrating resources.
- Use Bibliographic Level code "i" (Integrating Resource) when coding a record for an integrating resource. DO NOT use Bibliographic Level code "s" (Serial) or "m" (Monograph) for an integrating resource.
- For an electronic textual integrating resource, the typical Continuing Resource fixed field will be coded as follows:

Type: a	ELvl: I	Srce: d	GPub: _	Ctrl: _	Lang: III
BLvl: i	Form: s[1]	Conf: 0	Freq: _[2]	MRec: _	Ctry: III
S/L: 2[3]	Orig: s	EntW: _	Regl: _[2]	Alph: a	
Desc: I	SrTp: _[4]	Cont: ____	DtSt: c[5]	Dates: IIII,9999	

- [1] *Form:* For electronic integrating resources, continue to use code "s" in Form.
- [2] *Freq and Regl:* If the integrating resource is truly "continuously updated" (for instance, a constantly updating database, a newspaper's Web site that gets updated as news occurs, etc.), use the Frequency Code "k," which means "the item is updated more frequently than daily;" in that case, the correct Regularity code is likely to be "r" for Regular. More commonly, when the resource is updated less frequently than daily and none of the other Frequency codes apply, use "blank" for Frequency and "x" for Regularity.
- [3] *S/L:* In the continuing resources fixed field, use code "2" in Entry Convention (S/L, formerly Successive/Latest Entry) to indicate that the record was formulated using the revised rules for integrated entry.
- [4] *SrTp:* In the element SrTp (Type of Continuing Resource, formerly Type of Serial), use code "d" for updating databases, code "l" for updating loose-leafs, or code "w" for updating Web sites, as appropriate.
- [5] *DtSt:* For integrating resources that are currently published, use code "c" (rather than the former practice of code "m"). For

integrating resources that have ceased publication, use code "d" (rather than the former practice of code "m").

- Continue to include a computer file 006 and a computer file 007 field in records for electronic integrating resources. For a textual electronic integrating resource, the typical computer file 006 and 007 fields will be coded as follows:

COM 006:	Type: m	Audn:	File: d	GPub:
COM 007:	c $b r $d c $e n			

URIs and LCRIs 9.7B and 21.3B for Remote Access Electronic Resources

Two Library of Congress Rule Interpretations, 9.7B and 21.3B, offer some guidance about how to deal with remote access electronic integrating resources and the disposition of the resource's Uniform Resource Identifier (URI). When the original URI is no longer accessible, but the resource (or a new iteration thereof) is now accessible at another URI, you may edit the existing record to reflect this.

When the original URI is still active but now represents an entirely different resource, rather than a new iteration of the original resource, you may create a new record for the new electronic resource. In cases where you are unable to edit, or prefer not to edit the existing record, you are encouraged to report the necessary changes to OCLC.

SEPARATE RECORDS VERSUS SINGLE RECORD

Creating separate records for an item is preferable when both remote access electronic versions and tangible or direct access (including, but not limited to, print and other nonelectronic) versions exist.

You may, however, find a single record approach is better for your local environment. OCLC recommends that you verify the impact of these options with your local system vendor and other partners prior to implementation.

Use of the term "nonelectronic" in the options that follow is meant as shorthand for any tangible resource (including print, videocassette, videodisc, CD-ROM, etc.) and is not meant to exclude, for instance, tangible resources that may have electronic aspects.

In that light, elements of the recommendations may need to be adjusted to accommodate such aspects (for example, inclusion of fields 006 and/or 007).

Option 1: Separate Records

Nonelectronic item:

- Select the workform based on the current definition of "Type" and the primary aspect of the item.

- Do not input fields 006 and 007 and do not code "Form of Item" (008/23, 008/29, 006/06, or 006/12, depending on bibliographic format) for the electronic versio
- Note the availability of the electronic version in field 530.
- *Example:* Available also on the Internet.
- Add a 700-730 added entry field for the electronic version when the main entry differs.
- Optionally, link to the electronic record with field 776.
- Optionally, provide the location of any remotely accessible version(s) in field(s) 856. Use second indicator "1" when the address is for a version of the resource other than the one described in the body of the entry, or "2" when the address is for an otherwise related resource.

Electronic Item:

- Select the workform based on the current definition of "Type" and the primary aspect of the item.
- Include field 006 for computer file, if Type is not "m."
- Include field 007 for computer file.
- Code "Form of Item" (008/23, 008/29, 006/06, or 006/12, as appropriate, depending on bibliographic format) for "electronic" (code "s").
- Note the availability of the nonelectronic version in field 530.
- *Example:* Also available in printed form.
- Add a 700-730 added entry field when main entry for the nonelectronic version differs.
- Optionally, link to the nonelectronic version using field 776.
- Provide the location of any remotely accessible version(s) in field(s) 856. Use second indicator "0" when the address is for the resource itself, "1" when the address is for a version of the resource other than the one described in the body of the entry, or "2" when the address is for an otherwise related resource.

Option 2: Single Record with a Reference to the Electronic Item

You may create a record for the nonelectronic version and add an annotation about the existence of and access to the electronic version.

The nonelectronic version is the primary version and the electronic copy is secondary:

- Select the workform based on the current definition of "Type" and the primary aspect of the item.
- Do not input field 006 for the electronic version.
- Do not code "Form of Item"(008/23, 008/29, 006/06, or 006/12, depending on bibliographic format) for the electronic version.
- Optionally, include field 007.

- Note the availability of the electronic version in field 530.
- Add a 740 added entry when the title for the electronic version differs.
- Provide the location of any remotely accessible version in field 856. Use second indicator "1" when the address is for a version of the resource other than the one described in the body of the entry or "2" when the address is for an otherwise related resource.

Additional Separate Versus Single Record Considerations

If you are cataloguing an electronic item, you need not verify the physical existence of the nonelectronic version or whether it has been cataloged. Similarly, when you catalogue a nonelectronic item, you need not verify whether an electronic version exists.

In both cases, you need not apply these guidelines, and you may catalogue the item as if no other version exists. Apply the input convention in this document if you have verification that electronic and nonelectronic versions exist, and you want to record the existence of both.

In all cases, you may add references to electronic resources that are related to the item described in the body of the record when those references are thought to add value.

The CONSER Cataloguing Manual: Module 31—Remote Access Electronic Serials (Online Serials) permits a single record for a nonelectronic item to include information for the electronic version. OCLC's guidelines are currently compatible with CONSER's.

INTEGRATING RESOURCE OR MONOGRAPH VERSUS SERIAL

The decision to code an electronic resource as a monograph or as a serial is a decision made separately from the Type Code decision.

Note that for electronic serials where Type is not "a" or "m", two 006 fields will be necessary, one for the electronic aspects and one for the serial aspects. Apply the current AACR2 definitions of monograph and serial to electronic resources.

Treat as serials (Bibliographic Level: s (or b)) only those continuing resources issued in a succession of discrete parts with no predetermined conclusion. The parts may constitute an issue, or in some cases, an individual article.

Applying the current AACR2R definitions may result in different manifestations receiving different cataloguing treatment. For example, a manifestation in print form, such as an annual directory, is cataloged as a serial whereas it is cataloged as an integrating resource when the directory takes on the form of an electronic file that is continuously updated. LC and CONSER adhere to current definitions, and OCLC recommends its users do the same.

Remotely accessed electronic resources of a dynamic nature that are currently excluded from serial treatment are:

- Databases (including directories, A&I services, etc.)
- Electronic discussion groups (*e.g.*, SERIALST)
- Electronic discussion group digests (*e.g.*, AUTOCAT digest)
- Gopher servers (*e.g.*, LC-MARVEL)
- Online public access catalogues (*e.g.*, OCLC, RLIN)
- Online services (*e.g.*, America Online)
- Web sites (*e.g.*, the CONSER home page)

These electronic resources should be cataloged as integrating resources or monographs, as appropriate.

Electronic Reproductions of Items Previously Published in Print Form

In May 2000, the Library of Congress issued a revised version of LC Rule Interpretation 1.11A. The revision expands LC's "microform exception" to AACR2 to include remotely accessed electronic reproductions of works previously published in printed form (including electronic books). This practice applies only when the reproduction manifestation is represented by its own bibliographic record, separate from any record for the original.

In essence, LCRI 1.11A calls for users to:

- Transcribe the bibliographic data appropriate to the *original* work being reproduced in the following areas: title and statement of responsibility; edition; material (or type of publication) specific details; publication, distribution, etc.; physical description; series.
- If appropriate, give in the title and statement of responsibility area the General Material Designation that is applicable to the format of the reproduction (in the case of electronic reproductions, the GMD "[electronic resource]").
- Give in a single note (533 field) all other details relating to the reproduction and its publication/availability, including format of the reproduction, dates of publication and/or sequential designation of issues reproduced (for serials), place and name of the agency responsible for the reproduction, date of the reproduction, physical description of the reproduction if different from the original, series statement of the reproduction (if applicable), notes relating to the reproduction (if applicable).
- Use a physical description fixed field (007) applicable to the reproduction, and for electronic reproductions, also supply information about the electronic location and access (856 field).

In addition, OCLC users should include the appropriate field 006 and code "Form of Item" for "electronic" (code "s") as outlined earlier in these guidelines. Optionally, OCLC users may also include a field 539, following field 533, containing data about the reproduction in coded form.

DEALING WITH EXISTING RECORDS

These guidelines, of course, do not resolve all problems. OCLC's Duplicate Detection and Resolution software, for example, cannot always distinguish one version from another. Indexing and identifying a record as a computer file may not be possible if the local system does not index field 006 or field 007. The cataloguing of these electronic resources remains very much in flux, as do the resources themselves. The rules for dealing with them remain a work in progress.

OCLC users are encouraged to submit to the Library of Congress Network Development and MARC Standards Office (ndmso@loc.gov) examples of any electronic resources about which there is ambiguity concerning the coding of Leader/06, CF 008/26, and/or CF 006/09, and any instances not covered by LC's "Guidelines."

OCLC any needed Type and/or BLvl code changes, as well as any other changes to existing WorldCat records, either by phone, paper, or electronically, as appropriate. OCLC would prefer that you not add duplicate records in these instances.

Minimal-Level Upgrade continues to allow changes of BLvl only within the same bibliographic format, except:

- In records with Type Codes "a" or "t," BLvl "a," "c," "d," or "m" can be changed to BLvl "i"
- In records with Type Code "a" and BLvl "b" or "s," the BLvl can be changed to BLvl "i"

WorldCat Database Enrichment currently allows Full Mode users and above to add field 006 and/or 007 to most records through lock and replace. OCLC recognizes that the conversion of existing records for electronic resources is a significant issue for many groups within the OCLC membership. Through Minimal Level Upgrade, Database Enrichment, CONSER, and Enhance, many OCLC members have the ability to fix many of the records in question. OCLC encourages users to report other records that need to be converted, via any of the usual means.

DRAFT INTERIM GUIDELINES FOR CATALOGUING ELECTRONIC RESOURCES

BACKGROUND

The Library of Congress has become increasingly engaged in the world of those electronic resources requiring the use of a computer. In the early 1980s it began to assign International Standard Serial Numbers (ISSN) to directly accessed serial electronic resources and in 1988 to those that are online. In the early 1990's the Library, through the Cooperative Online Serials (CONSER) Programme, began to address the cataloguing of online serial resources, with an emphasis on those available on the Internet. It began to catalogue monographic computer files in the late 1980's. In the early 1990's, the Library began the digitization of original materials from its special collections under the aegis of the American Memory programme. In 1996 an informal group of staff members with interests in issues relating to digitization, not only of original materials in special collections, but also including some book materials, met on an irregular basis to begin exploring issues of common interest.

While the group's initial concern was the cataloguing treatment of materials that LC was digitizing from its own collections, it also encountered issues that relate to the bibliographic control of material in special collections, particu-larly "special format" material whose mode of expression is other than that of language material (non-manuscript language material) or whose modes of expression are mixed (*i.e.*, collections of mixed material). Even so, the issues are not solely the domain of these materials, as the group discovered with some of the collections of language materials (*e.g.*, various pamphlet collections; broadside collections).

Cataloguing electronic reproductions of material held by the Library as well as cataloguing other electronic resources, whether electronic manifestations of new or already existing material, raises several issues. One of the most important is the use of one record or two to describe closely related content. Thus a medium that spans both general and special cataloguing requires Library-wide application of a standard set of guidelines to ensure clarity in bibliographic records both for public catalogue users and for effective biblio-graphic control. It has been the intent of the Cataloguing Policy and Support Office (CPSO) to develop conceptual guidelines for the cataloguing of electronic resources.

That effort has been delayed for various reasons, and towards the end of 1996, stimulated by increased activities in the area of digitization, CPSO invited a small group of staff members to develop interim guidelines for cataloguing electronic resources. These guidelines are the result; they have been reviewed within LC by representatives of the units most directly concerned with cataloguing electronic manifestations, particularly by the staff members. Additional consultations were held with Copyright Office staff, and some changes were made to some of the terminology that had originally been proposed to accommodate the copyright perspective.

PURPOSE AND CHARACTER

The purpose is to establish an interim set of guidelines to be used for cataloguing electronic resources in the Library of Congress based on a common conceptual context and a common terminology. The intent of the guidelines is to apply to resources of divergent character produced under varying circumstances and managed by different entities, a set of conventions for bibliographic control that will enable genera-lized, standard practice to the extent judged practicable in a diverse, dynamic environment. It also endeavours to engage the electronic world on a broader scale by providing a conceptual framework for treating electronic resources. This framework is followed by the establishment and definition of concepts and terms appropriate to electronic resources in an attempt to ensure clear communication based on a common understanding.

The guidelines then include:

- Policies on when to use multiple records and when to use a single record;
- Conventions developed especially for the single-record technique;
- Directions for indicating the existence of other physical formats (530 field);
- Directions related to electronic location (856 field);
- Directions relating to collocating records (710 field) and linking them (76X-78X fields);
- Directions relating to identifying in MUMS those records related to a specific project (985 field; mandatory for American Memory projects).

The overall guidelines try to show how the cataloguing of all electronic resources fits together, but they do not cover the specifics of all resources. In meeting the needs of the Library of Congress in this regard, it remains to be seen whether the guidelines developed for these LC materials will necessarily be applicable elsewhere.

The one obvious lacuna in the current document is the absence of guidelines relating to the treatment of Internet resources—particularly with respect to which ones should be represented in the catalogue, under what circumstances, and in what detail. This is because the collection development guidelines for electronic resources are only now beginning to be formulated. Thus the issues related to cataloguing these materials have not been fully confronted.

One question of concern is the impact the nature of the medium itself will have. For tangible non-electronic materials, their very tangibility fixes the intellectual content. This tangibility is common across all items in a particular manifestation, thus allowing the description of one item to apply to all the others in the manifestation.

Changes in physical characteristics are used to surmise that there are changes in content, which is the basis of creating a new bibliographic record. With respect to cataloguing remotely accessed electronic resources, it will be interesting to see what the impact of the accessing mode will be, particularly, with regard to:

- The basis for determining that the content is "fixed," absent tangibility as a basis for doing this;
- The basis for determining that the content has changed, again, absent tangible characteristics for doing this.

On a more mundane level there are issues relating to:

- The disposition of information that is universal and that which is local;
- Determining who we are providing the information for (again universal/local);
- "Custody" (is it relevant?);
- Classification (should we attempt to classify?).

REASONS WHY THE GUIDELINES ARE INTERIM

The Guidelines are interim for the following reasons:

- Some of the copyright and collection development guidelines with respect to remotely accessed electronic resources are only now beginning to be formulated; the universe of material for which bibliographic control is to be applied will have a substantial impact on the resources available for this purpose and will in turn influence the nature of the conventions themselves (the larger the number of materials to be controlled the less labour intensive the conventions to control them can be);
- The dynamic nature of the environment of electronic resources is profoundly affecting the standards upon which current conventions of bibliographic control rest; it is necessary to monitor the changes that are developing in AACR2, in USMARC, and in such international activities as the ISBD (ER): International Standard Bibliographic Description for Electronic Resources and the IFLA study on the Functional Requirements for Bibliographic Records, and make adjustments accordingly;
- Experiments applicable to particular kinds of resources (*e.g.*, serials and CONSER policies; the BEONLINE project for business and economic resources) are under way with evaluation of results and implications for policy guidelines still to be determined;
- System considerations at LC are in a state of flux, particularly with the impending procurement of an Integrated Library System; hypertext links are still not available in the traditional interfaces to MUMS and SCORPIO; once this feature is more widely available, perceptions of which resources should be represented in the catalogue and how data need to be depicted may change.

CONCEPTUAL FRAMEWORK

The Interim Guidelines establish a common context through the use of entities and concepts derived from an entity analysis technique and based on work done heretofore in LC as part of information modelling and in the more recent work that resulted in an IFLA study: Functional Requirements for Bibliographic Records: Final Report. The following entities/concepts, applicable to all forms of material, are taken directly from the aforementioned IFLA study in a condensed but usually directly quoted form. They are stated here because they provide a vocabulary that clarifies conceptually what is currently embodied in a bibliographic record.

- *Work:* A distinct intellectual or artistic creation; a work is an abstract entity
- *Expression:* The intellectual or artistic realization of a work in the form of alpha-numeric, musical, or choreographic notation, sound, image, object, movement, etc., or any combination of such forms; an expression is the specific intellectual or artistic form that a work takes each time it is "realised"; inasmuch as the form of expression is an inherent characteristic of the expression, any change in form (*e.g.*, from alpha-numeric notation to spoken word) results in a new expression; similarly, changes in the intellectual conventions or instruments that are employed to express a work (*e.g.*, translation from one language to another) result in the production of a new expression
- *Manifestation:* The physical embodiment of an expression of a work; as an entity, manifestation represents all the physical objects that bear the same characteristics, in respect to both intellectual content and physical form; when a work is realised, the resulting expression of the work may be physically embodied on or in a medium such as paper, audio tape, video tape, etc.; the physical embodiment constitutes a manifestation of the work; in some cases there may be only a single physical exemplar produced of that manifestation of the work (*e.g.*, an author's manuscript, a tape recorded for an oral history archive, an original oil painting, etc.); in other cases there are multiple copies produced in order to facilitate public dissemination or distribution
- *Item:* A single exemplar of a manifestation; an item is a concrete entity; it is in many instances a single physical object (*e.g.*, a copy of a one-volume monograph, a single audio cassette, etc.); with respect to intellectual content and physical form, an item exemplifying a manifestation is normally the same as the manifestation itself; however, variations may occur from one item to another, even when the items exemplify the same manifestation, where those variations are the result of actions external to the intent of the producer of the manifestation (*e.g.*, damage occurring after the item was produced, binding performed by a library, etc.)

The entities shown in diagram "represent the different aspects of user interests in the products of intellectual or artistic endeavour. The entities defined as work (a distinct intellectual or artistic creation) and expression (the intellectual or artistic realization of a work) reflect intellectual or artistic content. The entities defined as manifestation (the physical embodiment of an expression of a work) and item (a single exemplar of a manifestation), on the other hand reflect physical form. The relationships depicted in the diagram indicate that a work may be realised through one or more than one expression (hence the double arrow on the line that links work to expression).

An expression, on the other hand, is the realization of one and only one work (hence the single arrow on the reverse direction of that line linking expression to work). An expression may be embodied in one or more than one manifestation; likewise a manifestation may embody one or more than one expression.

BASIC CONCEPTS/TERMS

The Guidelines use the following basic concepts and terms with their associated definition to establish a consistent vocabulary, recognizing that there may not always be full agreement in particular cases.

The basic concepts/terms are presented alphabetically for ease of reference. Some apply at a general level, others are more nearly related to electronic resources themselves:

- *Accessing Mode:* A concept that characterizes the means of access to an electronic resource; it is applicable at the item level.
  - *Direct Access:* The term used to characterize access to an electronic resource resident in a carrier such as a computer disk or a CD-ROM that a user physically inserts into a computer, typically a microcomputer.
- *Observation:* A tangible resource may also be accessed in an online mode as if remote (*e.g.*, networked CD-ROMS; data copied onto UNIX hosts).
  - *Remote Access:* The term used to characterize access to an electronic resource resident in a carrier that a user cannot physically handle, *i.e.*, a resource accessed, processed, executed, etc. remotely. Frequently this involves connection through a computer network. This type of access is often referred to as "online" access.

Adjunct see under Selected relationships:

- *Aggregates/Components:* Concepts pertinent to the make-up of a work. A work may be an integral unit or it may represent an aggregate of individual works (*e.g.*, a compilation), a set of individual monographs brought together by a common theme or topic (*e.g.*, a series), or a group of private papers organized by an archive as a single collection. A work may also represent an intellectually or artistically discrete component of a larger work, *e.g.*, an article in a journal, a monograph in a series. Entities at the aggregate or component level are seen as the same as entities at the integral unit level.

- *Compilation:* An electronic anthology whose constituent elements have been brought together and selected, coordinated, or arrnaged to form a new work.
- *Delineation:* A technique used in lieu of separately cataloguing a manifestation whereby detailed information about that manifestation is given in the bibliographic record for another manifestation; simply noting the existence of another manifestation does not constitute what is meant by delineation

Directly accessed electronic resource see under Physicality:

- *Electronic Conference:* A conference held in a virtual mode that takes place within the context of an interactive software environment running on the Internet. Headings for such conferences are treated the same as those for other conferences except headings for electronic conferences do not contain the name of the local place or other location in which the conference was held.
- *Electronic Discussion Group:* The term used to refer to a forum conducted electronically; these services, commonly called newsgroups and listservs, allow a computer user to post messages to, and read messages from, a group of people who have a common interest, usually by means of the Internet, a commercial online service, or electronic mail. For cataloguing purposes, treat such a discussion group as a work entered under title (X30 series of tags).
- *Electronic Resource:* The term used to refer to a manifestation of a work encoded for manipulation by computer. The manifestation resides in a carrier accessed either directly or remotely. It is the term used in the revised ISBD (ER) and serves in lieu of other terms currently in use such as computer file or digital resource. Some electronic resources may require the use of a peripheral device attached to a computer (*e.g.* a CD-ROM player). Note that for these Guidelines this term does not include "electronic" resources that do not require the use of a computer, *e.g.*, music compact discs, videodiscs.

BASE GUIDELINES (GENERAL)

Use the following base guidelines in determining the cataloguing treatment of a particular electronic resource. In general, the cataloguing treatment applied depends upon important factors related to the creation of the electronic resource itself, most importantly whether the resource is a sole manifestation or one of multiple manifestations and the realization of the work as a matter of time, *i.e.*, whether it is judged to be a monograph or a serial.

CONTENT VERSUS CARRIER (ELECTRONIC RESOURCES)

How to characterize records for electronic resources in terms of their primary form of material (the issue of "content versus carrier") has been widely discussed. AACR2 is oriented towards basing cataloguing treatment on carrier. Until 1997 the definition of computer file in USMARC (Leader/06 code"m") also indicated that the record would be coded for carrier. However, as a result of a change approved by MARBI in June 1997, Update No. 3 to the USMARC Bibliographic Format revised the definition of code "m" to allow for computer files to be coded for their most significant aspect.

That definition now reads:

- Code m indicates that the content of the record is for the following classes of electronic resources: computer software (including programmes, games, fonts), numeric data, computer-oriented multimedia, online systems or services. For these classes of materials, if there is a significant aspect that causes it to fall into another Leader/06 category, code for that significant aspect (*e.g.* vector data that is cartographic is not coded as numeric but as cartographic). Other classes of electronic resources are coded for their most significant aspect (*e.g.* language material, graphic, cartographic material, sound, music, moving image). In case of doubt or if the most significant aspect cannot be determined, consider the item a computer file.

In conjunction with this change, field 007 for computer files is now mandatory in any record representing an item whose carrier is a computer file. Directly accessed electronic resources have been treated as computer files at LC as have most of those accessed remotely. Directly accessed electronic resources have been represented in the COMPUTER FILES file, the BOOKS file (those that accompany books), and, with format integration, in the SERIALS file.

With respect to cataloguing remotely accessed electronic resources, LC has been most active in cataloguing electronic serials/journals and electronic counterparts or subsets of tangible, original items or collections. In most cases, the latter do not receive separate catalogue records; instead, they are delineated in records for the original items or collections.

The special format divisions are interested in providing an integrated approach to the bibliographic records for the materials of interest to them. Currently, that is done through the disposition of physical files under MUMS, essentially by type of material. Under an ILS it will be a requirement to be able to approach the catalogue in a similar way as at present but it will probably be a logical disposition instead of a physical one.

In the future when the shift in approach from carrier to content is implemented at LC, fundamental changes in the current LC environment will be required. Those electronic resources judged to have a significant aspect other than that of a computer file would now be represented in the file appropriate to what is judged to be the significant aspect. For example, if the significant aspect of a monographic electronic resource is judged to be language material, that resource would be represented in the Books file, not the Computer Files file (use of the GMD "[computer file]" will continue). As of the current writing, not all the details of the impact of this change have been worked out, but it is assumed that staff in the Computer Files/Microforms Team will continue to catalogue those general monographic electronic resources not pertaining to the materials of interest to the special format divisions.

However, they will do so by working in the file judged appropriate to the resource being cataloged. It is further assumed that special format divisions will continue to focus on cataloguing (except for Music, RBSCD) and servicing material acquired for the collections in their custody.

The change in approach that emphasizes content will, mean that electronic resources will now be represented throughout the files that constitute the catalogue, not just in the Computer Files file. An issue of potential significant impact relates to those computer-related electronic resources acquired by the special format divisions for their collections.

As of this writing, it is not clear how some of these materials will be treated with respect to:

- Who will catalogue these materials and
- What cataloguing treatment they will receive.

It is assumed that those judged to be cartographic materials will continue to be cataloged by staff in the Geography and Map Division (G&M); those judged to be serials will be cataloged in the Serial Record Division (SRD)). The treatment of other monographic materials is less clear. For example, will a directly accessed electronic resource manifes-ted in multiple copies whose significant aspect is judged to be moving image be cataloged in MBRS under the AMIM rules and, if circumstances warrant, added to the record for another manifestation?

This would be in lieu of being cataloged according to the general rules of AACR2 as a manifestation receiving a separate record by staff either in MBRS or in SMCD. The Library of Congress will develop/change workflow and cataloguing policies related to "content vs. carrier" issues and will make them available to the larger cataloguing community.

MONOGRAPH OR SERIAL

Apply the current AACR2 definitions of monograph and serial to electronic resources. Treat digitized texts, individual Web sites, and indeterminate works not issued in separate parts, particularly databases, as monographs. Treat as serials indeterminate works issued in separate, designated parts. The parts may constitute an issue, or in some cases, an individual article.

Applying the current definitions may result in different manifestations receiving different cataloguing treatment. For example, a manifestation in print form, such as an annual directory, is cataloged as a serial whereas it is cataloged as a monograph when the directory takes on the form of an electronic file that is continuously updated. This practice may change, but for the present LC and CONSER adhere to current definitions.

Remotely accessed electronic resources of a dynamic nature that are currently excluded from serial treatment are:

- Databases (including directories, A&I services, etc.)
- Electronic discussion groups (*e.g.*, SERIALST)
- Electronic discussion group digests (*e.g.*, AUTOCAT digest)
- Gopher servers (*e.g.*, LC-MARVEL)
- Online public access catalogues (*e.g.*, OCLC, RLIN)
- Online services (*e.g.*, America Online)
- Web sites (*e.g.*, the CONSER home page)

SINGLE MANIFESTATION

An electronic resource that exists solely in a single manifestation, *e.g.*, a publication that exists solely online, by definition is represented by a single bibliographic record in the same manner as other non-electronic resources that exist in a single manifestation. Currently, those judged to be monographs are cataloged as computer files by the Computer Files/Microforms Team of the Special Materials Cataloguing Division (SMCD) or as cartographic materials by staff in the Geography and Map Division (G&M) or, if judged to be accompanying material, by the general cataloguing divisions.

Those judged to be serials are cataloged in the Serial Record Division (SRD). Both monographs and serials are cataloged according to AACR2R, LCRIs, DCM, LCSH, SCM, LCC, USMARC, and supplementary documentation appropriate to each category of material.

MULTIPLE MANIFESTATIONS

An electronic resource that is another manifestation of a work is likely to be one of the following:

- A manifestation that is a counterpart or subset of a published resource (tangible or otherwise, usually directly accessed) or an adjunct to it;
- A directly accessed manifestation that is:
  - A counterpart or subset of a tangible resource (either at the collection level or item level or both);
  - A reproduction in electronic form done by or for the Library of Congress of a resource held by the Library;
- A remotely accessed manifestation that is
  - A counterpart or subset of a tangible resource (either at the collection level or item level or both);
  - A reproduction in electronic form done by or for the Library

of Congress of a resource (including material that may have been published) held by the Library.

Materials in categories a) and b) are usually cataloged by staff in the Computer Files/Microforms Team, SMCD (computer files), or in G&M (cartographic materials) or in SRD, depending upon whether the resource is judged to be a monograph or a serial.

Materials in category c) are usually delineated by staff in the special format division that has custody of the tangible, non-electronic resource. Note that a manifestation of conventionally published materials, including directly accessed electronic resources, usually consists of multiple copies. Unique collections usually occur in a single instance, although electronic manifestations of the original collection may be mirrored or copied and therefore exist at several storage locations.

The data elements contained in the USMARC biblio-graphic format are predicated on data elements common to all the copies of a manifestation. Those applicable to a particular copy are generally treated as "local" or as holdings information. This concept is less appropriate to a unique tangible resource such as an archival collection, although this does not preclude the concept of "copy specific" as applied to a particular item in a collection when the manifestation of the item itself consists of multiple copies.

Single/Multiple Records for Multiple Manifestations (Electronic Resources)

Criteria for Determining Single/Multiple Record Approach

Acquisitions/Initial Bibliographic Control (IBC) Criterion

Determine the processing state of the electronic resource from the perspective of acquisitions or the need for IBC data.

The degree of detail required for the management of initial and subsequent acquisitions actions may influence the employment of a single or multiple record approach as may the workflow steps required subsequent to the acquisitions process.

Citation Criterion

A user must be able to get to the manifestation cited in the record the user is observing. When a single bibliographic record includes one or more citations to multiple manifestations, each citation the user is observing must state clearly and succinctly the content of the manifestation(s) cited:

- For the directly accessed, the format of the manifestation more than likely requires a separate record to fulfil the citation criterion;

- For the remotely accessed, a separate record is less likely to be needed to fulfil the citation criterion unless the content among multiple manifestations varies substantially.

INTERLIBRARY LOAN (ILL) CRITERION

The receiver of a request must know which manifestation is being requested and the initiator of a request must know the manifes-tation(s) available for loan:

- For multiple directly accessed manifestations, multiple bibliographic records make it more clear which manifestation is being requested;
- Employment of a single bibliographic record that represents both tangible and remotely accessed manifestations is unlikely to cause confusion with respect to the manifestation available for loan, since it is unlikely someone would request the loan of a remotely accessed resource;
- When a single bibliographic record represents both a tangible manifestation (electronic or otherwise) and a remotely accessed one and the Library "holds" only the latter, it is more likely to cause confusion with respect to the manifestation held and whether it s likely to be available for loan.

Bibliographic Details Criterion

When there is more than one manifestation, the significant bibliographic details of each need to be recorded to identify and to access each. When using a single record that includes one or more delineations, it is necessary to find ways to indicate the significant bibliographic details of all the manifestations, not just those for the primary one.

In the past the Library of Congress has attempted to provide catalogue records not only for use in the catalogues of the Library of Congress but also of use in the catalogues of other libraries. For economic reasons, the present Guidelines now provide for the use of a single record to represent more than one manifestation in the cases. This necessarily focuses on the needs of the Library of Congress but may pose difficulties on other libraries that may wish to represent such resources in their catalogues.

Multiple Manifestations in a Single Record (Electronic Resources)

Two techniques are available for indicating the existence of an electronic manifestation in a record for another manifestation. Both are in lieu of LC's cataloguing the remotely accessed resource separately.

Delineate Another Manifestation

When using a single record to describe a tangible resource and also to delineate an electronic manifestation, consider the information provided in the delineation of the electronic resource as being in lieu of a separate catalogue record. Use the 530 field (Other Physical Form Available Note) to focus all the information about the electronic resource in one place.

Organize the delineation to include at least:

- An introductory phrase indicating the additional availability of an electronic manifestation;
- The name or title of the electronic manifestation if it varies from that of a tangible counterpart or subset;
- Information about the content of the electronic manifestation when it varies from that of the original, *e.g.,* a subset of the original or additional material;
- General information about access, particularly any restrictions on access or information about availability.

If a finding aid in electronic form is involved and it is the kind that incorporates actual material from the collection such that the finding aid itself becomes a remotely accessed electronic manifestation of the content of the collection or a subset of it, describe this special condition in the delineation.

The data making up a particular delineation are not prone to a structured presentation; therefore, the flexibility of the 530 field was chosen for delineation over the more structured 533 field. Also use of the 530 field avoids any implication that the original is not held, an implication often associated with the use of field 533.

When the electronic manifestation bears a title different from that of the tangible resource, provide uncontrolled title access through the title that differs. Do these by means of a 740 field with indicator values set to 0#? This is an exception to the general LC policy of providing title access through a controlled form (730).

Note the Existence of Another Manifestation

The cataloguing rules have long provided for indicating the existence of another manifestation in a note (field 530), usually in a very brief statement. With respect to serials, CONSER's Interim Guidelines for Online Versions allow CONSER institutions either to create separate records or to note the existence of an remotely accessed electronic manifestation on the record for the print (or other) serial.

Practically speaking, this policy is quite similar to delineating; however, there is a difference in the intent. The CONSER guidelines aim to retain the integrity of the print (or other) record in a shared database in which separate records for the remotely accessed electronic manifestation might exist or be created later.

Thus, field 007 is not given in such records and 530 notes tend to be less detailed than those given in records for LC's special collections. Field 740 may also be given when the title of the remotely accessed electronic manifestation differs from that of the original. LC applies the CONSER single record option only for one-to-one reproduc-tions of serials and in other cases creates separate records.

Multiple Presentations of the Same Electronic Resource

If an electronic resource is available in multiple presen-tations that may be generated from different underlying digital representations, *e.g.*, images in TIFF or JPEG format, it is not necessary to acknowledge the condition.

Electronic Resources in Bibliographical References

With respect to bibliography notes, interpret the term "bibliographical references" to include all kinds of resources, including electronic resources; do not give any special treatment to, or provide special mention of, the latter.

Electronic Manifesatation–original in Non–Electronic From–specific Guidelines

General

This is the condition in which an electronic resource is the digitized counterpart to, subset of, or an adjunct to, a tangible manifestation of a work, and the decision has been made to represent the electronic manifestation in the catalogue. Determine whether it is preferable to do this by a single-or multiple-record approach (the single-record approach requires a record for the original, tangible manifestation; one may already exist or it may need to be created). For remotely accessed manifestations of tangible LC materials, a general reference to the Library of Congress Web site is sufficient, since the specific location is always given in an 856 field.

For uniformity of presentation, use the terminology illustrated in the following examples to the extent practicable:

- 530 ## $a Available also through the Library of Congress Web site under title: America's first look into the camera: daguerreotype portraits and views... This finding aid in electronic form, with reproductions, captions, and subject indexing for each image, was produced in 1995 for the National Digital Library Programme, American Memory collections.
- 530 ## $a Available also through the Library of Congress Web site under title: Colour photographs from the FSA and OWI, ca. 1938-1944. This finding aid in electronic form contains reproductions with full caption information and subject indexing for each image.
- 530 ## $a Available also through the Library of Congress Web site under title: Documents from the Continental Congress and the Constitutional Convention 1774-1789. At least one facsimile image of each broadside is presented along with a narrative introduction.

- 530 ## $a Available also as part of a microfilm with title: Continental Congress and Constitutional convention Collections. Washington, D.C.: Library of Congress Photoduplication Service. 1 microfilm reel; 35 mm.
- 530 ## $a Available also through the Library of Congress Web site in two forms: as facsimile page images and as full text in SGML.
- 530 ## $a Available also through the Library of Congress Web site as a raster image.
- 538 (System Details Note)

11

Principles in Library Automation and Networking

INTRODUCTION

We live in an increasingly globalized and interconnected world. Barriers in trade, commerce, banking, industry, science, technology, education, etc., are breaking down and will continue to become more and more borderless with time. Globalization also means increased dependency on one other in various domains. Globalization also has increased competition; consumers of all kinds now, more than ever before, have a number of choices. Globalization is in a sense synonymous with networking. Computers, telecommunications infrastructure and the Internet are not only essential but indispensable in the world we live in today.

The library and information world has traditionally been borderless long before others. However, the Internet and the worldwide web have pushed libraries to be even more interdependent than before, because of the bewildering array of sources and providers of information from which they draw their information. Equally, libraries are now facing competition from other players. The place of libraries as centres for the acquisition, description, organization, preservation and access to information has been challenged by new players such as Google, Yahoo!, etc., and subject portals, digital libraries and open access repositories.

These services use new methods to acquire, analyze, display and organize information and are undoubtedly a threat to the traditional role of libraries and librarians. How libraries can get an edge over competing services and continue to be relevant, different, wanted and useful has engaged the attention of many library professionals. Even before the advent of the Internet and the web, libraries sought to automate and network with each other so that their clients could have easier and wider access to resources. The proliferation of resources such as other library catalogues, online databases, full text publications, electronic serials, learning resources, discussion forum postings, etc., on the web has posed a considerable challenge to librarians. How to cope with these new resources and newer forms of older resources is a question that requires to be addressed by all libraries. Library automation and networking, which until the 1990's was considered to be adequate, today do not provide all the answers.

Library automation and networking is all about connecting to other libraries and information centres, search engines, peer groups, databases and experts. Thus the sceanrio today is one of many dispersed digital collections. The need is to move to inter-operable digital libraries. This requires that we focus on standards of many kinds. Of these, metadata standards have assumed the highest importance. To put it in simple words, libraries and networks of all kinds use different hardware and software platforms. To enable interconnectivity to such a diversity of systems and to enable mutual sharing of resources and exchange of data between them requires that all of them follow internationally agreed upon standards.

Networks operate at different levels in respect of:

- The variety of resources they handle,
- The computer hardware they use,
- Operating system platforms,
- The language used to describe subject content,
- The support to protocols and standards they provide, and
- The back-end software in use.

The one element in all library automation and networking today that has assumed highest priority is the use of (wherever possible) international standards for the following.

- Metadata standards which includes standards for data elements as well as identification, description and representation standards
- Information exchange standards
- Communication standards
- Content representation standards
- Interoperability standards.

The above categorization is only used for convenience and it must be emphasized that there is considerable overlap in the purpose and function of these standards. It is important that these should be understood and used in library systems if there is to be effective automation and networking. This tutorial attempts to:

- Describe briefly the various metadata and interoperability standards, and
- Emphasize the importance of these standards when planning library Automation and more importantly networking of libraries.

WHAT IS METADATA

Metadata may be described as having the following characteristics:

- Structured Data about data used to aid identification, description, management and location of resources

- Also may include physical resources, e.g., metadata embedded in web pages

The earliest form of metadata records are 5" x 3" card catalogue records

METADATA STANDARDS

Metadata standards comprise the following types:

- Standards for data elements needed to describe different types of information objects — some well known, some new and some newer forms of existing objects,
- Library cataloguing standards such as the AACR2R and ISBD comprising rules on how to describe the data elements constituting information objects and rules for the determination and establishment of headings (or access points) (and sequence with separating symbols as in ISBD) under which the descriptive information is to be presented to catalogue users, and with the making of references to those headings.
- Standards (or languages) on how to represent the metadata in computers,
- Standards to represent subject content

THE MARC-21 BIBLIOGRAPHIC METADATA FORMAT

Records structured in the MARC-21 format are the most widely used ones in bibliographic databases. MARC-21 is a data element standard as well a standard that specifies how different data elements are recognized by a computer via numeric tags, numeric indicators and alphanumeric subfield codes.

This format is ideally suited for variable length records, and to accommodate all the idiosyncrasies of bibliographic records such as the presence of a variable number of repeatable fields, presence of fields in some records and not in others. The MARC record was designed as a standard format for the exchange of bibliographic data between organizations, e.g., two national libraries, a national library and other academic libraries.

MARC formats exist for:

- Bibliographic data,
- Authority data and
- Holdings data.

The MARC format has undoubtedly been one of the most successful and durable metadata standards in the library environment. Most western library automation software support the MARC format for import of records into a local catalogue database (also called copy cataloguing) into their local databases.

More than a billion metadata records are available in the MARC format with large national libraries such as the Library of Congress (LOC) and cooperative networks such as OCLC and RLN. Many sources of MARC-21 catalogue records are available free for use and download by other libraries worldwide. It makes good sense therefore for Indian libraries to use these resources within their library's.

There are several advantages in doing this:

- The efficiency of cataloguing is greatly improed and therefore the cost of cataloguing can be considerably reduced
- Metadata imported from an authoritative MARC source ensures more completeness and accuracy in library catalogues.
- Use of authority files with MARC sources enhances the consistency of library catalogues.
- Exchange of a library's catalogue records is possible with other libraries via a common standard format.
- Moving from one integrated library management software (ILMS) to a more sophisticated one is more easily accomplished than if a library has to move from a non-standard structure to a standard one such as MARC-21.

Irrespective of how an integrated library management software (ILMS) represents its catalogue database records internally, e.g., using a relational database management system (RDBMS) or as a flat file structure, it is important that the software should allow import of records from one or other MARC data source, e.g., the national library or a cooperative network such as OCLC. In other words when considering library automation, it is important to examine the extent to which the The MARC format is supported by the ILMS.

The MARC format has been an important element in the development of many union catalogues and for ensuring the exchange of data between and across library systems through out the world. In fact, the MARC format is the bedrock on which global cooperative networks such as OCLC and the RLN are founded. Most Indian libraries by default do not use the MARC format in their catalogue databases. Similarly, most Indian library automation software do not provide the capability to seamlessly import and/or export records from and to the MARC format. This has led to many shortcomings. Some of these are given below.

- It is not possible to use copy cataloguing by downloading MARC-21 cataloguing data from authoritative sources such as the Library of Congress and other freely available web sources to build online catalogues.
- There is considerable duplicated effort across libraries apart from inconsistent entries in catalogues leading to difficulties in building union databases.
- Large libraries in India such as University libraries have not been able to act as providers of authoritative cataloguing data to smaller

libraries, e.g., colleges. Common use of the MARC format across libraries would enable such sharing.

- Indian libraries cannot participate in global cooperative networks such as OCLC and RLN. Indian intellectual input is thus not adequately represented in global databases.

Closely linked with the MARC-21 format are standards (actually rules) such as AACR2R and ISBD. ISBD is a set of rules produced by the International Federation of Library Associations (IFLA) to describe a wide range of library materials, within the context of a catalogue.

ISBD defines a number of areas, e.g., title and statement of responsibility, edition, material-dependent information (for example, the scale of a map or the duration of a sound recording). These rules organize the bibliographic description of an item. Librarians use the AACR2R and ISBD in conjunction with MARC.

AUTHORITY AND HOLDINGS RECORDS

It is important to emphasize that MARC-21 is a format not only for bibliographic records. MARC-21 formats exist for authority records and holdings records. Good ILMS software provide support to both these formats. There are several advantages of adhering to these formats in addition to the bibliographic formats.

- Local authority file records can be created via imports from an authoritative source such as the LoC.
- An ILMS could ensure that new entries of data are validated against the local authority data to ensure better consistency in the use of personal names, subject terms, etc.

It is high time that Indian libraries embrace the MARC format and look for software solutions that support this format if they wish to effectively contribute and benefit from networked resources within India and outside it. Equally importantly, today's ILMS should also provide crosswalks to and from other metadata standards.

DUBLIN CORE METADATA ELEMENT SCHEME (DCMES)

The emergence of a variety of new digital information objects and digital formats of traditional materials (e.g., images, text, sound) required adaptations of traditional descriptive methods and this triggered the development of a metadata description scheme which would be simple and also cover a wide range of materials.

Work on defining such a metadata element scheme which later became known as the Dublin Core Metadata Element Scheme (DCMES) began in 1995 in an invitational workshop convened by the Online Computer Library Center (OCLC) and the National Center for Supercomputing Applications (NCSA), at Dublin, Ohio. The workshop was attended by professionals from librarianship, computer science, text encoding, and related areas to advance the state of the art in the development of resource description of records for networked electronic information objects.

The inititaive, now known as the Dublin Core Metadata Intiative (DCMI) has had the benefit of consultations from specialists from many countries over the years. DCMES is now an international standard (ISO 15836:2003) and is also used as a national standard in countries such as New Zealand, Australia, USA, and the UK among many others.

Some of the other reasons for a new metadata schema for today's needs cited are:

- New types of information objects, (e.g., web pages, computer programs, discussion forum postings) require new methods of description to accurately describe their unique content.
- Increasing technological capabilities allow delivery of richer and more complex 'objects' (e.g., an interactive learning object may have text, video and sound objects embedded into it). Such objects will need more complex descriptive methods.
- Search methods have changed. Users rely more and more on keywords than on field-directed searches, e.g., personal name or title searches. Advanced searching, browsing, text-mining algorithms and relevance ranking are being employed in addition to the use of hyperlinking between two or more objects to ensure better search results and resource discovery.
- Users no longer feel limited to the resources of their institution or institutional network. They expect virtual access to resources wherever they may be available.
- The preservation needs of digital objects are very different from those of physical objects. Digital objects require to be monitored actively and detailed documentation about these is useful in helping to preserve these objects as compared to paper-based objects.
- Many new systems for direct use by authors and other professionals are now becoming available, e.g., document management systems (DMS) and digital archives applications. These require that authors of various types of information objects should themselves create the metadata for the objects they author. A simpler scheme is called for in such situations and DCMES is an answer to such a need.

DCMES is a simple yet effective element set for describing a wide range of networked resources. The Dublin Core (DC) standard defines two levels: Basic and Qualified. *Basic Dublin Core* comprises fifteen elements; *Qualified Dublin Core* includes an additional element, Audience, as well as a group of element refinements (also called qualifiers) that refine the semantics of the elements in ways that may be useful in resource discovery.

The semantics and grammar of Dublin Core have been established by an international, cross-disciplinary group of professionals from librarianship, computer science, text encoding, the museum community, and other related fields of scholarship and practice. Most elements also have a limited set of qualifiers or refinements, attributes that may be used to further refine (not extend) the meaning of the element. Each of the elements is optional and may be repeated as many times as needed to describe an instance of a digital resource, e.g.,

the full text of a journal article or an annual report; a digital image of an insect pest. Standard ways to refine elements have been defined by the Dublin Core Metadata Initiatitive (DCMI) and they encourage the use of encoding and controlled vocabulary schemes.

A metadata scheme is expected to serve the following purposes:

- Description of the intellectual content (descriptive metadata) of an information object. The purpose of this metadata is to facilitate resource discovery.
- Management of the digital file and the maintenance of a digital object. This is especially important for successful preservation – that is to insure that it will be accessible even after the original hardware and software become obsolete.
- Definition of the internal structure of an information object (structural metadata). This metadata provides the connection between the intellectual organization of the information object and the digital representation of that organization.
- Provide information related to rights and use, i.e., the social and legal restrictions on how the information object can be used, including copyright information, intellectual property and breeders rights, and usage guidelines (administrative metadata). Information on rights of use is important since many copyrighted digital objects have become accessible via the web.

Although Dublin Core (DC) was originally developed to describe document-like objects, DC metadata can be applied to other resources as well. Examples of the use of DC in many projects, some of which are quite unique in that they integrate text, images, videos, sound, and multimedia resources using Dublin Core as the basis for description.

APPLICATION PROFILES

The DCMES is more like a framework and allows domain-specific extensions. In other words, an information agency that needs to describe resources in a specific domain need not re-invent metadata elements. They can use the basic elements, the element refinements of the DCMES and add domain specific extensions together with content rules, encoding schemes and controlled vocabularies.

These domain-specific schemes also have come to be known as schemas or Application Profiles. The use of DCMES as the underlying basis of different metadata schemas or Application Profiles (AP) enables the easy exchange of data between two or more metadata databases.For instance, if closely related information centres dealing with rural development, agricultural research, agricultural statistics, fisheries, agricultural universities, agricultural extension centres, etc., all use a common AP such as the AGRIS-AP, they will all be able to exchange information (at least at the level of common elements) with each other much more easily than if each of them follow their own metadata schemes.

An Application profile is defined as a type of metadata schema comprising data elements drawn from one or more namespaces, combined together by implementors, and optimised for a particular local application. This model allows different communities to use the DC elements for core descriptive information with extensions which make sense within a more limited area or discipline.

The idea is to ensure many metadata databases to be able to exchange data with each other because all of them have the same core elements. In view of the fact that there are more than one internationally accepted metadata scheme in use, e.g., MARC-21, DCMES, there are computer programs which allow the transformation of data in one scheme to another. This allows the exchange of data at the base level.

Inevitably, however, when data from one metadata schema is converted into another, there is bound to be loss of data. In today's globalized, networked world, the use of DC is widespread in many digital repositories and especially those subscribing to concepts of and the software compliant with the protocols of the Open Archives Initiative (OAI). Effective information networking today requires that libraries utilize software that supports newer metadata standards such as Dublin Core and become capable of contributing to and participate in such initiatives. As a result library automation solutions now need to provide support to interoperable standards such as DCMES Libraries in India seeking automation solutions need to take into account the need for software to support

MARKUP LANGUAGES

How should metadata be actually represented within a computer is another area which has received considerable attention. For instance in MARC-21, the metadata is represented using tags, indicators and subfield codes. The idea is that it should be possible for a computer program to easily identify the title of a resource, its creator, kind of resource, etc. The tagged structure was invented in the 1950's when on-line storage was expensive. In fact this structure was well suited for variable length records such as bibliographic records on magnetic tape.

However, the emergence of the web and formats such as HTML which are Markup langauges and the fact that many computer applications, especially Internet browsers, can easily interpret data in such formats. The fact that on-line storage has become cheap thanks to hard disk technology, has made markup languages as the preferred way of representing data in computers. More recently the development of XML and its advantages over HTML have made XML as the *lingua franca* of data on the web.

XML representation of data in a computer has several advantages:

- There is clear demarcation between content and display unlike with HTML
- Each application area (e.g., banking, e-commerce, libraries, chemistry, geophysics, etc.,) can define Markup tags specific to their area. The XML tags and their definitions in each application area is agreed upon internationally (or as W3C standards) and these definitions are all provided as what is known as a Document Type Definition (DTD). The DTD is accessible at a web site and all XML documents in the area are validated against such DTDs to ensure consistency of data transmitted across the web.
- XML data is textual data and is therefore not subject to the quirks of proprietary software such as word processing. Thus XML data is readable by computer programs irrespective of the operating system platform being used by a computer that connects to the data over the web. In a sense therefore XML data is future-proof.
- Due to the wide spread use of XML in web-based systems, there are standard open source computer programs (freely downloadable from the web) that can handle (search, index) such data.
- Many library-related metadata standards such as MARC-21 and Dublin Core have already developed DTDs for the storage of data in XML form and for inter-conversion of data, e.g., there is a DTD which allows MARC-21 data to be converted into MARC-XML form using a DTD that has been developed by the LoC and vice-versa.
- Of special interest to libraries: XML's fixed character set is Unicode (and its extensions), which allows diacritics, special characters, and non-Roman data to be handled like ordinary text. HTML was heavily oriented to English and did inhibit its use in other languages.
- Due to Unicode and platform neutrality, XML offers the greatest promise of data longevity (or future proofing), as hardware, software, and network protocols continue to change.
- XML also provides for the unambiguous identification of complex data structures that can be treated as objects, well suited for bibliographic data.

Many of the new metadata standards such as Dublin Core and Application Profiles, expose their data as XML files due to the advantages of XML mentioned above. The LoC also has made available a DTD to convert MARC records to XML. New ILMS are expected to provide the import of data in XML formats to local structures. As of today, the thinking is that it is not a question of choice between XML and MARC, or between XML and relational databases. The attempt will be to see how these technologies can be used synergistically to enable greater and seamless integration of library resources with the many other web resources. There is little doubt that effective library and information networking requires that libraries pay more and more attention to software that will allow them to use the new markup languages in their database and networking transactions.

INTEROPERABILITY STANDARDS

A simple definition of the term interoperability is the ability of software and hardware on different machines (and on different networks) from different vendors to share data. Interoperability may also be said to be an approach for dealing with the diversity and heterogeneity of the marketplace. Interoperability includes the exchange of data, records, and messages between computer systems across different hardware, operating systems, and networks.

The greater the ease and seamlessness of the exchanges, the greater is the interoperability. Interoperability is sought to be achieved by establishing standards that different vendors of software and hardware can adopt so that they can share data and information. When two or more organizations exchange records on a regular basis, such as the transfer between shared cataloguing services and local systems, these arrangements are manageable. Similarly, when libraries migrate from one library automation system to another, they can plan and implement a one-time data transfer. Today's requirements are much more complex, however.

Ideally, libraries would like to treat multiple bibliographic databases as comprising an online, real-time, virtual digital library. Such a structure would enable libraries to exchange records on a casual, ad hoc basis, and would enable information seekers to search one or more external digital libraries as though all were one single resource. Only recently has it become possible to support generic clientserver relationships between information systems. The most advanced is the z39.50 standard that is being implemented for online catalogues and other bibliographic retrieval systems.

THE Z39.50 STANDARD

ANSI/NISO z39.50 is the American National Standard Information Retrieval Application Service Definition and Protocol Specification for Open Systems Interconnection. Version 3 of the standard with new facilities and services was released in 1995. ANSI/NISO z39.50 defines a standard procedure for two computers to communicate for the purpose of information retrieval. z39.50 makes it easier to use large information databases by standardizing the procedures and features for searching and retrieving information.

Specifically, z39.50 supports information retrieval in a distributed, client and server environment, where a computer operating as a client submits a search request (i.e., a query) to another computer acting as an information server.

Software on the server performs a search on one or more databases and creates a result set of records that meet the criteria of the search request. The server returns records from the result set to the client for processing. The power of z39.50 lies in its ability to separate the user interface on the client side from the information servers, search engines, and databases. Z39.50 provides a consistent view of information from a wide variety of sources, and it offers client implementors the capability to integrate information from a range of databases and servers.

ANSI/NISO z39.50 can be implemented on any platform. In other words z39.50 enables different computer systems—with different operating systems hardware, search engines, database management systems—to interoperate and work together *seamlessly*. A z39.50 implementation enables one interface to access multiple systems, providing end users with nearly transparent access to other systems. Users access multiple systems with the familiar commands and displays of their own local systems, without having to learn new commands and search techniques.

Such searches are called Federated Searches. The results of the searches are presented on the local system - again, in the formats and styles that users are accustomed to. Originally developed for use in computer communications networks using Open System Interconnection (OSI) protocols, z39.50 is now successfully operational in the environment of the Internet. Interoperability testing of various z39.50 implementations has made it clear that the transport services (i.e., the TCP/IP) of the Internet could be used successfully for the protocol.

Using z39.50 over the Internet is a major step forward. Z39.50 implementations are available both as standalone applications as well as integral parts of an integrated library automation system (ILMS). In today's networked world, a library automation system that provides federated searching capabilities for its users will obviously be at a great advantage than others.

WEB SERVICES PROTOCOL-BASED APPLICATIONS FOR LIBRARY NETWORKING

Although the z39.50 protocol has been around since before the Internet era, there are several problems with this implementation of federated searching.

Some of these are:

- Z39.50 is a complex and high-level protocol
- The implementation barrier is high for present web-based systems
- Federated search results from different servers are retrieved at various times depending on the availability of the server and

network resources. In other words, this protocol is very information resource and band width sensitive.

As a result of these limitations, a new generation of services have been developed using web services protocols for federated searching. The two new services are SRW (Search and Retrieve Web Service) and SRU (Search and Retrieve URL Service).

These two new protocols have several advantages:

- All the advantages of Z39.50
- Implementation barrier is very low for web based systems, since this is based on high level web-based protocols
- SRW works with all high level protocols, viz., http, ftp and smtp

SRW and SRU are web Services-based protocols for querying Internetaccessible databases and returning search results. SRW and SRU requests and results are similar, their difference lies in the ways the queries and results are encapsulated and transmitted between client and server applications. SRW uses existing, well tested and easily available technologies such as Simple Object Access Protocol (SOAP) and XPath in order to perform what has been done in the past using proprietary solutions.

The design has had the benefit of 20 years of experience with the Z39.50 information retrieval protocol, and is both robust and easy to understand while still retaining the important aspects of its predecessor. A SRW query is represented in CQL, the "Common Query Language", designed for human readable, human writeable, intuitive queries. It supports very simple queries — for example an unqualified single term (e.g. "cat") — but maintains the expressiveness of more complex languages, to represent arbitrarily complex queries.

Many libraries in the west using specialized software and/or a new generation ILMS have begun implementing SRU/SRW protocols. Similarly, many libraries have also made their databases accessible via SRW/SRU servers. Indian libraries must become aware of these developments as they will undoubtedly increase a library's capability to provide easier access to specialized databases in single or federated mode. Provision of such access is a clear way of differentiating libraries from their competitors.

OPENURL

More and more full text resources are now becoming accessible on web sites of publishers, libraries, professional bodies. These resources are identified by a URL. However, when the web site decides to move the resource to some other location within the site or even remove it from their site, the old URL captured in a database will no longer point to the resource. This leads to frustration for the user.

This is particularly so when users search journal article databases or when they access e-journals. Access to the full text of articles is sought and this is where the concept of a persistent URL becomes necessary. However, users, working as they do in an organizational context, have defined access and view privileges for e-serials and databases. For instance, the organization they work for may not have access to an e-journal's full text but only to the abstract of articles. The OpenURL standard is a protocol for interoperability between an information resource, e.g., an on-line or CD-ROM database and a service component, referred to as a link server, which offers localized services.

The underlying concept of the OpenURL standard is that links should lead a user to appropriate resources. A link server, such as the SFX server from the ILMS, ExLibris, defines the context of the user. When the link server accepts an OpenURL as input, it acts on it to provide users with services that comply with their institution's collections and policies. The OpenURL standard enables a user who has retrieved an article citation, for example, to obtain immediate access to the "most appropriate" copy of that object through the implementation of extended linking services (also called context-sensitive linking).

The selection of the best copy is based on user and organizational preferences regarding the location of the copy, its cost, and agreements with information suppliers, and similar considerations. This selection occurs without the knowledge of the user; it is made possible by the transport of metadata with the OpenURL link from the source citation to a "resolver" (the link server), which stores the preference information and the links to the appropriate material.

A *link resolver* interprets incoming OpenURLs, takes the local holdings and access privileges of that institution (usually a library) into account, and displays links to appropriate resources. A link resolver allows the library to provide a range of library-configured links and services, including links to the full-text, a local catalogue to check print holdings, document delivery or ILL services, databases, search engines, etc. Many of today's information providers can generate and output OpenURLs. Libraries that have access to an OpenURLcompliant link server such as SFX, must furnish an OpenURL for their full text resources, e.g., their own monographs, reports, etc., in digital form.

The OpenURL system works in conjunction with a body called CrossRef, an independent membership association, founded and directed by publishers. CrossRef's mandate is to connect users to primary research content, by enabling publishers to do collectively what they cannot do individually. CrossRef establishes Digital Object Identifiers (DOI), an identifier using an open standard, to scholarly and professional publications. CrossRef operates a cross-publisher citation linking system that allows a researcher to click on a reference citation on one publisher's platform and link directly to the cited content on another publisher's platform, subject to the target publisher's access control practices.

The citation-linking network today covers millions of articles and other content items from several hundred scholarly and professional publishers. CrossRef DOIs link to publisher response pages, which include the full bibliographic citation and abstract, as well as full-text access (for authenticated users or at no charge, as determined by the publisher). The publisher response page often includes other linking options, such as pay-per-view access, journal table of contents and homepage, and associated resources. CrossRef is a collaborative membership network, and not a product for purchase. DOI, an open standard, is an alphanumeric identifier for digital content, such as a book or journal article.

The DOI is paired with the object's electronic address, or URL, in an updateable central directory, and is published in place of the URL in order to avoid broken links while allowing the content to move as needed. DOIs are distributed by publishers and by CrossRef, and there is no end-user charge associated with their use. As an identifier, the DOI can be incorporated into many different systems and databases. The DOI system provides a framework for persistent identification, managing intellectual content, managing metadata, and linking customers with content suppliers.

The key benefits of the CrossRef DOI for libraries are:

- Truly persistent links
- Increased usage of acquired resources
- Expanded access to content not owned
- Enhanced and customizable localized linking
- Metadata retrieval privileges at no cost to most libraries

Although these new fangled standards seem complex at first glance, it is important that Indian libraries become familiar with these and look for solutions which will support these new standards. The move towards provision of access to full text, the fact that more and more digital resources are on the web, the emergence of the open archives initiatives (OAI) and digital repositories has made it absolutely vital that libraries embrace these new standards and technologies if they wish to differentiate themselves from their competitors.

12

Network Browser

INTRODUCTION

It has long been known that many kinds of technological devices possess subtle but measurable variations which allow them to be \fingerprinted". Cameras, typewriters, and quartz crystal clocks are among the devices that can be entirely or substantially identified by a remote attacker possessing only outputs or communications from the device. There are several companies that sell products which purport to fingerprint web browsers in some manner, and there are anecdotal reports that these prints are being used both for analytics and second-layer authentication purposes.

But, aside from limited results from one recent experiment, there is to our knowledge no information in the public domain to quantify how much of a privacy problem fingerprinting may pose. In this paper we investigate the real-world effectiveness of browser fingerprinting algorithms. We defined one candidate fingerprinting algorithm, and collected these fingerprints from a sample of 470,161 browsers operated by informed participants who visited the website https://panopticlick.eff.org.

The details of the algorithm, and our collection methodology, are discussed in Section 3. While our sample of browsers is quite biased, it is likely to be representative of the population of Internet users who pay enough attention to privacy to be aware of the minimal steps, such as limiting cookies or perhaps using proxy servers for sensitive browsing, that are generally agreed to be necessary to avoid having most of one's browsing activities tracked and collated by various parties.

In this sample of privacy-conscious users, 83.6% of the browsers seen had an instantaneously unique fingerprint, and a further 5.3% had an anonymity set of size 2. Among visiting browsers that had either Adobe Flash or a Java Virtual Machine enabled, 94.2% exhibited instantaneously unique fingerprints and a further 4.8% had fingerprints that were seen exactly twice. Only 1.0% of browsers with Flash or Java had anonymity sets larger than two. Overall, we were able to place a lower bound on the fingerprint distribution entropy of 18.1 bits, meaning that if we pick a browser at random, at best only one in

286,777 other browsers will share its fingerprint. Our results are presented in further detail in Section 4. In our data, fingerprints changed quite rapidly. Among the subset of 8,833 users who accepted cookies and visited panopticlick.eff.org several times over a period of more than 24 hours, 37.4% exhibited at least one fingerprint change.

This large percentage may in part be attributable to the interactive nature of the site, which immediately reported the uniqueness or otherwise of fingerprints and thereby encouraged users to find ways to alter them, particularly to try to make them less unique. Even if 37.4% is an overestimate, this level of fingerprint instability was at least momentary grounds for privacy optimism. Unfortunately, we found that a simple algorithm was able to guess and follow many of these fingerprint changes. If asked about all newly appearing fingerprints in the dataset, the algorithm was able to correctly pick a \progenitor" finger- print in 99.1% of cases, with a false positive rate of only 0.87%.

FINGERPRINTS AS THREATS TO WEB PRIVACY

The most common way to track web browsers is via HTTP cookies, often set by with 3rd party analytics and advertising domains. There is growing awareness among web users that HTTP cookies are a serious threat to privacy, and many people now block, limit or periodically delete them. Awareness of super-cookies is lower, but political and PR pressures may eventually force firms like Adobe to make their super-cookies comply with the browser's normal HTTP cookie privacy settings. In the mean time, a user seeking to avoid being followed around the Web must pass three tests.

The first is tricky: find appropriate settings that allow sites to use cookies for necessary user interface features, but prevent other less welcome kinds of tracking. The second is harder: learn about all the kinds of super-cookies, perhaps including some quite obscure types, and find ways to disable them. Only a tiny minority of people will pass the first two tests, but those who do will be confronted by a third challenge: fingerprinting. As a tracking mechanism for use against people who limit cookies, fingerprinting also has the insidious property that it may be much harder for investigators to detect than super-cookie methods, since it leaves no persistent evidence of tagging on the user's computer.

FINGERPRINTS AS GLOBAL IDENTIFIERS

If there is enough entropy in the distribution of a given fingerprinting algorithm to make a recognisable subset of users unique, that fingerprint may essentially be usable as a 'Global Identifier' for those users. Such a global identifier can be thought of as akin to a cookie that cannot be deleted except by a browser configuration change that is large enough to break the fingerprint. Global identifier fingerprints are a worst case for privacy. But even users who are not globally identified by a particular fingerprint may be vulnerable to more context-specific kinds of tracking by the same fingerprint algorithm, if the print is used in combination with other data.

FINGERPRINT + IP ADDRESS AS COOKIE REGENERATORS

Some websites use Adobe's Flash LSO super-cookies as a way to 'regenerate' normal cookies that the user has deleted, or more discretely, to link the user's previous cookie ID with a newly assigned cookie ID. Fingerprints may pose a similar 'cookie regeneration' threat, even if those fingerprints are not globally identifying. In particular, a fingerprint that carries no more than 15-20 bits of identifying information will in almost all cases be sufficient to uniquely identify a particular browser, given its IP address, its subnet, or even just its Autonomous System Number. If the user deletes their cookies while continuing to use an IP address, subnet or ASN that they have used previously, the cookie-setter could, with high probability, link their new cookie to the old one.

FINGERPRINT + IP ADDRESS IN THE ABSENCE OF COOKIES

A final use for fingerprints is as a means of distinguishing machines behind a single IP address, even if those machines block cookies entirely. It is very likely that fingerprinting will work for this purpose in all but a tiny number of cases.

METHODOLOGY

A BROWSER FINGERPRINTING ALGORITHM

We implemented a browser fingerprinting algorithm by collecting a number of commonly and less-commonly known characteristics that browsers make avail- able to websites. Some of these can be inferred from the content of simple, static HTTP requests; others were collected by AJAX . We grouped the measurements into eight separate strings, though some of these strings comprise multiple, related details. The fingerprint is essentially the concatenation of these strings. In some cases the informational content of the strings is straightforward, while in others the measurement can capture more subtle facts.

For instance, a browser with JavaScript disabled will record default values for video, plugins, fonts and super-cookies, so the presence of these measurements indicates that JavaScript is active. More subtly, browsers with a Flash blocking add-on in- stalled show Flash in the plugins list, but fail to obtain a list of system fonts via Flash, thereby creating a distinctive fingerprint, even though neither measurement explicitly detects the Flash blocker. Similarly many browsers with forged User Agent strings are distinguished because the other measurements do not comport with the User Agent.

In fact, the modal fingerprint among browsers that included Flash or Java plugins; it was observed 16 times from 16 distinct IP addresses. There are many other measurements which could conceivably have been included in a fingerprint.

Generally, these were omitted for one of three reasons:

- We were unaware of the measurement, or lacked the time to implement it correctly including the full use of Microsoft's ActiveX and Silverlight APIs to collect fingerprintable measures; detection of more plugins in Internet Explorer; tests for other kinds of super-cookies; detection of system fonts by CSS introspection, even when Flash and Java are absent; the order in which browsers send HTTP headers; variation in HTTP Accept headers across requests for different content types; clock skew measurements; TCP stack fingerprinting; and a wide range of subtle JavaScript behavioural tests that may indicate both browser add-ons and true browser versions.
- We did not believe that the measurement would be sufficiently stable within a given browser—including geolocation, IP addresses as detected using Flash or Java, and the CSS history detection hack.
- The measurement requires consent from the user before being collectable—for instance, Google Gears super-cookie support or the wireless router {based geolocation features included in recent browsers. In general, it should be assumed that commercial browser fingerprinting services would not have omitted measurements for reason 1 above, and that as a result, commercial fingerprinting methods would be more powerful than the one studied here.

DATA COLLECTION AND PREPROCESSING

We deployed code to collect our fingerprints and report them—along with simple self-information measurements calculated from live fingerprint tallies—at panopticlick.eff.org. A large number of people heard about the site through websites like Slashdot, BoingBoing, Lifehacker, Ars Technica, io9, and through social media channels like Twitter, Facebook, Digg and Reddit. The data for this paper was collected between the 27th of January and the 15th of February, 2010. For each HTTP client that followed the \test me" link at panopticlick. eff.org, we recorded the fingerprint, as well as a 3-month persistent HTTP cookie ID, an HMAC of the IP address, and an HMAC of the IP address with the least significant octet erased.

We kept live tallies of each fingerprint, but in order to reduce double-counting, we did not increment the live tally if we had previously seen that precise fingerprint with that precise cookie ID. Before computing the statistics reported throughout this paper, we undertook several further offline preprocessing steps. Firstly, we excluded a number of our early data points, which had been collected before the diagnosis and correction of some minor bugs in our client side JavaScript and database types. We excluded the records that had been directly affected by these bugs, and other records collected while the bugs were present. Next, we undertook some preprocessing to correct for the fact that some users who blocked, deleted or limited the duration of cookies had been multi-counted in the live data, while those whose browsers accepted our persistent cookie would not be.

We assumed that all browsers with identical fingerprints and identical IP addresses were the same. There was one exception to the rule. If a tuple exhibited \interleaved" cookies, all distinct cookies at that IP were counted as separate instances of that fingerprint. \Interleaved" meant that the same fingerprint was seen from the same IP address first with cookie A, then cookie B, then cookie A again, which would likely indicate that multiple identical systems were operating behind a single firewall.

We saw interleaved cookies from 2,585 IP addresses, which was 3.5% of the total number of IP addresses that exhibited either multiple signatures or multiple cookies. Starting with 1,043,426 hits at the test website, the successive steps de- scribed above produced a population of 470,161 fingerprint-instances, with minimal multi-counting, for statistical analysis. Lastly we considered whether over-counting might occur because of hosts changing IP addresses.

We were able to detect such IP changes among cookie- accepting browsers; 14,849 users changed IPs, with their subsequent destinations making up 4.6% of the 321,155 IP addresses from which users accepted cookies. This percentage was small enough to accept it as an error rate; had it been large, we could have reduced the weight of every non-cookie fingerprint by this percentage, in order to counteract the over-counting of non-cookie users who were visiting the site from multiple IPs.

RESULTS

The frequency distribution of fingerprints we observed. Were the x axis not logarithmic, it would be a strongly \L"-shaped distribution, with 83.6% in an extremely long tail of unique fingerprints at the bottom right, 8.1% having fingerprints that were fairly \non rare", with anonymity set sizes in our sample of 10, and 8.2% in the joint of the L-curve, with fingerprints that were seen between 2 and 9 times.

The distribution of surprisal for different browsers. In general, modern desktop browsers fare very poorly, and around 90% of these are unique. The least unique desktop browsers often have JavaScript disabled. iPhone and Android browsers are significantly more uniform and harder to fingerprint than desktop browsers; for the time being, these smart phones do not have the variety of plugins seen on desktop systems.

Sadly, iPhones and Androids lack good cookie control options like session-cookies-only or blacklists, so their users are eminently trackable by non-fingerprint means. The sizes of the anonymity sets that would be induced if each of our eight measurements were used as a fingerprint on its own. In general, plugins and fonts are the most identifying metrics, followed by User Agent, HTTP Accept, and screen resolution, though all of the metrics are uniquely identifying in some cases.

GLOBAL UNIQUENESS

We know that in the particular sample of browsers observed by Panopticlick, 83.6% had unique fingerprints. But we might be interested in the question of what percentage of browsers in existence are unique, regardless of whether they visited our test website. Mayer has argued that it is almost impossible to reach any conclusions about the global uniqueness of a browser fingerprint, because the multi-nominal theorem indicates that the maximum likelihood for the probability of any fingerprint that was unique in a sample of size N is:

$$P(f_i) = \frac{1}{N}$$

A fingerprint with this probability would be far from unique in the global set of browsers G, because $G \gg N$. This may indeed be the maximum subjective likelihood for any single fingerprint that we observe, but in fact, this conclusion is wildly over-optimistic for privacy. If the probability of each unique fingerprint in the sample N had been $\frac{1}{N}$, the applying the multinomial expansion for those 392,938 events of probabilty $\frac{1}{N}$ it would have been inordinately unlikely that we would have seen each of these events precisely once. Essentially, the maximum likelihood approach has assigned a probability of zero for all fingerprints that were not seen in the sample N, when in fact many new fingerprints would appear in a larger sample G. What we could attempt to meaningfully infer is the global proportion of uniqueness.

Then, we could employ Monte Carlo simulations to estimate levels of uniqueness and fingerprint entropy in a global population of any given size G. Furthermore, this method could offer confidence intervals for the proposition that a fingerprint unique in N would remain unique in G. We did not prioritise conducting that analysis for a fairly prosaic reason: the dataset collected at panopticlick.eff.org is so biased towards technically educated and privacy-conscious users that it is somewhat meaningless to extrapolate it out to a global population size. If other fingerprint datasets are collected that do not suffer from this level of bias, it may be interesting to extrapolate from those.

HOW STABLE ARE BROWSER FINGERPRINTS?

Many events can cause a browser fingerprint to change. In the case of the algorithm we deployed, those events include upgrades to the browser, upgrading a plugin, disabling cookies, installing a new font or an external application which includes fonts, or connecting an external monitor which alters the screen resolution. By collecting other tracking information alongside fingerprints, we were able to observe how constant or changeable fingerprints were among Panopticlick users.

In particular, we used cookies to recognise browsers that were returning visitors, and checked to see whether their fingerprints had changed. Our observations probably overstate the rate at which fingerprints change in the real world, because the interactive nature of the Panopticlick website encourages to experiment with alterations to their browser configuration.

CHANGING FINGERPRINTS AS A FUNCTION OF TIME

Among our userbase, rates of fingerprint change for returning cookie-accepting users were very high, with 37.4% of users who visited the site more than once exhibiting more than one fingerprint over time. The time-dependence of fingerprint changes, which plots the proportion of fingerprints that was constant among cookies that were seen by Panopticlick exactly twice, with a substantial time interval in between.

The population with precisely two time-separated hits was selected because this group is significantly less likely to be actively trying to alter their browser fingerprints. Upon first examination, the high rate of change for fingerprints—even if it overstates the rate of change in the wider Internet population—appears to constitute a powerful protection against fingerprinting attacks.

FOLLOWING CHANGING FINGERPRINTS

We performed a simple test to see whether a connection can be inferred between the old and new values of fingerprints that change over time. We implemented a very simple algorithm to heuristically estimate whether a given fingerprint might be an evolved version of a fingerprint seen previously. The algorithm operated on an input fingerprint q, where

$$F_i(g), i \in \{1..8\}$$

are the 8 fingerprint components, and G is the set of all browsers observed in our dataset. The algorithm did not attempt to guess a preceding fingerprint if q indicated that the browser did not have Flash or Java installed. We ran our algorithm over the set of users whose cookies indicated that they were returning to the site 1{2 hours or more after their first visit, and who now had a different fingerprint.

Excluding users whose fingerprints changed because they disabled javascript, our heuristic made a correct guess in 65% of cases, an incorrect guess in 0.56% of cases, and no guess in 35% of cases. 99.1% of guesses were correct, while the false positive rate was 0.86%. Our algorithm was clearly very crude, and no doubt could be significantly improved with effort.

DEFENDING AGAINST FINGERPRINTING

The Paradox of Fingerprintable Privacy Enhancing Technologies Sometimes, technologies intended to enhance user privacy turn out to make fingerprinting easier. Extreme examples include many forms of User Agent spoofing and Flash blocking browser extensions. The paradox, essentially, is that many kinds of measures to make a device harder to fingerprint are themselves distinctive unless a lot of other people also take them. Examples of measures that might be intended to improve privacy but which appear to be ineffective or even potentially counterproductive in the face of fingerprinting include Flash blocking, and User Agent alteration.

A small group of users had \Privoxy" in their User Agent strings; those User Agents alone averaged 15.5 bits of surprisal. All 7 users of the purportedly privacy-enhancing \Browzar" browser were unique in our dataset. There are some commendable exceptions to this paradox. TorButton has evolved to give considerable thought to fingerprint resistance and may be receiving the levels of scrutiny necessary to succeed in that project. NoScript is a useful privacy enhancing technology that seems to reduce fingerprintability.

ENUMERATABLE CHARACTERISTICS VS TESTABLE CHARACTERISTICS

One significant API choice that several plugin and browser vendors made, which strengthens fingerprints tremendously, is offering function calls that enumerate large amounts of system information. The navigator.plugins object is one example, as are the font lists returned by Flash and Java. Microsoft Internet Explorer deserves an honourable mention for not allowing plugin enumeration, and even though we collected version numbers for 8½ plugins, the plugin entropy on IE was 16.5 bits, somewhat lower than the 17.7 seen in non-IE browsers.

The benefits of allowing Java and Flash to read exhaustive system font lists is questionable. Any website that cares whether someone has the \False Positive BRK" font installed could surely test for it explicitly. There are probably stronger ease-of-development arguments for making plugins enumeratable, but the example of IE shows that it is not strictly necessary. We recommend that browsers switch to confirm-only testing for fonts and plugins, with an exponential backofi to prevent exhaustive searches by malicious javascript.

FINGERPRINTABILITY $\propto$ DEBUGGABILITY

Much of the entropy we observe in browsers comes from the precise micro-version numbers of all of their plugins. This is somewhat true even in IE, where we were limited to testing the version numbers of 8½ common plugins using PluginDetect and custom JavaScript. A similar, though less severe, problem comes from precise micro-version numbers in User Agent strings. The obvious solution to this problem would be to make the version numbers less precise. Why report Java 1.6.0 17 rather than just Java 1.6, or DivX Web Player 1.4.0.233 rather than just DivX Web Player 1.4? The motivation for these precise version numbers appears to be debuggability.

Plugin and browser developers want the option of occasionally excavating the micro-version numbers of clients when trying to retrospectively diagnose some error that may be present in a particular micro-version of their code. This is an understandable desire, but it should now be clear that this decision trades o_ the user's privacy against the developer's convenience. There is a spectrum between extreme debuggability and extreme defense against fingerprinting, and current browsers choose a point in that spectrum close to the debuggability extreme. Perhaps this should change, especially when users enter \private browsing" modes.

FONT ORDERS AS AN UNNECESSARY SOURCE OF ENTROPY

When implementing our fingerprinting code, we observed that Adobe Flash and Sun's Java VM not only report complete lists of fonts installed on a system, but return them in non-sorted order, perhaps due to a file system walk. We tested the hypothesis that font orders are informative, by checking to see if any returning, cookie-accepting users had font lists whose order had changed. We found that only 30 returning browsers had font lists that were different solely with respect to order. Interestingly, these font lists only varied in the ordering of certain fonts from the \Lucida" family, and there was a related population of about 200 browsers where the same fonts varied in ordering and surrounding whitespace.

All of these browsers had Mac OS X User Agent strings, so we concluded that some application on OS X overwrites these font _les, either during upgrades or at other times. Aside from this group, our hypothesis that font list orderings were stable turned out to be correct. Next, we investigated whether a substantial reduction in font list entropy could be achieved if plugins like Flash and Java began sorting these lists before returning them via their APIs. Among browsers where the fonts were detectable, the entropy of the fonts variable was 17.1 bits. We recalculated this quantity after sorting to be 16.0, a decrease of only 1.1 bits.

Confounding this calculation slightly is the fact that the maximum possible entropy we could detect for either of these numbers, given our dataset, was only 18.4. It is possible that sorting the font lists would have made a much larger difference if the sample size had been large enough for the font entropy and its conceivable ceiling to diverge further. In contrast to the font case, our pre-launch testing seemed to indicate that the ordering of navigator plugins was not stable in all browsers, so, we sorted the plugin list before recording it. We subsequently read Jonathan Mayer's claims that Mozilla actually exposes two different plugin orderings based on different inode timestamps. Unfortunately, having sorted our plugin dataset, we cannot test his claims.

13

Data Information

DESIGN AND DEVELOPMENT OF WEB-ENABLED DATABASES

Application of computers certainly has improved the ways in which we acquire, process, store and disseminate information in libraries. As a result, we have automated house-keeping operations, catalogue and, user services in libraries. Moreover, with the advancement in the network technology during last decade, we have started providing user services through various online modes viz. e-mail, FTP, Telnet, etc. These static/ interactive modes of data/information sharing over network have improved the library services and, their popularity among the users. During 1994, libraries began to show their presence on the internet by setting up their web sites. In the beginning, libraries built their web pages by providing mainly static information.

However, in the late 1997, libraries began re-engineering their web pages with the intention of providing information from databases in a dynamic manner . Today the advancements in web and database technology have enabled the libraries to share/publish the data/information directly from the databases over the internet. Now web has become a dynamic platform for information delivery over the internet and very useful for libraries to provide various user services. This paper intends to provide an overview of the database tools available for designing in-house databases in the libraries as well as the web technology for publishing such databases over the web. Besides, the paper discusses the need of developing in-house databases in libraries, advantages of web-enabled databases, and selection of database tools from RDBMS commonly available.

IN-HOUSE DATABASES IN LIBRARIES

There are a number of ready-made library automation software packages in the market which can be used to automate the library functions and user services. However, many of these packages lack web interface and, thus, do not provide library database access (OPAC, etc.) through web. Moreover, these commercial packages provide less flexibility to librarians for making desired changes to the existing databases and to publish the same on the web. An in-house designed database system provides full flexibility to the developer/ administrator/librarian and is simpler to install, maintain and, use without having to rely on external support, and also is highly customizable and can be designed to meet local needs . Librarians can also participate in design/ development process as now a days easy and user-friendly database tools are available with in-built web interface. As per the survey conducted in order to get a clear understanding of the current role of library web master, 100 percent of the respondents felt that librarians should have some role in web site design and maintenance .

BENEFITS OF WEB-ENABLED DATABASES

Web-enabled databases have certain advantages over other means of sharing/publishing information over internet. These advantages are common to bibliographic databases also where libraries can put their OPACs and other databases on web.

According to L.J.Haravu ; Kristin Aantelman and; Chong Ho Yu , the benefits of web-enabled databases are as follows:

- Global/wide ac cess to data with a sin gle user in ter face
- Format in dependent ac cess of data (text, graph ics, au dio, video, etc.)
- Up-to-minute up dated ac cess of data in real time
- Dynamic updation of data from many locations
- Cost-effective way of data sharing
- Instant feedback from users
- Seamless links from resource to resource
- Unlimited download/printing
- Environmental friendly.

Besides, Ortiz-Repiso and Norm Medeiros have written excellent papers on differences between traditional v/s innovative means (web OPACs) of library catalogs, while B. Ramesh Babu, *et al* have presented an overview of web OPACS with their advantages in libraries.

DATABASE TOOLS

In the early days of database development, it was the flat-file system to store data in a single file by using field separators and record separators. Later, such flat-file systems were facilitated by an index in which a single index file stored keywords and pointers to the records that were stored in main file. This made retrieval more efficient, still flat-file systems were seriously inefficient. It showed data-redundancy, poor data control, and did not supported complex data types (audio, video, graphics, etc.) . After 1960s, two database models were developed in quick succession to solve the limitations of flat-file systems. These database models were Hierarchical Database Model and Network Database Model. The Hierarchical Database composes of a root segment, parent segments and child segments. This model depicts a set of one-to-many relationships between a parent and its children.

However, this model has number of limitations. It does not include ad hoc querying capability and, a multi-parent relationship is difficult to implement, as in a many-to-many relationship. The Network Database Model attempted to deal with many of the hierarchical model's limitations. The network database structure easily accommodates the multiple child, although, its structural complexities often limit its effectiveness and efficiency. Both of these database models are obsolete now mainly because of their incompatibility with web environment and have been replaced by RDBMS. RDBMS is the current database implementation standard being used for publishing information on the web.

It includes the following features which make it suitable for web environment:

- Provide extremely useful tools for database administration;
- Adhere to powerful query language SQL (structured query language) developed by Microsoft Corporation;
- Compliant with ODBC/JDBC and other database interface tools;
- Work in client/server mode;
- Offer distributed database and distributed processing options; and
- Have referential integrity controls to ensure data consistency and, thus, suitable for web environment.

It is easier to design applications in RDBMS due to the following features:

- Requires less programming skill
- Availability of third party tools, and
- Inbuilt web interface.

These all features of RDBMS have made them ideal for library applications to setup bibliographic database solutions and publishing them over the web. In the early days of library systems development, vendors have designed library applications software by using pre-relational database technology. Still some library systems suppliers are continuing to maintain and develop such products. These proprietary library applications software have their own advantages and disadvantages. However, in the library management systems marketplace, there is a growing trend towards the use of RDBMS.

As per the Gartner list of database management systems, there are 140 products from 67 vendors ranging from pre-relational, relational and, object-oriented databases (OODBMS). The RDBMS accounted three-quarters of the total database market.

Some of the common RDBMS which can be used to design in-house databases in libraries are *MS Access, SQL Server, Oracle, Informix, Sybase, File Maker Pro, SAS,* etc. However, the selection of suitable RDBMS for library applications depends on the particular library requirements, kind of applications (bibliographic/full-text/numeric), the application level (database level/data warehouse level), magnitude of data (number of records/length of fields), nature of data analysis (basic statistics, i.e., sum, average, mean/ advance statistics) and, comprehensiveness and inter-operability. Other points to be considered while selecting database tools for library applications are easiness, user-friendliness, flexibility and low cost.

In most of the cases in libraries where bibliographic databases are dealt with, commonly available consumer database products such as *MS Access*, and *File Maker Pro* are sufficient. These products can support up to 1GB of data and provide cheaper solutions.

However, these database tools are suitable for small databases and not useful for large databases, hence provide limitations in web environment. There are specific database solutions for large databases available from *MS SQL Server, DB2, Oracle, Informix, Sybase,* etc. These database tools support up to several terra byte of data; permit thousands of simultaneous users; work in client/server mode; show natural affinity towards web environment and, thus, suitable for large bibliographic, web-enabled databases in libraries.

However, to design full-text databases in libraries where large files are to be stored and retrieved, these tools do not offer good solutions as most of these tools support 200-255-400 characters field length. Although, many of these tools allow unlimited entries in memo field, the data inside a memo field are not searchable and thus, offer limited utility. In this respect, *MS SQL Server* has extended the searchable field length up to 8063 characters and thus, provide solutions for moderate full-text databases. As a common trend , a number of libraries have been using open source software available either free or on nominal prices.

These database management systems include the most common *mySQL, mSQL* and, recently updated *PostgreSQL*. These database tools are easy to work and run on various platforms such as UNIX, Lynux, NT, etc. Besides, there are some library specific text retrieval database tools for management of full-text large files, generally known as 'Free Form Databases', provide powerful search engine. Although, in some ways they are at the opposite end of the RDBMS, little database structure imposed on the designer and, thus, provide an easy and readymade database structure. However, they provide some limitations in achieving integration in the modules other than searching such as cataloguing, classification, management module, etc. These software are *BRS/Search, Basis Plus, Status,* etc.

WEB TECHNOLOGY

World Wide Web or WWW or web, sometimes wrongly mentioned as synonymous to internet, is a sub-set of it and is a most promising mode of publishing/sharing of data/information. Now, the web has emerged as the dominant protocol over internet due to its special features like easy interfacing of diverse platforms/technologies; provision to incorporate text, graphics, audio and video, etc.; permitting to access data/information in a non-linear way and; jumping from one document/resource to another through hyperlinks. The superiority of www over other modes of online sharing viz. e-mail, FTP, Telnet, Gopher, etc., has been well explained by Paul Scully . In fact, web has provided a single user interface to facilitate the user interaction with the databases or systems resources.

The web uses unique URL (universal resource locator) address which facilitates the access of information seamlessly across the diverse platforms in a client-server mode. The actual data represented in a structured way reside in a powerful computers called server, while the latter is equipped with server tools/software to populate the information over web. The client/user equipped with web browser such as Microsoft Internet Explorer (MSIE) and Netscape Navigator, etc., which interact with the server through common communications protocol TCP/IP over high speed network/internet. In fact, the client/user sends its query to the server while the latter processes the request and gets the response/results from the database and sends it back to the client/user over the web.

COMPONENTS OF WEB-BASED SYSTEMS

Following components are required for web-based systems:

Web Browser

It is a software that helps users to interact with the server for sending queries and getting results over the web. MSIE and Netscape are the most popular web browsers, both of these are available free.

Web Server

Web server is the software that helps in sharing the system resources/ files over the internet through web browsers. The latter communicate with a web server via the standard Hyper-Text Transfer Protocol (HTTP). In fact, web servers receive queries from the client, process it, get data from databases and send it back to the client over web. The popular web servers are Apache, Microsoft IIS, iPlanet from Sun-Netscape alliance, and newly developed *Zeus* from Zeus Technology Ltd. Although web servers are increasingly found as components within full-featured server operating systems, there are some basic selection points that should be highlighted.

These points are scalability and performance; high availability and reliability; interoperability and open standards; system administration and; security . In fact, there are not much choice in the web server segments as many of them come along with database tools, show natural affinity with the database tools from same vendor, and some other work better with certain platform/operating systems. According to the widely followed Netcraft web survey, approximately 60 percent of web servers run Apache, with Microsoft's IIS and the Netscape/iPlanet web server as its major competitors. However, Gartner studies have given Netscape/iPlanet a larger share of public web sites, followed by Apache and Microsoft/IIS. Apache is being used for the public sites of companies such as Merck, American Express, Texaco, Chrysler, and others.

However, it is easier to find both Microsoft/IIS and Netscape/iPlanet as the servers for large corporate public web sites when using the lookup facility offered by Netcraft. Also, for intranets, most counts credit Microsoft/IIS and Netscape/iPlanet as the leaders, followed by Apache, IBM's Lotus Domino Go server, and others. Among hot e-commerce sites, E*Trade runs the Netscape/ iPlanet server, eBay runs Windows/IIS, and Amazon runs Apache (the Apache-based Stronghold Secure Server), according to the Netcraft web survey .

WEB AUTHORING TOOLS

Basic web server software does nothing except it sends HTML data in response to a browser request. However, certain other web-authoring and scripting tools are required to extend the functionality of web server to extract the data from databases. These web-authoring tools (*HTML* and its derivatives; and other Markup languages, etc.) and scripting tools (*Perl, C++, Java Script, JScript, VBScript,* etc.) are required to write web pages and scripts to interact with back-end databases.

In early days of web-based applications, *CGI* (common gateway interface) programs were used extensively to extend the server functionality by allowing web users to interact with the web server to request specific data from the databases. Although, writing *CGI* program is difficult and requires programming skill, however, it works with high reliability. Now a days, a number visual editors are available to generate the web pages and write scripts automatically. The common editors are *Microsoft Front Page, Visual Interdev, Netscape Composer, Web Builder,* etc. Besides, other technologies have been introduced to communicate with the back-end databases.

These technologies are Microsoft *Active Server Pages (ASP*) and *Java Server Pages (JSP)* from Sun Micro Systems. Both the technologies have combined the HTML codes with the scripts in a single page and thus, making it easier to interact with back-end databases. During last few years, object-oriented and component based solutions were added to further make it easier to interact with the back-end databases.

These solutions include:

- Microsoft COM/DCOM,
- ActiveX Data Objects (ADO);
- OMA and CORBA (Common Objects Request Broker Architecture) from Object Management Group;
- Sun's EJB (Enterprise Java Beans),

- Java Applets (for client) and
- Java Servlets (for server), etc.

Besides, some database connectivity tools such as ODBC and JDBC have also emerged as in-built features of operating systems, etc.

FREE WIZARDS AND THIRD PARTY TOOLS

Writing HTML codes and scripts for database interaction is the most difficult part, requires programming skill, systems logic and manipulation planning, especially for non-computer professionals. However, a number of free wizards and third party tools are available on internet which can generate hundred of lines of codes automatically with a single click, thus, making it easier for non-skilled users to set up web-enabled database solutions in libraries. Some of the free wizards are Rule Zero, Power ASP, Active Server Pages Tools & Components, etc. Besides, *Microsoft FrontPage* also provides database wizard to generate *ASP* pages/*VBScripts* automatically to interact with back-end databases, while *Visual InterDev* provides a visual interface to develop a web-enabled web site with minimum efforts.

DATABASE SEARCHING IN CENTRAL UNIVERSITY LIBRARIES IN INDIA

In consequence of the recommendation of the National Knowledge Commission, each of the Indian states has at least one fully-funded central university. Now there are 39 central universities. Privately funded and owned statelegislated universities are also being established to cater to the increased demand for higher education. In between there are many universities that are not legislation-based but are authorized by the University Grant Commission to award degrees. Central universities are better-equipped in terms of financial resources, faculty, and infrastructure, and thus have an edge over the usually fund-starved state universities.

The libraries across the globe are challenged to integrate e-resources into their collection, services, and patrons' lives and academic libraries face obstacles when virtual learning environment (VLEs) become "the primary means of interaction between students and universities. Providing access to electronic journals and other e-resources is an important area of librarianship. The design of usable online interfaces is a crucial issue. Traditional library services and printed material are still more effective to researchers in Indian universities than web-based information and resources. Barriers to progress in this area in university libraries in India cannot be overlooked.

NETWORK INFRASTRUCTURE AND STRENGTH

Fast and effective information retrieval to support information sharing requires sound and wide network with adequate bandwidth. The UGC-sponsored Infonet is the mainstay of the academic info-network infrastructure.

The UGC has constituted a national committee called the Central Monitoring Committee (CMC) for smooth implementation and execution of information infrastructure. The CMC has chosen ERNET India (Education and Research Network) to establish information network in universities. The committee has recommended high bandwidth campus wide networks for Internet and external connectivity. So far 149 universities have been provided connectivity with raw bandwidth ranging from 512 KBPS to 20 MBPS. The Inflibnet is administering and funds its cost for all these universities.

ONLINE DATABASES

Out of the eight universities surveyed, seven are members of the UGC-Infonet consortia. The IGNOU, due to its unique character, subscribes to 17 databases of its own. There are 77 databases in all in these eight universities. But strangely enough only one online database, namely Project Muse, is common to all the universities, and 69 databases are subscribed by single universities. The following Databases are available in seven of the eight university libraries: ACS, AIP, APS, Annual Review, BWP, CUP, IOP, ISID, JCCC, JSTOR, OUP, RSC, SIAM, Springerlink and Taylor & Francis.

These are further categorized as:

- Full Text e-Journals - 72
- Bibliographic Databases 15
- E-Books 29
- Total Databases 116

Of these there are 15 bibliographic/indexing databases, while 29 are e-book databases. There is no single common e-book database available in all eight libraries. Among the bibliographic databases, DELNET and ISID are most popular, which are available in seven libraries, while MathSciNet is subscribed by six university libraries. Exemptions are Assam and Viswabharati Universities. It is natural and normal as each central university located in different region has its own requirements based upon its courses of study and areas of research.

The subject needs of the JNU differ from that of Delhi University, while Jamia has its own needs. Need and Specialization of IGNOU are of quite different nature. Still some of the databases are very common to all universities especially the Project Muse, JSTOR, American Chemical Society, American Institute of Physics, American Physical Society, Annual Review, Blackwell Publishing, Cambridge University Press, Institute of Physics, Oxford University of Press, Royal Society of Chemistry, SIAM, Springerlink and Taylor & Francis.

Retrieval Techniques

Net Server and CD-ROM mirror servers are very popular among the universities. The university libraries under study no longer provide CD-ROM services. Multimedia databases are available only in DU and JNU, while all the eight libraries own and provide access to full text and bibliographic databases. For academic libraries the two most important consortia are the UGC-Infonet and Indest. All the libraries have self-subscribed as well as consortia based databases, whereas the DU and JNU have also developed in-house databases.

Being traditional and general universities under the preview of the UGC, all are members of the UGC-Infonet, while DU is also member of AICTE Indest consortia. All the universities use commercial as well as open source databases while DU and JNU have also their home grown databases. Open source databases are also available there, but the study found that only DU, BHU, IGNOU and JNU host important open source online databases on their websites. Other universities are not able to create this kind of facility for their users merely because the staff of these libraries are not conversant with open access sources on the Internet. Databases can be accessed through login and password, but the misuse of these is a common complaint.

Therefore, IP access is more suitable. Now most of the universities allow online access to databases either through their intranet or directly from the Web. Experienced librarians prefer a campus-wide facility for providing access to databases. AU, IGNOU, Jamia, JNU and Viswabharati allow access from limited and specified terminals within campuses. Assam, IGNOU, Jamia, JNU and Viswabharati allow access through campus wide Intranet or Internet with identification and password. Many busy scholars and faculty have less time to visit the library. Therefore, access to online information must be provided on their desktops. This requires campus wide Internet accessibility. Further it was found that AU, BHU, DU, Jamia, JNU, PU and Viswabharati allow IP enabled access while IGNOU databases are password based.

Download Facility

Downloading of the required files is a critical issue. In case of commercial databases it is costly as the host library has to pay per download. But indeed it is an essential facility. It has been found that all the libraries provide downloading of PDF and HTML files, while image downloading facilities are available in all except at BHU and DU. RTF downloading is not permitted by BHU, DU and Jamia Millia Islamia, Whereas word file are not downloadable at BHU, DU and Jamia. DU and JNU provide DBMS software to download the data oriented information.

Data Retrieval Techniques

Some of the universities provide common databases linked through federated search. Only DU has the federated search engine GIST find. In this survey, only DU and PU revealed their online search techniques while the other libraries kept these confidential. DU uses Boolean, Interactive, and

Proximity searches, while PU uses quick search. Simple search Advanced/ Boolean search in addition to menudriven searches are provided by their vendors. Both these libraries provide facilities for further refinement of large chunks of search output to make the search more precise and relevant. Nevertheless, none of the universities use data mining.

Complexity of Information Retrieval

Indeed information retrieval techniques vary from university to university system. It depends upon both internal and external factor of database. In the questionnaire about 48 aspects or facilities for information retrieval were identified and the users of these eight libraries were asked to mark their ease of use on the Likert scale as:

- Easy 3
- Challenging 2
- Difficult 1

The mean value of university wise pattern is given below:

User Orientation

For optimum use of all resources and services of a library, user orientation programmes, especially of new users, are a proven effective measure. User orientation is the most important component in the online databases for the users to gain knowledge and enhance usability of databases. All the university libraries in this study have positively voted for provision of such programmes to help users in the effective use of the retrieval system for information access. This survey found that orientation programme are conducted by all except AU, BHU, IGNOU, and Viswa Bharati.

It is important to note that regular orientation programmes are required to make the users familiar with new feature of new databases. DU conducted programmes as "How to search the online databases," while the Pondicherry library provides instructions in the use of library resources including eresources and effective online searching. BHU conducts programmes on Science Direct and Proquest. DU provides need-based instruction and PU provides general instruction in effective search and the publishers also conducted such programmes to faciliatets searching of their supplied databases.

DU conducts such programmes throughout the years, while PU organizes orientation of the users at the beginning of the academic years. PU also offers need based person to person training. It is clear that there is no uniform pattern of conducting user's orientation programmes. Indeed we need a dedicated library staff for online training of library users, especially in the electronic environment. There are posts of information scientist in universities funded initially by the by UGC. Those hired are mostly from computer science and not conversant with library philosophy and routine. There is an urgent need of a designated post for an online librarian who can provide assistance in using e-resources and may also take care of any aspect of user orientation for sharing and dissemination of library e-resources. The survey showed that none of the library staff has any formal education and training in online searching. Most have learned it on the job, and most have learned by trial and error.

XML AND RELATIONAL DATABASES: USES AND OPPORTUNITIES FOR LIBRARIES

Extensible Markup Language (XML) is becoming an indispensable tool for virtually every type of content that is digitally produced. The advantages of XML for libraries have been well described by others.

On a general level, XML has at least three key advantages:

- *XML is standard*: XML is a subset of Standard Generalized Markup Language (SGML), a well established and highly regarded ISO standard. XML also offers mechanisms (document type definitions, and more recently, XML Schema) to encourage and enforce common definitions of the logical structure of a document so that standards for the documents themselves are easier to apply.
- *XML is extensible*: XML has no limits on the number of markup languages that can be defined using it, and each of these languages can consist of an unlimited number of tags. This flexibility is essential for fostering the widespread adoption of XML and helps explain why XML has been utilized for markup languages in every conceivable subject area, ranging from chess playing to mind reading.
- *XML is well supported*: It seems that almost every serious Web technology is now expected to define its relationship to XML, and XML has fostered an explosion of related technologies. The W3C has made many tools and toolkits freely available to Web developers, and utilities and applications for XML are being developed by a worldwide community of vendors, open source contributors, and other groups that seek to move information across the Web.

XML has been used extensively for authoring standalone documents, but database solutions for storing and managing large collections of materials in XML format are becoming more common. As Bourett, a researcher who tracks developments in XML databases, points out, choosing between an RDBMS and other database options for storing XML often comes down to whether you are working with data or documents.

If the XML content is usually manipulated at the individual field level, needs to be accessed with standard query and reporting tools, and pulls together information from sources that are updated and maintained separately, then a Relational Database Management System (RDBMS) approach may make the most sense.

Examples of this kind of "data-centric" content include purchase orders, flight schedules, and scientific data. If the XML content is largely contained in individual documents, and the content will be edited and updated at the document level, then Object Orientated Databases (OODBMS), Object/ Relational Databases, and other solutions that can maintain XML documents as a more complete unit on the backend will be preferred. Most RDBMS solutions for storing XML assemble XML representations of the data on the fly. Object relational databases and some RDBMS addons.

This allows the document to be stored with all tags and ordering preserved. Of course, the data and document distinction is not absolute, and there are other factors that can influence the choice of a database. An organization may have built up a high level of Oracle experience, for example, and that would have a huge impact on any data management decisions. Libraries are also in a somewhat unique situation in that they house collections of both data-centric and document-centric materials that may require database solutions.

For example, libraries with finding aids in Encoded Archival Description (EAD) format or full text materials marked up with Text Encoding Initiative (TEI) are more likely to favor "document-centric" solutions and require extensive full text searching capabilities that are more prevalent in OODBMS and Object/ Relational Databases. Libraries are even more likely to deal with content that is "data-centric", such as purchase orders and circulation records; they may already have RDBMSs in place to support the processing activities associated with this data.

MARC AND XML

The difficulty in separating data from document-based content can be seen in the Machine Readable Cataloguing (MARC) format, one of the library community's most successful and durable standards. Like many document-centric formats, MARC records can carry a lot of text-intensive information. Libraries may even choose to convert MARC records to standalone XML documents in order to take advantage of mainstream XML tools for indexing or for presentation purposes.

On the other hand, MARC records are "data-centric" in the sense that they can often bring together data sources that are maintained outside of the bibliographic description of an item. Authority, holdings and item records, for example, play a key role in helping to define the bibliographic view of the physical and virtual objects in the library's collection, yet these records are often processed and updated separately.

Libraries have begun to explore the use of XML for MARC. Lane Medical Library at Stanford University has created a DTD and released conversion software for converting MARC records to XML documents in an initiative called XMLMARC. K.T. Lam has also proposed a DTD for MARC and suggests that the use of a decentralized authority repository may one day be possible with XML linking technologies. This would allow libraries to "point" to established names and subjects that could be maintained remotely rather than replicated by each individual library.

Clearly, there is interest on the part of libraries in bringing MARC fully into an XML environment. The challenge is to define an XML infrastructure that can handle the amount of materials that libraries catalogue without isolating the content from the transactional processes that libraries use for acquiring and circulating the collection. Cataloguing records are typically maintained by dozens of library staff and are linked to ordering and circulation processing procedures that involve many updates. Any application of XML that is tied directly to where cataloguing records are maintained and use XML as a means of updating content may need to be "transaction aware" and support a high level of multi-user access.

MIDDLEWARE ALTERNATIVES

The middleware typically uses Structured Query Language (SQL) to pull together the fields needed for the XML input/output. The advantages of this approach are that this greatly increases the number of database systems that a library can select from because all major RDBMSs support SQL, and that this allows great flexibility for moving from one database to another. For formats like MARC, these tools also offer the possibility of using XML technologies without losing the robustness of relational databases for maintaining content and linkages that are updated by multiple users.

The disadvantages of this approach include the overhead required to assemble and disassemble XML documents as they move in and out of the database, and the extra groundwork to define an XML representation that takes full advantage of both the RDBMS and XML technologies. good example of an XML mapping tool for relational databases is Castor, an open source project from Exolabs.

The mapping file in Castor determines how the XML will be produced from the contents of the RDBMS. Castor is very "Java-centric," which can be an advantage or disadvantage depending on how comfortable an organization is with the Java platform. By working with Java, a developer can use Castor to render the records in an RDBMS accessible and updatable as XML documents. Databases that can be used with Castor include Oracle, MySQL, and PostgreSQL.

THE WEB AS THE WORLD'S BIGGEST RELATIONAL DATABASE

A Web page is, in some ways, much like an RDBMS "view" of disparate data. From a user perspective, the content is brought together based on a predefined logic and a series of "keys" or "pointers" that identify relevant material. A dynamically generated Web page comes even closer to the conceptual model of an RDBMS, particularly if much of the content of the page is based on remote network resources retrieved through URLs. For example, a search of a library catalogue on the Web typically involves a cgi-bin program that dynamically displays results using HTML. Each result record is usually linked to a fuller display via a URL that specifies from where the information is to be retrieved.

The linking mechanisms of the Web have recently been leveraged to support the OpenURL framework. The OpenURL framework has been proposed as an architecture for retrieving references to scholarly works by enabling third parties to provide links for a referenced item. Although OpenURLs have typically been deployed to provide links to the full text of scholarly works, the framework can also be utilized to identify a catalogued item in an ILS. Ex Libris' ALEPH500 System, for example, directly supports OpenURL, and exploratory work has been carried out to generalize the OpenURL framework beyond reference linking scholarly environments.

If the Web can be thought of as an ever-growing RDBMS, and OpenURLs can be utilized to provide "RDBMS-like" standard and precise links between specific items in information systems, then there are possibilities for providing extensive distributed search and retrieval functions in Web-based library services. For example, a remote database consisting of Library of Congress names and subject headings could be searched within a browser environment, and the results could provide links to items in the local catalogue . Web-based union catalogues support standardized indexing and searching at a central location.

With OpenURLs, links can be made to point to holdings and other localized information within the member library's Integrated Library System. All of this fits within the RDBMS notion of creating and maintaining data with as little duplication as possible, and linking it together to provide a logical view of the content itself. XML plays a role by greatly enhancing the linking mechanisms of the Web. XML technologies such as Xinclude, Xpath, and Xlink, provide sophisticated methods for drawing on network resources. Xinclude allows the contents of a separate XML resource to be inserted into an XML document based on a link .

Xpath will be familiar to anyone who has worked with XSTL and other XML stylesheet tools. It allows the creation of expressions for specifying every visual and interface portion of a document. Xlink is the XML linking language and offers much more sophisticated types of linking than currently offered by the familiar HREF and NAME elements found in HTML. Xlink's extended element can name one or more linked resources. The arc element in this example tells an application about the behavior expected when moving through the linked resources.

The role and title attributes are used to describe the function of the linked resource in the context of the local resource. Role is meant to be descriptive to the application and title is meant to be descriptive to the user. In this case, the roles are meant to identify an author's works and biographies. The *acutate* element describes how the resources should appear. The value "onRequest" specifies that the resource should appear when the link is selected, and the value "embed" for the *show* attribute tells the application to insert the specified resource inline within the current document.

Finally, an *item* element is used to represent where this particular resource can be found in physical form in the library. If an XML representation of an RDBMS-based library catalogue or other library database is made available, the library can make use of XML linking technologies and other XML tools for manipulating database contents. OpenURL lays the groundwork for using links as virtual keys to content that goes far beyond individual tables, and the content can be as broad as the diversity of the Web itself.

STANDARDS FOR CREATING BIBLIOGRAPHIC DATABASES

The concept of "standard" in the field of library and information science is interpreted as codes of cataloguing rules, classification schemes, subject headings and various other documents contained recommendations for good library practice, all of which are subject to varying interpretation. But, for another professionals, standards are extremely precise technical specifications for communication between software and machines in an automated information-processing environment.

For example, Operating Systems, TCP/IP etc. Standards are documented agreements containing technical specifications or other precise criteria to be used consistently as rules, guidelines, or definitions of characteristics, to ensure that materials, products, processes and services are fit for their purpose Field of bibliographic standards are not limited to the rules only but spread up to the authority files such as person names, corporate names, subject headings, classification schemes, series names, institution names, software and standardization form and format etc. In beginning, during the initiation of automation to library professionals, there was not much focus on bibliographic standards and were creating databases in any formats.

That affected to the automation of their libraries, which forced them to think over the issue. Now, gradually, the libraries and information centres are realizing the importance of bibliographic standards. Centres like Information and Library Network (INFLIBNET), Ahmedabad is playing important role in bringing all libraries together to work on a single platform of standards with linking under one huge national network i.e. UGC-Infonet.

INFLIBNET Centre is an Inter-University Centre of University Grants Commission (UGC), working on Academic library system in India. In 1990, UGC launched it as a programme for five years on pilot basis. On June 1996, the programme was recognized as a full-fledged Centre. To know more about the Centre, kindly visit the website http://www.inflibnet.ac.in. UGC-Infonet is a project of UGC being implemented by INFLIBNET Centre in collaboration with ERNET (Education and Research Network), New Delhi. It is an Intra-Network of Indian universities and colleges across the country based on the Open IP platform, employing state-of-the-art technologies like IP or TV, enabling online response to queries. The network facilitates Intranet and Internet access to its users on high data rates.

STANDARDS FOR BIBLIOGRAPHIC DATABASE

Well-known simple definition of database is a set of records and record is a set of fields, where, field is a combination of different pieces of information. Bibliographic database is a database of resources available at libraries in print format. With the revolution of information technology in the field of libraries, bibliographic catalogue has come up into the form of bibliographic database.

For making compatible with these changes, there, many library institutions have come up with different standards and formats such as CCF, AUSMARC, CANMARC, UKMARC, USMARC, UNIMARC, MARC21, AACR2, ISBD, LCSH, MeSH etc. Some of the Internationally recognized standards and formats being used by many libraries of different countries for creating databases. As per the INFLIBNET's guidelines following standards are recommended for use:

Standardized Bibliographic Formats

During the inception of the Programme, The Task Group on "Union Catalogue, Data Capturing and Standardization" was constituted by UGC. The Task Group was assisted by a Sub-Committee on implementation of Common Communication Format (CCF) for data capturing and data exchange. Later on, the Sub-Committee formalized some fields based on CCF and named it as "Guidelines for Data Capturing: a user manual".

During the initial stage of automation, Micro CDS/ISIS software (developed by Unesco) were suggested to use for creating bibliographic databases based on the format recommended by the Centre. Standards for Creating Bibliographic Databases Simultaneously, other DBMS such as DBase, FoxPro, FoxBase etc.

were also being used by different libraries for creating the databases. In addition, the Centre had also the library house keeping software called "ILMS – Integrated Library Management System" developed on COBOL language on Unix platform, and was distributed freely to the member libraries of the Centre. Later in February 2000, Centre developed another library house keeping software called "SOUL – Software for University Libraries" on Power Builder language on Windows platform by using the client-server architecture to keep in mind the shortcomings being faced in ILMS software.

The software is developed based on the format formalized by Sub-Committee of the Task Force. Later, early 2001, The Ministry of Human Resource Development (MHRD), Govt. of India visualizes building up a national database of library holdings in the country based on the MARC21 format. Further, after approval the committee directed INFLIBNET Centre to implement the MARC21 format in all libraries of the country. In this regards, the Centre formed the MARC21 Core Group during December 2001, which formalized the fields for implementing it with the SOUL library house keeping software.

The main reason for preferring MARC21 over CCF and other formats was that most of the countries in the world use MARC and it is comprehensive having number of fields. Also there is constant development taking place in MARC21 and is updated regularly whereas CCF has become stagnant. In the first meeting MARC21 Core Group were come out with the following results

- MARC21 Code list for field identification. Available on following website:
- http://web.inflibnet.ac.in/info/dwld/marc21_codelist.pdf
- Field list for Name and Subject Authority Database. Accessible through:
- http://web.inflibnet.ac.in/info/dwld/auth_tag_lst.pdf
- Fields for the Indian Manuscript Database. Available at:
- http://web.inflibnet.ac.in/info/dwld/finalmanuscript.pdf

STANDARD FOR RENDERING INFORMATION / BIBLIOGRAPHIC DESCRIPTIONS

AACR2R, ISBD and CCC are standards for bibliographic descriptions. But, INFLIBNET Centre suggests their participating libraries to follow the Anglo American Cataloging Rules-II (AACRII) Revised version for rendering bibliographic information.

STANDARDIZED SUBJECT HEADINGS

Different subject headings list are available, developed by different institutions such as LCSH, Sear's List of Subject Headings, MeSH, Thesaurus etc. But INFLIBNET suggests to its member library to use LCSH (for generalized subject headings) and Engineering Index, MeSH and thesaurus (for specialized Subject Headings).

STANDARD FOR CLASSIFICATION SCHEMES

There are various classification schemes have been developed by different organizations for classifying the books on different subjects. Functionally, most of the libraries are using the Dewey Decimal Classification (DDC) for assigning the Classification Number to the documents. But, under INFLIBNET umbrella, all the libraries are free to use any classification scheme for classifying the document, as it is very difficult for any library to reclassify the entire collection based on any new scheme. As per the library practice any classification scheme can be used as MARC21 has capability to adopt any kind of classification schemes.

ISO–2709 INFORMATION EXCHANGE FORMAT

This standard specifies the requirements for generalized interchange format that will accommodate data describing all forms of material. It describes a generalized structure designed specifically for exchange of data between processing systems and not necessarily for use as a processing format within systems. The format may be used for the interchange of records using various communication media. INFLIBNET Centre recommends to follow this Exchange Format for contributing records to the Centre. The exchange format has implemented too with the in-house developed software SOUL for exchanging records. Physical structure of the implemented information exchange format is given below:

Physical Structure

Leader

Each record begins with a leader of fixed length of 24 character positions and is the first instance of the ISO 2709 format of a record.

It contains:

- Record length (5 characters): The length of the record includes the leader, directory, data fields and record separator.
- Record Status Code (1 character): Always '0' for output files, ignored on input files.
- Implementation Codes (4 characters): These codes are defined for each specific implementation of the ISO 2709 format. Second character position represents Bibliographic level codes (i.e. s- serials, m- single volume monographs, c- multivolume monographs, a- component part) and rest of the character positioned not used. Here, Bibliographic level is defined here as per the INFLIBNET's use. For the MARC21 based records, it follows the description defined for bibliographic level in MARC21 bibliographic format.
- Indicator length (1 character): This is always '0', because here at INFLIBNET database indicator is not being used. But the value is '2', when we export records from SOUL to MARC21 in ISO 2709 format.
- Subfield identifier length (1 character): '2' The subfield identifier length. This shows the number of characters being used for the subfield identifier.
- Base address of data (5 characters): A decimal number indicating the number of control characters (length of leader plus directory and field separator) which precede the variable data fields. This number, when added to the starting address of the record, gives

the address of the first character of the variable fields.

- For user systems (3 characters): These character positions are not used. Always '000' in output files.
- Length of "Length of Datafield" field (1 character): '4' the length of "Length of Datafield" in the directory. (Use of 4 characters permits datafields as long as 9,999 characters)
- Length of "Starting character" position (1 character): '5' the length is "Starting character position" in the directory.
- Rest (2 characters): These character positions are not used. Always sets on '00'.

Directory

A directory entry in this bibliographic record is made up of a tag, length-of-field, and field starting position.

It is of variable length and consists of a series of fixed fields, referred to as "entries". One directory entry is associated with each datafield present in the record.

Each directory entry is 12 characters in length and is divided into three parts:

- *Tag*: A three numeric ASCII character code identifying the datafield, which corresponds to the directory entry. In software, names of the fields are being used in alphabetical name, but during the export in ISO 2709 format and display on screen, it converts in three-numeric digit ASCII character code.
- *Length of datafield*: A four digit number showing how many characters are occupied by the datafield, including datafield separator but excluding the record separator code if the datafield is the last field in the record.
- *Starting character position*: A five-digit number giving the position of the first character of the datafield relative to the base address of data, i.e. the first character of the first of the datafields.

Datafields

A datafield consists of subfield and datafield separator:

- Subflield : A subfield consists of a subfield identifier followed by a data string, which is terminated by either another subfield identifier or a field separator. A subfield identifier consists of a subfield identifier flag i.e. cap (^) sign followed by one another character, that can be alphabet a to z (small or capital) and numeric 1 to 9, INFLIBNET Centre uses here small alphabets. For MARC21 based records "$" graphical sign is used as a subfield identifier.
- Datafield Separator : The datafield separator i.e. hash (#) sign constitutes the final character of every datafield. ASCII value 30 (character 1/14 of ISO 646) is being used as a field separator in MARC21 based data.

Record Terminator / Separator

The record terminator is the final character of the record i.e. hash (#) sign. It follows the field separator of the final datafield of the record. ASCII 29 (character 1/13 of ISO 646) is being used as record separator in MARC21 based data.

OTHER STANDARDS RELATED TO BIBLIOGRAPHIC DATABASE

There are some other standards related to the bibliographic databases, are given below:

Z39.50 Retrieval protocol

Z39.50 refers to the International Standard, ISO 23950: "Information Retrieval (Z39.50): Application Service Definition and Protocol Specification", and to ANSI/NISO Z39.50. The standard specifies a client/serverbased protocol for searching and retrieving information from remote databases. More can be found on http://lcweb.loc.gov/z3950/agency/.

OAI (Open Archive Initiative)

The Open Archive Initiative (OAI) for metadata harvesting is a new protocol dedicated to solving problems of digital library interoperability by defining simple protocols, most recently for the exchange of metadata. Although, Z39.50 Information Retrieval Protocol is also one of the harvesting protocols. Some digital library systems are using for retrieving and searching the records for example Maxwell System.

It is crucial to explain, discuss, and disambiguate the concepts and terminology used among OAI implementers to harvesting approach to interoperability. The harvesting protocol defined by the OAI is a request / response protocol with 6 request types, viz. *Identity, ListMetadataFormats, ListSets, GetRecords ListRecord, and ListIdentifiers.* It has defined in such a way to support a common set of principles and a technical framework to achieve interoperability. Although, both the standards are not being used with the INFLIBNET database right now, but being explored to implement it in near future.

PURPOSE OF THE BIBLIOGRAPHIC STANDARDS

Mostly, purpose of using these standards for creating bibliographic databases or suggesting using it at libraries of India, has following reasons behind it:

- Pursuing Universal Bibliographic Control
- Exchange of information among union databases for the purpose of global resource sharing
- Cooperation at the local level, transferring data from one system to another

IMPORTANCE OF THE BIBLIOGRAPHIC STANDARDS

Following bibliographic standards for creating the databases produces following importance:

- It makes uniformity in records
- It provides better resource sharing between different resource centres
- It helps in exchanging of records and facilitates it without data loss
- It helps in creating national / International bibliographic union database
- It helps to adopt any system and provides platform interoperability

14

Organizational Change and Library Automation

The University Libraries of Notre Dame closed their library system, NOTIS, during Christmas break in 1998. In January of 1999, they brought a new library system, Aleph, into production. The NOTIS system is based on a large IBM mainframe with text-based terminals. Library patrons and staff use the same terminal connections to access the catalog. The system is command driven, and all computation activity takes place on the mainframe. Aleph is a client-server system, using an ORACLE database mounted on a UNIX server. The library staff use a Windows client on PCs to access the database. This client uses a graphical interface, with drop-down menus and buttons. Staff edit records on PCs, and send them back to the server when they are finished. The library patrons do not use the same software to access the catalog. Instead, they connect with their web-browsers, using virtually any computer platform they like.

IDENTIFICATION OF THE ISSUE

The above example is only one instance of the large-scale changes that affect people's work lives. These types of changes raise many important issues for managers, from the level of director to unit supervisor. Some issues are primarily technological. What equipment will be needed? Is the technological infrastructure in place? Will the system crash when the date changes to January 1, 2000? Other issues are more social. How will the employees react? Will they accept the change or resist it? Can the change process be made easier? Unfortunately, this second group of issues can be easily overlooked. Managers often do not address human issues adequately, even though they are aware of them, and even though they consider their employees, clients, and other people to be important (Backer). This paper will focus on human aspects of change, particularly in the context of library automation projects.

CHANGE ISSUES IN THE PUBLIC AND PRIVATE SECTORS

While the specific issue of library automation is located principally in the public sector, the processes and challenges of change are common to both areas.

HUMAN FACTORS IN LIBRARY AUTOMATION

Librarians, staff and patrons must make a number of adjustments as a result of any library automation project, whether it is an original implementation or a migration. One key area is the relationship between people and technology. People have to change the way they behave and think to work effectively in an automated environment. They skim through cards to find a catalog record in a manual system. To find a catalog record in an automated system they use computer commands (Smith). In a migration scenario, this might be a change from typing keyboard commands to choosing buttons or menu items on a graphical interface.

For long-term employees, this requires yet a third "mental map." These demands for change easily lead to stress reactions of fear or anger, especially when they are large-scale or frequent. Smith mentions several sources for these emotions, such as loss of control, worries about identity and security in the workplace, and breakdowns in interpersonal relationships. It is no wonder that people often resist change. However, Smith cautions against regarding human responses solely as a barrier to change. For leaders who pay attention to social issues, these responses provide valuable feedback and help to implement a more successful system.

HISTORICAL PERSPECTIVE

The early history of library automation can be divided into three phases, the Developmental Phase, the Operational Phase, and the Integrative Phase (Montague). The development phase was the period of early experimentation up to the early seventies.

During this period a small number of institutions engaged in automation projects. While management hoped that systems could be transferred from one institution to another, this was not the case with these early efforts. Libraries did not have similar computer operating systems, they did not have standardized procedures, and they could not agree on outputs.

However, the development of the MARC record was a significant development that allowed libraries to communicate bibliographic records in a standard format. The operational phase, in the mid-to-late seventies, saw the expansion of automation in a wider variety of libraries.

Vendor-supplied systems, shared computer resources, and networking made this possible. Since libraries were no longer forced to develop their own systems from scratch, it was an easier and less expensive task. During this phase most library automation projects still focused on discrete tasks, such as check-in or circulation.

Operational areas were not integrated, and the overall workflow stayed basically the same, "it has been utterly possible to use the automated system as inefficiently and ineffectively and with as little knowledge of what is going on as with the manual system" (Montague). Montague proposed that the next phase would be an integrative phase, in which the automation systems would cut across operational lines, actually change the way libraries do business, and improve service.

There were a number of obstacles during these stages of library automation:

- Lack of direction and oversight from library managers to systems staff
- Lack of technical training for library managers
- Failure to develop long-range plans (including a cost analysis of the manual systems and the automated replacements)
- Lack of up and down communication between managers and staff
- Lack of staff input
- Lack of staff training
- Lack of feedback mechanisms

Overall, it appears that the several problems, training, oversight, input, feedback, all involved a general lack of communication.

MIGRATION: SECOND GENERATION SYSTEMS

Since many libraries, including Notre Dame, have or plan to migrate to second generation library systems, it is important to consider whether the obstacles are the same. One view (representing a system vendor) is that they are not the same. Migrations are said to be easier than initial implementations. Although there may be some staff apprehensions, staff morale is reported to improve.

A significant advantage is that second-time buyers have a better understanding of what they want in a system, and focus more on quality and customer support, instead of low bids. There is one potential source of resistance, which is never present in an initial automation project, that is a hostile "soon-to-be former vendor."

Another important distinction is whether the library is migrating after successful implementation of a system which simply no longer meets their needs, or whether the library is desperately seeking a new system after a failed effort (Sybrowsky). The reaction of librarians to this viewpoint is to be mixed. Some libraries have reported a very similar degree of "technostress" during migration projects, with similar emotional responses (stress, fear and anxiety). Staff are required to change procedures, and in many cases the new procedures are not clear-cut — of course, the procedures in the "old" system were not clear-cut in the beginning either (Saunders).

On the other hand, the majority of directors in a survey of 33 libraries that had undergone system migrations felt that "promoting" the system change to the staff was unnecessary. This seems to be primarily due to staff frustration with the old systems, providing a clear motivation for change. The worse the original system, the less staff resistance there was to migration. However, there were still some symptoms of technostress. Many found the vendors training programs to be inadequate, consisting of "canned" presentations were did not apply to local needs. Due to "rush jobs," the staff at many libraries did not have adequate time to become familiar with the new system before it was made available to the public. In one particularly egregious case, the staff and patrons were given access to the system at the same time. The staff "hated this." A two-month lead-time between staff and public access gave optimum results (Hallmark).

PRIVATE SECTOR EXPERIENCES

While library automation, per se, is not a major issue in the for-profit world, automation in general definitely is. As such, experiences in the private sector provide helpful comparisons. One very familiar theme from corporate settings in the need to consult with users prior to any sort of migration or automation project. This is true even with systems that are not central to the users' jobs. Gaudin relates several stories of companies that tried to implement new systems without consulting users.

One case involved replacing a mainframe email system with a desktop system. After the company spent $3 million, the employees rejected it because it was not fast or stable enough. In another case, FedEx introduced a scheduling system (which had been very popular with employees at *other* airlines) without consulting their *own* employees. This became one of the issues in a potential strike against the company. One manager pointed out the importance of remembering that "users might like their old systems" (Gaudin). This is an important lesson for library managers to remember in a migration, especially when the original system was basically successful.

Even a failed system may have features the employees liked. Another illustration is provided by Norman's study of a failed automation effort. An attempt to introduce the CASE (computer-aided software engineering) system in a management information firm provides valuable lessons for both sectors. The goal of the CASE project was to establish a 2-1 ratio of CASE workstation usage among the MIS staff and achieve a 10 to 15% increase in productivity. The project is considered to be a failure, because people are not using it. The company has lost business to competitors who do use the system (Norman). Norman identifies a number of factors in the CASE implementation, which contributed to its failure.

From the beginning, the decision to implement CASE was made by a small high-level committee, without involving staff. There was a successful pilot project, following which the company attempted to expand the system. Their main methodology was a staff-training program. Management assumed that if they provided training, the programmers would use the system. While the training was described as "adequate," it was informational only, and there was no effort made to change attitudes. The most critical barrier identified in the study was the high learning curve for using CASE. Management did not make any effort to reduce this learning curve. Instead, each work group that attempted to use the system had to learn it on their own. There was no sharing of tricks or shortcuts, or any help given by those who had already started using the product to new users.

Interdepartmental friction and a rigid chain-of-command that stifled communication between units prevented this type of cooperation. A related factor was the lack of any visible benefits or rewards for using CASE. Instead rewards were based on completing projects under-time and under-budget. Since CASE is intended to increase productivity, it might seem that this would reward its use.

But "this means that the rewards are indirect and totally dependent upon the *successful* use of the tool" (Norman, emphasis added). In conjunction with the high learning curve, this becomes a negative incentive – the system is likely to slow production in the short-term, until the learning curve is past. If the programmer fails to learn it quickly, rewards are lost rather than gained.

THEORIES AND STRATEGIES FOR CHANGE

In discussing theories of organizational change, many theorists divide changes into different types. Before delving too deeply into specific strategies for change, I would like to examine the relationship between library automation projects and descriptive theories. Continuity In the Age of Unreason, Handy tells us that "Change is not what it used to be". He distinguishes continuous and discontinuous change. Continuous change is gradual and predictable, with one situation leading into the next. This is relatively comfortable for most people. But he asserts that the changes in the workplace now (and in life in general) are discontinuous.

That is, changes are abrupt and unpredictable, and hence, far less comfortable. Handy frequently links discontinuous change to technology. As such, it is easy to reach the conclusion that a library automation project is a discontinuous change. People who worked with paper switch to online systems, and their jobs are altered or even eliminated. But we should not be too quick to classify it this way.

Particularly in the early automation projects, automated tasks were substituted for manual tasks on a one-to-one basis. Because of this, there was no drastic change in the overall workflow; even when specific tasks were drastically altered (Montague). It could be argued that automation has had a more significant impact since that time, as library systems have become integrated.

CALM AND TURBULENT WATERS

Robbins focuses on the frequency of change. He uses two metaphors, "calm waters" and "whitewater rapids." In the calm-waters scenario, change is the exception. Most of the time is spent in a state of equilibrium, until some crisis (the storm) forces a change. After the change is past, the organization regains a new (albeit different) state of equilibrium. In the white-water scenario, change is continuous, though in a different sense than Handy uses the word. There is no state of equilibrium; instead one period of change is followed directly by another.

It is very tempting to identify library automation projects with the "calm water" metaphor. In fact, Saunders uses a very similar model in her article on library system migration. First various forces bring about a need for change, which requires unfreezing process. This is followed by a period of instability (the actual time of the change). When this is over, the library establishes a new state of equilibrium, as new patterns and procedures are frozen into place. Because automation efforts are not made frequently, this model appears to be a good match.

In an original automation project, the library has been using a manual system as long as it has been in existence. Once the project has been completed, the library will continue to use the new system indefinitely. Even in a migration project, the library may have been using its old system for many years, and certainly would hope the new system would be long-lived. One potential problem with this model is that it ignores the wider picture of overall changes. At the same time as a library is contemplating an integrated library system, the staff may be dealing with new (and ever-changing) online indexes, electronic journals, email systems, computer operating systems, and even (in Notre Dame's case) a building renovation.

Taken in this larger context, the white water metaphor seems more appropriate to the library environment. It is often not just the project at hand that causes problems for staff and users, but the "unrelenting demand" of changes in many areas. Another issue is the continuing change following the implementation of an automated system due to new releases and upgrades to the system. Even after a new system is fully implemented, it may not be as "calm" as the old manual system.

One significant problem with the white-water model as a model for change is that it suggests a reactive style of management with unplanned changes. But most library automation and migration projects are planned, as are many (not all) of the other changes affecting the library staff. This model seems most apt for dealing with the external changes impacting an organization.

THE FOUR MOTORS OF CHANGE

Van de Ven and Poole give a more fully fleshed taxonomy of change. They identify two crosscutting distinctions, the level and the mode of change. The level of change is whether the change involves single or multiple entities (an entity being anything from an individual to an institution). The mode of change is either prescribed or emergent. A priori changes are planned, predictable or follow set rules or patterns (what Handy would describe as continuous). Emergent change is discontinuous and unpredictable. This combination yields four "motors of change."

- Life-cycle (single entity, prescribed)
- Teleological (single entity, emergent)
- Dialectical (multiple entities, emergent)
- Evolutionary (multiple entities, prescribed)

While these motors can be separated in theory, most real-life changes involve interaction between them (Van de Ven). The four motors model provides a more complete description of organizational change, and avoids oversimplification problems. If we examine library automation projects in this e context of the four motors of change that Van de Ven describes, we will find rather complex interactions.

The teleological theory, which is characterized by planning and goal setting, provides the closest description of the first stage in an automation project. Libraries may have a variety of motivations for undertaking an automation or migration project.

In the case of migration, this might include negative factors, like dissatisfaction with the current vendor, as well as positive ones, like a desire to expand capabilities (Hallmark). These motivations provide the Aristotelian final cause for the project. Most libraries engage in goal setting activities, such as compiling lists of desired features (Begg). This stage may be described as teleological in Van de Ven's scheme because it primarily involves one entity (the library) and the process is emergent. At the beginning of this stage, it is not clear where it will finish.

Although the process is planned (rather than reactive) the goals are identified during the process, and may provide a dramatic break (or discontinuity) with the existing manual or automated system. The dialectical motor may be present to a lessor extant, as different stakeholders (such as work units) interact with each other, and occasionally present conflicting goals.

This teleological description fits most, but not all migration projects. For 79% of cases in a migration survey, the projects were planned. But in some cases, the libraries did not have time to develop plans due to legal or financial problems. In those cases, the teleological motor would only apply in a trivial sense, if at all.

Those cases are obviously not ideal scenarios (Hallmark). Towards the end of the selection process, the library must compare its goals and desires to the actual systems available. At this point, the process could be described as dialectical, involving the library and the vendors who would like to supply the system. Vendors and librarians both regard this process as different for migration projects compared to first-time automation efforts. In a first-time automation, libraries tend to rely on numerical evaluation of vendors' proposals and claims.

In migration projects, libraries find site visits to be the most effective way to evaluate quality and hands-on work issues (Begg, Sybrowski). At some point either during the final selection process or shortly after a vendor is chosen, the process shifts to a life-cycle model. The life-cycle motor is also primarily concerned with the library as a single entity. At this point, the plan, which was developed in earlier stages, becomes the guide for the process. The library engages is a series of steps that were laid out in the plan, possibly on a strict timeschedule.

This includes all of the steps technically necessary to implement the system (e.g., data mapping and test conversions) as well as steps to prepare the users. This process is imminent in, or prescribed by the plan, and is much more predictable than the earlier stages. The library may have even planned for contingencies. Once the actual conversion in done, and the new system is live, the process become somewhat less predictable. Procedures that worked on paper or in test may fail under the pressure of real-life use.

While none of the motors seem to be completely dominant at this point, the evolutionary theory is closest. Procedures that work "survive" while others are discarded. The changes may still be described as imminent, however, because they are constrained by the system. The others motors continue to play some role, as plans are made and carried out, and different stakeholders disagree on various issues. The dialectical motor may become dominant from time-to-time as the vendor announces new releases, or the library recommends enhancements for the system. At these times the possibilities for change are less constrained, and the results become more emergent.

STRATEGIES

The authors who describe actual automation projects also list key lessons and make recommendations. There are a number of general, and some very specific, suggestions along with a couple of common threads. One of the common threads is communication. Whether it is between management and employees, between systems and users, or between the employees at large, it seems that more communication is always better.

A related thread is the need to involve the users in the process as early as possible. Several of the authors suggested that users should be involved at the very beginning, during the selection process. Montage, Norman, Gaudin, Hallmark and Smith all cite lack of user involvement in the selection or planning stage as an obstacle to successful implementation. Since these two threads stand out, we may conclude that if any overall strategy is too be effective, it must include a high level of communication and user participation.

STRATEGIES FROM THE CASE IMPLEMENTATION

Norman described three change strategies in his evaluation of the CASE implementation. These strategies could be used independently or in conjunction with each other. *Rational-empirical* This strategy focuses on training (i.e., how to use the system) and information (the benefits of the system). It is presumed that teaching people to use the system and providing a rational explanation of why it is better will lead them to use it. This strategy could easily be applied to a library automation or migration project, as many of the authors indicated the importance of training programs.

Normative-educational

This strategy focuses on group strategies for promoting acceptance of the new systems and providing motivation to use it. First, identify the attitudes that create resistance, and then develop programs to change them. This is similar to developing training sessions in the rational-empirical strategy. The difference is that the sessions are intended to develop positive attitudes instead imparting information.

Power-coercive

In this strategy individuals are induced to use the new system by the threat of loosing their job or other benefits (e.g. promotion opportunities). This can be a fairly direct approach to implement change, but it also runs a high risk creating bad feelings, job dissatisfaction, and tension between management and employees. Threats, whether explicit or implicit, will also add to the fear and anxiety already identified as an obstacle to change. A variation of this strategy can be applied in a positive way by offering employees incentives for change.

While this is can be regarded as a power-exercise (the employees who do not use the new system will not get the new benefits) it is less confrontational. In the CASE implementation, the main strategy that was applied was the rational-empirical strategy. The normative-educational strategy was largely ignored, and the power-coercive strategy was inconsistently applied. Management made statements that employees were required to use the system, but did not follow-up when it was not used. Management also did not provide any direct positive incentives. This strategy may also be applied to library systems in the sense that when the old (manual or automated) system is shut-off, employees will not be able to perform their duties without using the new system.

PHASED IMPLEMENTATION

Saunders recommends a strategy of phased implementation. The idea of this strategy is to minimize the impact of the new system has on staff by introducing modules in a gradual fashion. For example, a library might implement cataloging or acquisitions functions first, and circulation latter. This strategy has some advantages. Successful implementation of one module should increase staff willingness to use another. Also, management can deal with the staff in smaller groups, concentrating on the area currently being automated, instead of dealing with all areas at once. The chief drawback of this strategy is found when the current system is already well integrated. In this case, phased implementation may mean that user's (staff and patrons) are initially presented with a system that has *fewer features* than their previous system.

There may also be technical difficulties that preclude phased implementation, as the two systems are not likely to communicate with each other well, if at all. Where it is usable, this strategy should also be combined with other strategies. Saunders specifically emphasizes the importance of training and communication issues.

PARTICIPANT ORIENTED CHANGE

Zeffane advocates the strategy of participant oriented change, which is based on the premise that change works best when comes from the bottom up rather than from the top down. One reason for this premise is that if the employees introduce change, then they will not have an authority figure to rebel against. It is also based on the idea that collegial affiliation is a positive motivation for change.

That is, employees will be more motivated to help with a changes initiated by someone at, or close to, their level. To use participant oriented change, management needs to shift the responsibility for change away from themselves and towards the employees. This strategy goes beyond considering the users' needs, or soliciting input, to actually delegating authority to the participants.

This strategy takes advantage of the fact that the employees who are closest to the hands-on work have the most detailed knowledge about it. This also frees the upper management from concentrating on this level of detail, and to concentrate on overall strategic planning. This strategy may not be effective in all types of organizations.

There are some essential elements for participative strategies to work. First, the employees given responsibilities for change must be well informed. Second, the employees must understand and agree with the mission of the organization.

Unless these requirements are met, management cannot expect that the decisions will be beneficial to the organization. The third requirement is that this style of change must be supported by the organization culture. The management must be comfortable with this type of delegation (Zeffane).

MANAGEMENT FUNCTIONS

The traditional roles of management are planning, organization, coordination and control. These can be applied to these change strategies.

RATIONAL-EMPIRICAL

The rational-empirical strategy is primarily concerned with dispensing information, presuming that the plans for change have already been made. It involves the organizing function of management, in the sense that the managers determine what information needs to be given to which employees in order to implement the changes. It also involves the control function, in that the management is seeking to influence behavior through the information it dispenses (or withholds).

NORMATIVE-EDUCATIONAL

The normative-education strategy is concerned with influencing attitudes and behavior. As such, it involves the control function of management, but in an indirect manner. That is, rather than controlling behavior directly, the management attempts to instill attitudes which are likely to result in the desired behavior. Like the rational-empirical strategy, it also involves the coordinating function, as managers decide who should be involved in which programs.

POWER-COERCIVE

The power-coercive strategy concerns the management role of control in a straight- forward fashion. It is mainly concerned with seeing to it that the change decisions (which have already been made) are carried out as directed. To ensure this, it dispenses rewards or penalties to individuals or groups depending or whether they have implemented the changes. In the extreme, employees who fail to change are fired.

PHASED IMPLEMENTATION

Phased implementation involves both the planning and coordinating functions to a large degree. Planning includes determining the order in which to implement the modules and setting timetables for each phase. Coordination includes meshing together the efforts of different groups associated with each phase, and ensuring that each module is integrated with the previous ones when it is brought into production. As more modules are brought into the "live" mode, coordination becomes essential in order to see that the different areas function smoothly.

PARTICIPANT ORIENTED CHANGE

Participant oriented change involves the coordinating function of management. Since much of the planning and decision making is delegated downward to the staff, management must integrate these plans and decisions. This is particularly important when implementing an integrated library system (either in an initial automation, or in comparison to a less integrated system), as the activities of staff in one area will have more impact on other areas than they are accustomed to. The actual delegation of these responsibilities to employees involves the organizing function. Determining how and to whom these responsibilities are delegated is in important part of the change process. This may involve organizing employees into self-managed teams, work groups, or interdepartmental task forces. How these groups are organized, the amount of authority they have, and how they will interact with each other are crucial decisions.

CONCLUSIONS AND RECOMMENDATIONS

The participant oriented change strategy provides the best overall approach to managing library automation and migration projects. Of the strategies which have been outlined, it offers the highest degree of employee communication and participation. These are the same areas that caused the most problems if they were inadequate. One of the chief advantages of this strategy is that it involves the users of the system at the earliest possible stage of the project. That is during the teleological process of identifying reasons for the project and setting goals or criteria for a new system. Involving the employees at this stage reduces the need for normative attitude-adjusting sessions latter in the process.

This is not to say that managers who adopt this strategy can just ignore employee attitudes later on. Change will still be stressful, and people may still resist it at various points. But, management will not have to invest as much effort in convincing staff that the new system is better if the staff were involved in selecting it. The rational-empirical strategies of employee training programs will still have a role to play, as the process moves on. As was demonstrated in the failed attempt at implementing the CASE system, this strategy is not sufficient by itself. But users must learn how a new system works if they are to use it at all. Within the overall context of participant oriented strategy, other employees provide much of that training.

With their hands-on experience, employee led training can be more effective than vendorsupplied "canned presentations" (Hallmark). This also promotes an atmosphere in which employees will be comfortable sharing their learning experiences, tricks and shortcuts following implementation (Norman). The other two strategies, phased implementation and power-coercive can not be recommended across the board. The power-coercive strategy is divisive, and is likely make the change harder instead of easier. This strategy aggravates fears about job security, which is one of the sources of change anxiety.

While a degree of control needs to be maintained, a threatening approach is not desirable as a general strategy. The strategy of phased implementation will be helpful for some situations, but not for all. For libraries currently using manual systems or automated systems that are not integrated, this method may help to ease the transition. For libraries that already have a well-integrated system, it could create even more chaos. Within the context of participant oriented change, the choice of whether to include it rests with the employees who actually work with the system.

Index